David R. Nornvorthy

CAPITAL
PUNISHMENT

D0974150

Readers in Social Problems

DONALD R. CRESSEY, CONSULTING EDITOR

UNIVERSITY OF CALIFORNIA, SANTA BARBARA

CAPITAL PUNISHMENT

EDITED BY

THORSTEN SELLIN

CENTER OF CRIMINOLOGICAL RESEARCH
UNIVERSITY OF PENNSYLVANIA

HARPER & ROW

Publishers

NEW YORK, EVANSTON, AND LONDON

CAPITAL PUNISHMENT / Copyright © 1967 by Thorsten Sellin. Printed in the United States of America. All rights reserved. No part of this book may be used or reproduced in any manner whatsoever without written permission except in the case of brief quotations embodied in critical articles and reviews. For information address Harper & Row, Publishers, Incorporated, 49 East 33rd Street, New York, N.Y. 10016.

Library of Congress Catalog Card Number: 67–13476

CONTENTS

PART IV/THE DEATH PENALTY AND JUDICIAL ADMINISTRATION

PART V/SUMMATION

PREFACE

THE DEATH PENALTY occupies a peculiar place in discussions of punishments. No one today questions the propriety and necessity of depriving some offenders against the law of their freedom for periods of time or of their property in the form of fines. When these penalties are discussed, the only questions raised concern when, how, and to whom they should be applied. It is different when capital punishment is debated. Its very existence is questioned. Those defending it believe it is legitimate and necessary; those opposed to it regard it as unjustifiable, impotent, and outdated.

In this small book an attempt has been made to assemble the arguments for and against the dealth penality and to present some of the facts on which they are based. Most of the readings have not previously been gathered together, and half a dozen have been written specially for inclusion in the compilation.

The readings are grouped under five general headings. Part I opens with an article by Justice Marc Ancel of the Supreme Court *(Cour de Cassation)* of France, eminent student of comparative criminal law and author of the report on capital punishment issued by the United Nations in 1962. There follow an article on crimes punishable by death in the United States by Robert H. Finkel, assistant district attorney of Philadelphia County, Pennsylvania, and a brief article by the editor on the statistics of executions in the United States.

Part II includes a series of articles on the general theme of abolition of capital punishment. The first reading is a section from the famous treatise on *Crime and Punishment* by Cesare Bonesana, Marquis of Beccaria, published in 1764. This treatise provided the chief impetus for the abolition movement in Europe. That the debate on the question was not a novelty is proved by the article on the Roman debate between Caesar and Cato by Professor William McAllen Green, University of California (Berkeley). Beccaria's views were adopted by the drafters of the criminal code presented to the French Constituent Assembly in 1791. The ensuing debate is summarized and compared with the debate in the British House of Commons in 1956 by Finn Hornum of the staff of the American Foundation, Philadelphia. The most recent parliamentary debate on the question of abolition took place in March and April, 1966, in the Canadian House of Commons; the views on both sides are illustrated in selections from nine speeches by members of the House. The other articles in this section are: one on the history of abolition in the United States by Louis Filler, professor of American civilization, Antioch College; a brief survey of the effects of temporary experiments with abolition in American states by the editor; and a case history of such an experiment in Missouri by Ellen Elizabeth Guillot, now deputy director of the Office of International Surveys, United States Department of Health, Education and Welfare.

In Part III special attention is given to the problem of deterrence. The first of the five readings, prepared by the editor and illustrated graphically, compares homicide death rates in abolition states with those in bordering retentionist states. The next two articles, by the editor, test the claim of the police that they are exposed to fewer hazards to life in states with the death penalty and the claim that if imprisonment were substituted, the staff and inmates of prisons would be exposed to increased danger. The latter belief is further examined in a study of homicides and serious assaults in Canadian prisons by Dogan D. Akman, now a Canadian Commonwealth Scholar at Oxford University. The risk of recidivism among paroled murderers is studied in an article by G. I. Giardini, late superintendent of Parole Supervision, Pennsylvania State Board of Parole, and R. G. Farrow, now chief, Division of Youth Rehabilitation, Bureau of Children's Services, Pennsylvania Department of Welfare.

Part IV touches on some aspects of the administration of justice in capital cases. The problem in general is discussed by Herbert B. Ehrmann, Boston attorney. The question of judicial errors, usually alluded to by opponents of capital punishment, is treated by Otto Pollak, professor of sociology, University of Pennsylvania. Walter E. Oberer, professor of law, Cornell Law School, deals with an interesting argument concerning the effect on capital trials of the custom of debarring from juries persons who are opposed to the death penalty. Solie M. Ringold, judge of the Superior Court of King County (Seattle),Washington, writes about the exercise of clemency by the state executive in capital cases.

The last part of the book consist of an article by the editor which, in a manner of speaking, summarizes the ideas about capital punishment and examines the varied and numerous aspects of the problem it presents.

A short selected bibliography is included.

The editor expresses his gratitude to all those authors and publishers who freely granted permission for the inclusion of certain of the writings. When applicable, specific acknowledgment is made in a footnote on the first page of the selection.

THORSTEN SELLIN

December, 1966

PART I

The Death Penalty,
Past and Present

The Problem of the Death Penalty

MARC ANCEL

At the end of the last or at the beginning of this century, the problem of the death penalty appeared to be a subject typically suited to academic discussion. Enrico Ferri, the founder of criminal sociology, had declared the topic to be "worn out from an intellectual point of view," while Adolphe Prins saw in the death penalty nothing but "a survival of the ancient theory of deterrence."[1] Enlightened opinion limited itself to watching, without impatience, its gradual disappearance.

Since then, the disorganization caused by two world wars has again made acutely poignant the violent and deliberate taking of human life. Nazi crimes, the spectacular "purges" of the East European countries during the Stalin era, and some notorious trials and bitterly debated executions in the western countries have attracted the attention of jurists and sociologists, of intellectuals and the public at large, and the matter is again being passionately debated.

We know the repercussions of the labor of the English Royal Commission on Capital Punishment, appointed in 1949,

This article is an enlarged version of a paper presented June 27, 1963, to the Belgian League for the Defense of Human Rights. Authorized translation from the French original in the *Revue de droit pénal et de criminologie*, 44th year (1963–1964):373–393, February, 1964.

All footnotes appear in the Notes section, grouped by article, at the end of this book.

whose report was made in September 1953.[2] More recently, and perhaps even concurrently, the European Committee on Problems of Crime and the Economic and Social Council of the United Nations have been concerned with the matter, and two reports on the present status of the question have been published by these international agencies.[3]

This is no doubt the essential point. It is a question of where we are in regard to this problem which no "honest man" can disregard in the future. From this point of view we would like to make some observations without pretending to exhaust the question and without wishing to renew the old controversy pro and con, on which, in fact, all has been said for two centuries. Nevertheless, it is not useless to try to comprehend, as objectively as possible, the place assigned today to the death penalty and what role could or should be reserved for it in the society of the second half of the 20th century. Such a task is really quite arduous, and we might try to accomplish it by successively discussing the past, the present, and the future.

I

The present situation is, in this matter as in many others, largely linked with the past. There is no intention here to engage in an historical study of the death penalty or, in that connection, to yield to the seductions of the philosophy of history. One can be satisfied with choosing some interesting points which are essential for an up-to-date comprehension of the problem.

First, it will be noted that for centuries the death penalty was not debated so far as its legitimacy or its practical utility was concerned. Its acceptance, general in ancient societies, seems to have depended on three principal causes.

The first of these was the insignificant value attached to human life, or, at least, to the life of any particular individual. Greek and Roman antiquity, though having given us the basis of our civilization, unhesitatingly sacrificed both slaves and captives.

In primitive societies and even in the more developed societies which succeeded them, from the Greco-Roman civilization to the Middle Ages and the Renaissance up to the 17th century, one notes the persistence of the idea of talion under the form of individual or tribal vengeance. When the respect for life began to be widely admitted, one tried to show that the death of the criminal was its complement in such a way that it could be said to be both just and necessary.[4]

Finally, the death penalty was to find natural support by the arrival or gradual establishment of an all-powerful state where the sovereign, considered so by divine right, was both the only source of justice and the guardian of peace or of public security. One of the attributes of this absolute sovereign that caused the disappearance of both private vengeance and private wars was precisely the right granted to him to inflict death in the name of the organized society he incarnated.

These three reasons, historical and ideological, contributed to make recourse to the death penalty appear necessary, in the original sense of that word. But, people had failed to note that certain primitive or ancient societies did not know the death penalty or accorded it an extremely restricted place. Such was the case of the very ancient Chinese law, as revealed in the famous Book of Five Punishments.[5] The death penalty was ignored also by the Islamic penal law for the most serious crimes punished and curbed by the Koran and later among punishments assessed by the judge provided by the customary law derived from the *Shariah*,[6] because these punishments were conceived of as "correctional" and meant to reform the offender. It was unknown in Slavic customary law before the ukases of the Tsars and even then it was found only exceptionally in certain population groups, such as the Cossacks, where it was only provided for the theft of horses. Finally, we know that it was rejected by the Canon Law, which only worried about penitence and left the death penalty to the secular branch.[7] It was, to repeat, royal or imperial authoritarianism that ended by imposing it as a legal punishment and, for a long time, as normal punishment.

The abolition movement can doubtless point to ancient precursors and, in that connection, one should not forget the activity of George Fox in the 17th century.[8] But, it was with the publication of the treatise *Of Crimes and Punishment* by

Beccaria two hundred years ago that the movement brilliantly asserted itself. For the first time, an authoritative and widely heard voice raised a doubt about the very legitimacy of the death penalty. Success was prompt and considerable, not among philosophers alone (Voltaire attached a celebrated commentary to the French translation of Beccaria's little book) but among sovereigns who prided themselves on being practitioners of an enlightened despotism. In 1767 Catharine II ordered the commission that she appointed to draft a new code to exclude the death penalty. In 1786 and 1787, respectively, Leopold II of Tuscany and Joseph II of Austria removed the death penalty from their *Corpus Juris Criminalis*.[9] In France, early in its deliberations, the National Convention decided on its suppression "the moment peace would be re-established." Soon, in England, Sir Samuel Romilly began his famous campaign for reducing capital crimes, which at the time numbered over 200, and in 1829 the first association for the abolition of the death penalty was formed in London.[10]

This generous movement which united enlightened rulers and the ideologists of the Declaration of the Rights of Man was soon to be slowed by the wars of the Revolution and of the Empire and the troubles following the political revolution that appeared in France and the industrial revolution marking the beginning of the 19th century. After a return to authoritarianism, underscored by the Austrian code of 1805, the French code of 1810 and the Bavarian code of 1813, the abolition movement recovered strength. It soon found itself fortified by three important currents of thought of the time. First, there was the humanitarian current tending to the mitigation of punishments and especially the removal of corporal or humiliating penalties. This trend was reinforced by the sentimentality and the romantic humanitarianism which, in France, found eloquent advocates, especially in Lamartine and Victor Hugo.[11]

The liberal current which developed especially after 1830 also tended to limit the absolutism of the state, to abolish the crime of lese majesty, and to render any appeal to "reasons of State" unpopular. In France, Guizot and Charles Lucas represented this movement, which in 1848 ended by removing the death penalty for political crimes. Many other countries, from Switzerland to Portugal and Latin America, felt its repercussions.

Finally, the utilitarian current, which, in diverse forms, was evident from Bentham to Stuart Mill or to Spencer, and among jurists to Rossi, affirmed that it was proper to search for happiness and not for pain. In particular, punishment should be "no more than just, nor more than necessary"; this led one logically to ask if it was ever really necessary to punish any offender by death regardless of his crime.

Under the influence of these diverse currents of thought, the criminal policy of the second half of the 19th century seemed to be tending toward the gradual elimination of the death penalty. From 1848 on there are clear signs of it in many European states and, after impassioned discussions, the movement received brilliant support in the Italian code of 1889, which contained no capital punishment. From 1863 on England had only three capital crimes, of which only one, murder, had meaning in practice. At this point, then, it seems as though we should agree with Ihering, who said that the history of punishment and, in particular, of the death penalty is one of continuous abolition.

At the turn of the century, however, there arose three counter-currents in favor of retention of the death penalty and even of its re-institution. The first was a current which one might call conservative. A spectacular increase in criminality during the last years of the 19th century aroused public opinion and disturbed the tranquility of the liberals, humanitarians, and utilitarians of the preceding generation. From those soon to be referred to as "apaches" to anarchists whose activity threatened the calm of the bourgeoisie of the Victorian era, new forms of criminality appeared that seemed to pose a serious threat to established order. Soon the exploits of some great criminals stopped, in France, the attempt at abolition *de facto* which President Fallières had made by a systematic use of commutation.[12]

The current just mentioned was fortified by another which might be called scientific. In publishing his famous work, *The Criminal Man,* in 1878, Lombroso developed the idea of a born criminal fatally destined to commit crime because of his bio-psychological constitution. Garofalo, in his *Criminology,* evolved the concept of social dangerousness, and the positivists taught that society must be defended by appropriate and vigorous means. Therefore, one must oppose the humanitarian or sentimental indulgence of judges and especially of juries. One was even led to ask if the death penalty should not be considered as a scientific procedure of social selection in line with Darwinian ideas.[13]

Finally, at the start of the 20th century, Europe experienced a strong authoritarian current of thought of which German national socialism and Italian fascism were only the most blatant examples. The central idea of authoritarian regimes and especially of the totalitarian ones was that the new social order, produced by a revolution which, depending on the case, was called national or popular, should be ruthlessly defended by all available means. In this perspective the death penalty again became a normal part of criminal policy. The crime of lese majesty reappeared in new forms. The execution of a culprit marked for public vengeance was the tangible sign of the absolute power of the state. Every political enemy appeared as a criminal, every nonconformist became suspect, every offender an outlaw. Death was a means of government.

However, by its very excesses totalitarianism provoked a reaction which made itself felt immediately after the Second World War. It was shown in the prosecution of war crimes, even if, here and there, at the time, it was marked by a temporary recrudescence of capital executions. The Universal Declaration of Human Rights of 1948 proclaimed anew to the world the rights of individuals and the eminent dignity of the human being.[14] The abolitionist movement was invigorated and scored successes even—and sometimes especially—in the countries where totalitarianism had imposed a return of the death penalty. Free from fascism, Italy returned to the great tradition of Beccaria and of the Zanardelli code. Austria, which had been forcibly incorporated in the Hitlerian system, returned to its earlier condition, which also had repudiated capital punishment. The German federal republic in turn excluded it by a constitutional provision. Great Britain, which the partisans of the death penalty had for a long time thought of as their strongest bastion of resistance, began to question it and soon became troubled by it. A considerable literature, two abolitionist victories in the House of Commons, and the already mentioned effects of the work of the Royal Commission resulted in the compromise Homicide Act of 1957 which still further reduced capital crimes, distinguished between capital and non-capital murder and introduced into the English system the concept of limited responsibility, which the Scottish law had already known for a long time.[15]

Now, international congresses and researches in criminology and penology are raising the question of abolition anew in a form both pointed and up-to-date, and to take one's stand on it again becomes unavoidable.

II

After the preceding review of history, the exact measurement of the present status of the question requires, no doubt, an attempt to present what might be called the "geography of capital punishment." Afterward one should specify the crimes to which it is applied in the countries concerned, the jurisdictions assessing it, the manner of its execution and the different procedures by which execution may be prevented, and, finally, the problems of procedural practice or correctional administration created by its existence.

It obviously is impossible to deal with these diverse matters exhaustively and, therefore, reference is made to the reports published by the Council of Europe and by the United Nations in which a survey of the present situation may be found. It would seem both sufficient and necessary to make a few comments on the law involved that have not, it seems, hitherto always been stressed as much as required.

So far as the "geography of capital punishment" is concerned, strictly speaking, we realize that distinctions should be made between countries which have retained the death penalty and apply it, the countries which have struck it from their laws, and the countries which have preserved capital punishment in the list of legal punishments but have abolished it in practice by never executing it. In certain cases, the death penalty is pronounced in accordance with the law, but traditional practice demands a commutation to prevent the execution. Belgium is surely the best example of this system. In other instances, the death penalty, though established in law, is never pronounced by the competent courts. It may happen, finally, in certain countries and at certain times, that executions are temporarily suspended provisionally and in some way experimentally either by legislative act or, as happened in England before the vote on the Homicide Act, by executive decision. These few observations make clear that a number of appreciable nuances may exist between the *legal* existence of the death penalty and its real application.

If one casts a panoramic eye on the different parts of the world, one is struck by the fact that at the present time all the countries of Africa and Asia have and use the death penalty. It appears that in most of these countries, and especially in the states which have newly gained independence, the death penalty is still considered fully justified in itself to such a degree that its abolition is not seriously proposed.

The countries of Oceania present a much more differentiated situation. Certain territories remain attached to the death penalty. But, after some fluctuations, New Zealand has again joined the abolitionists. In Australia the death penalty is found in five of eight states, the three abolitionist states being Queensland, *de jure*, and New South Wales and Victoria, *de facto*.

North America remains altogether rather in favor of the death penalty, although this punishment evokes, especially in the United States, great controversy and serious opposition. Canada kept it in its 1955 penal code, but the reform in 1961 which distinguished capital from non-capital murder has been regarded by many as a step toward abolition.[16] In the United States, 42 out of 50 states still have the death penalty, but it has ceased to be mandatory, which means that the court dealing with a capital crime is not compelled to impose it upon a convicted defendant.[17] This is important to note from the point of view of penal policy, because we know that the movement to reduce the death penalty tends first to make its imposition by the court involved discretionary.

Latin America, on the other hand, is abolitionist by a wide margin. The death penalty is still known and even employed in Chile, Cuba, Guatemala, El Salvador, and in four of Mexico's 29 states. Everywhere else it has been removed from the roster of punishments, and it is remarkable that all Latin American countries which have abolished it are abolitionist *de jure*. The elimination of the death penalty there has been done as a matter of principle. At times, the affirmation has taken the form of a constitutional rule.

Finally, in Europe the death penalty is used only in the Eastern countries and in Spain, France, Ireland, the United Kingdom, and Turkey. But one should mention that it is everywhere an exceptional sanction either because the law so states, as in the Soviet penal code of 1960, or because the practice and regulations governing the death penalty recognize its exceptional nature. Belgium, Luxembourg, and Lichtenstein are abolitionist *de facto*, as well as Monaco, until it recently rejoined the camp of *de jure* abolitionist countries,[18] which include essentially the Nordic nations, the Netherlands, Switzerland, Italy, Austria, and the German federal republic.

It would be interesting to study the technique of abolition at one's leisure. It would be necessary to show that it has taken successively different forms. To begin with, the problem consisted in reducing the incidence of the death penalty; the 19th-century movement tried above all to restrict the supreme punishment to aggravated murder alone. At times, a variant aimed at suppressing this sanction for political crimes by using the technique of alternative penalties in order to achieve partial abolition. One notes also that most of the time abolition *de jure* has followed abolition *de facto*, so that in many countries the law officially removing capital punishment has provoked no serious contest; the penalty had already disappeared from the positive law in force. Finally, one should mention that in this matter the trend is not irreversible and that various circumstances of political, economic, and social nature can lead to a resumption of a capital penalty previously abolished. Flagrant examples of this are found in the abolitionist countries of Europe which, at the close of the last war, temporarily re-established the death penalty in order to strike at the most serious cases of treason and collaboration with the enemy. Political changes, such as the advent of fascism in Italy, have in certain cases led to such a re-introduction of the death penalty. Elsewhere, as in certain states of the United States or in New Zealand, the abolition or the return of the death penalty may have been the consequence of a change in parliamentary majorities.[19]

We cannot, unfortunately, give the attention to all these points that they perhaps deserve, but we should mention that the exact catalogue of capital crimes is, in spite of what one may assume, always difficult to establish for any country at a given time. First of all, there often exist in a country's legislation crimes theoretically punishable by a death which is never, in fact, imposed, even if the country continues to execute certain criminals. In such cases, legal nomenclature does not reflect sociological reality.

Second, when the death penalty exists, something which American sociologists correctly refer to as "panic legislation" often occurs; faced with certain spectacular crimes laws are passed to punish them with death.[20] It is a matter of appeasing public opinion or satisfying an instinctive feeling of fear or a primitive one of vengeance. This has been the case, for instance, with the laws on kidnapping, statutes fixing the death penalty for certain crimes committed by groups or with the aid of automobiles, and, more recently in the Soviet Union, for certain economic offenses regarded as especially grave, such as illegal currency deals. The suppression of terrorism or, at least, of what passes as such also creates a serious problem for certain countries or at certain times in deciding what acts should be punished by death. The definition of capital crimes can thus vary both at the legislative and the judicial levels, and these differences can defy an analysis which is focused on the legal texts or on the data of criminal statistics alone.

These different aspects of the matter would really require long explanations, but in concluding this discussion of the present status of the problem I shall limit myself to three remarks, based on my previous observations, but requiring, in my opinion, more specific formulation.

First of all, even though the catalogue of capital crimes is difficult to establish with precision, it is certain that its recent development is marked, in a rather large number of countries, by a curious movement to revive or extend the death penalty to cases other than those to which the legislation of the liberal era had confined it. We have noted that the 19th century tried to reserve the supreme penalty for particularly serious cases of murder. The Anglo-American division of murder into capital and non-capital (or murder in the first and the second degree) was but one manifestation of this legislative movement. Now, the troubles that followed two world wars—economic crises, uneasiness of mind, the appearance of certain new forms of criminality—have often led the legislator to restore the death penalty for crimes which do not necessarily imply danger to human life; the most recent economic legislation of the East European countries and especially of the Soviet Union testifies to this fact.[21] One is therefore tempted to wonder if, by a curious paradox, the death penalty, which is seeing its traditional domain—murder—being more and more narrowed, may not be finding an expanded domain by a return to the system which in earlier days punished such crimes as burglary or counterfeiting with death.

This word "counterfeiting" leads us by a natural transition to our second observation. We know that in almost all abolitionist countries the death penalty has been kept for military crimes in wartime. Now, the difference between wartime and peacetime seems to be fading away somewhat: witness the practices of not only the "cold war" but of certain external and internal wars which are not officially called wars. Decolonization has furnished sad examples of this. Furthermore, parallel with this the difference between political crime and common law crime is equally fading. One is then led to think that in many countries, notably but not exclusively in those of Eastern Europe, one can be virtually in a state of war while at the same time conserving the economic and legal regime of a time of peace; that, besides, the enemy within is no less dangerous than the enemy without and that the same means of defense should be used toward him. Now, the external enemy is in wartime normally marked for death. Finding oneself in a condition resembling wartime, it is then easy to apply the same system to the "enemy within."

The re-introduction of the death penalty in France in 1960 for political crimes was evidently inspired by this kind of thinking. Theoretically it finds its justification in the special legislation governing states of emergency, national peril, or exceptional circumstances, whatever may be their official name. One can thus pass from a normal to an "exceptional" regime without disturbing the juridical equilibrium of times of peace. On the other hand, if one is ingenious enough in providing for a recourse to a "state of urgency," this suffices to re-introduce the death penalty even in the countries which are abolitionist *de jure;* this appears to be the actual aim today of a certain German doctrine.[22]

This movement of ideas, propagated today in certain groups and in various countries, ends rather curiously in a weakening of the contrast between abolitionist and retentionist camps. It can also be rather cleverly used to create a confusion by upholding an abolitionist position while in fact maintaining a regime where the death penalty would be retained—in reality retained in order to protect the political order established by the regime in power.

The dual evolution to which we have just called attention really tends to reduce the significance of earlier abolition, whether of crimes punishable by death or of the possibility of imposing a death sentence. Furthermore, this movement is often—especially in cases of emergency or peril—attended by a recourse to special courts and expeditious repressive procedures. The result is—and this is my last observation—that while the liberal law of the 19th century tended to increase the guarantees of the defense in capital cases, the modern trend instead consists in reducing the rights of the accused to a minimum in such cases in order to arrive as quickly as possible at executions meant to impress public opinion. Here the old concepts of intimidation and exemplarity are being upheld, but since the First World War, we have, as a matter of fact, been witnessing a new offensive by a criminal policy and almost by a mystique which do not fail to remind us of those

of the *ancien régime*. We are, in any case, in the presence of
a revival of the "reason of State" so clearly manifested by
special procedures which the men of 1789 wished to proscribe
by prohibiting the withholding of the citizen from his "natural
judge."

To me it seems necessary to keep in mind these different
traits of modern evolution if one is to think lucidly about the
future solution of the problem of the death penalty.

III

In order to simplify this aspect of the problem, one would
be tempted to say that it poses two questions: Where are we
coming from? and Where are we heading?

After what has been said earlier, the point of departure may
appear rather somber to the partisans of the abolitionist thesis.
The death penalty is still solidly ensconced in most criminal
legislations and seems even to be expanding through the in-
direct forms we have noted. Public opinion generally seems to
favor it, both in the countries using it and in some completely
abolitionist countries, such as federal Germany.[23] Finally, the
development during the last thirty years has seen the list of
capital crimes increase instead of diminish. The recourse to
the death penalty may have appeared, at certain moments
and in certain countries, as the great resource of threatened
governments, but sometimes it also provides an easy means
for journalists eager to tickle the instinct for vengeance and
the hidden taste for blood that lie dormant in many readers or
radio listeners.

Nevertheless, in spite of these outward appearances, one can
claim that the death penalty is on the defensive today. It is
so already, as we have seen, because of the exceptional character accorded to it nowadays by countries as different and as
clearly "users" as are the Soviet Union and Spain.[24] It is so
also in that people everywhere try to limit its application. Even
those who envisage its retention usually hasten to add that it
reaches actual execution only in extremely rare cases and
that numerous procedures exist to avoid the execution of the
condemned. The suppression of public executions, now the
rule in all civilized countries, is evidence enough that the

states using the death penalty are doubtless more concerned with the conviction than with the execution of the offender. One might ask oneself what the real moral value might be of this public vindictiveness that wants to be impressive but hides itself when it executes its task.

It is curious to note that for more than a century a rather strange reversal of ideological positions has recurred. During the romantic period, not Lamartine and Victor Hugo alone but even Charles Lucas were sentimentalists moved by a feeling of social pity. Partisans of the death penalty, in the tradition of Joseph de Maistre, portrayed themselves as the only ones having cool heads. Today, as Sir Ernest Gowers,[25] chairman of the English Royal Commission (of whom we know that although he was a partisan of the death penalty when he was appointed to that post he gradually became a convinced abolitionist as the work of the Commission progressed), has properly said, it is the "retentionists" who are carried away by a sentimental anger or a superstitious mysticism. That is why it is becoming more and more difficult to find speakers favoring the death penalty at round tables, colloquia, or discussions. Generally, the debates evoke the increasingly deep resonances of the abolition movement. It is not rare to find that in the course of a particular debate many participants reverse their original positions and finally join the abolitionist majority.[26]

Others are content to say that since the death penalty exists it should be retained, even though there may be doubts. This is precisely the position which seems to be most debatable, for if there *is* a doubt of the propriety of taking the life of a human being, can an actual execution be justified? Whatever the case may be, this doubt is widespread today in the sense that the basic and traditional justifications of the death penalty are now commonly rejected. Partisans of the death penalty no longer dare to invoke the idea of expiation, which may still have the support of a part of the population but which leads to the re-establishment of the punishments of the Middle Ages. All our civilization rejects this expiatory justice as it rejects that infamous and purely quantitative justice, the talion.

Retribution, often invoked, seems equally inadequate as justification. All present systems support—and properly so—a social disapproval of the offense committed. But it does not follow that the punishment should or even could consist of the taking of life. It has finally been realized that human justice is relative. Informed criminologists and penologists now teach that it is less important to strike blindly than to reform thoughtfully. The death penalty reforms no one.

Human justice is also relative in that, no matter what we do, a judicial error is always possible. It was in England that, as a consequence of some cases such as that of Evans-Christie, a sudden awareness of this possibility provoked the great movement of abolitionist opinion reflected in the vote in the House of Commons. Had an opinion poll been taken the day after Caryl Chessman's execution, the percentage of partisans of abolition, especially in France, would have been clearly in the majority.[27]

Of course, the idea of deterrence is also stressed; it would be absurd to deny this theory completely. But it is no less absurd and certainly risky to claim that deterrence operates in an absolute manner. The intimidating power of punishment is, everything considered, only a presumption, if not a mere hope, unless it be a fiction.[28] Here, too, modern criminal science recognizes relativity. We know that criminal statistics and criminological research on the evolution of criminality demonstrate that the abolition of the death penalty has never brought about an increase in crime. Thorsten Sellin, specialist in such matters, thinks that changes in criminogenic factors have no direct or even apparent relationship to the presence or absence of the death penalty.[29] Besides, criminal psychology leads us to believe that intimidation particularly influences the calculating offender but is practically ineffective on the murderer and still less on the "terrorist" who willingly accepts the risk or even finds in such risk an additional reason and a justification for his deed.

Furthermore, when we begin to reflect on it we cannot fail to note that retribution and intimidation, which partisans of the death penalty invoke simultaneously, are really contradictory. One pretends, in fact, to punish certain serious criminals by death because such a punishment would be "just," and at the same time one says that other offenders should be executed in order to deter potential criminals. Sir Lionel Fox liked to refer to the formula of an English 18th-century judge who told the defendant at the bar that "you are to be hanged, not because you have stolen a sheep but in order that others may not steal sheep."[30] In such a case intimidation is no longer retributive and hence, whether one likes it or not, it is unjust. If we take a closer look, however, what is really deterrent in the death penalty if not its execution, which is to serve as an example? Can this truly be a justice that satisfies our modern conscience and can we, then, keep talking about punishment proportioned to the crime?

Finally, we must not forget that many criminologists and penologists have stressed the criminogenic nature of the death penalty, which lowers public respect for human life. It may even constitute a morbid stimulus to crime. Many criminal justice specialists, at any rate, stress in their turn the deleterious and demoralizing character of capital punishment both on the public in general and on the administration of justice itself. It disturbs the serenity and objectivity of the trial, which it causes to degenerate into a kind of macabre game with the life of an individual as its stake.[31]

Prison administrators have often shown how the death penalty deteriorates the prison atmosphere, whether staff or inmates are in question. Modern correctional procedure today . . . tries not to cause the offender suffering or humiliation or to eliminate him but to reclaim him. Pope John XXIII personally proclaimed the importance and necessity of the "social reintegration" of the offender.[32] In this concept of punishment, where the relative character of the sanction serves as the starting point for a differentiated process of re-socialization,[33] what could be the justification and even the practical utility of the death penalty?

The great Swedish penal reformer, Karl Schlyter, resolute adversary of the death penalty, tried to promote a "protective criminal law" and this is, as we know, the deep meaning of the modern social defense movement.[34] Even though society is necessary to man, it is created by him and for him, not against him. It should no doubt defend itself but it is not scientifically proved that it should do so by means of the death penalty, and from an ethical point of view it is more than doubtful that it could do so.

Such is the meaning of modern socio-penal humanism, which emphasizes the eminent dignity of man as an irreplaceable individual. Therefore it highlights the irreducible ignominy of the execution, whatever its method. This social humanism refuses, as Albert Camus proclaimed, to grant a deified society, i.e., the State or its representatives, a right over the life and death of it citizens that would be justifiable only in the ritual killings of primitive societies.[35]

All these ideas explain the revival and the vitality of the present abolitionist movement. Can we then conclude that, barring inhuman catastrophes or antihumanist revolutions, we are logically and necessarily moving toward the suppression of the death penalty? I would personally be rather tempted to think so, in spite of the obstacles of the present and in spite of the fact that the effort is being made to raise two final barriers to a definitive abolition of capital punishment.

The first barrier is the incontestable difficulty of planning an adequate substitute penalty. There is no time here to deal with this difficult problem in its entirety. At the start of the 19th century one sought to solve it by a grading of prison sentences, the most serious of which took on a frightful aspect. Does the movement to unify punishments of imprisonment that characterizes the penology of the 20th century really complicate the question of a penal substitute? We do not believe it, because the logic of penal imprisonment in its modern connotation requires it to be re-educational, not perpetual. One convicted of a crime once capital should not, in an abolitionist regime, lose all hope of some day regaining freedom, but this does not mean that he should be set at liberty after a brief time and that no precautions should be taken before his release. An offender is, from many points of view, accountable to society not for his crime alone but also for his dangerousness, and the problem no doubt consists first in preventing the one "condemned to death" from being freed, in some way or other, of all debts and impediments too quickly from the public's point of view.[36]

Partisans of a humane criminal policy do not forget, besides, that there exist "social misfits," and that some persons are socially unadjustable. They only deny that this justifies their being put to death because, in so doing, society would not be punishing their crimes but would only be trying to defend itself by means worthy, at most, of primitive communities or Nazi regimes.

The second and last barrier facing the modern abolitionist movement is that of the *special case* for which people say that the death penalty should be reserved, just as Beccaria once claimed. In this connection, we must make an essential distinction.

From an historical and sociological point of view it is incontestable that when certain peculiar circumstances appear they fatally produce the re-establishment or the expansion of the death penalty. But the problem is to decide if this fact is enough to furnish an ethical-social justification for using the death penalty under normal conditions. Can one claim that the anticipation of such special cases is so difficult that a rather selective use of the death penalty is justifiable? We cannot but wonder, recalling what has already been said about certain recent currents of thought, if this is not a covert attempt to retain or re-introduce the death penalty behind the mask of a hypocritical and officially confirmed abolition. Whether one wants to or not, one has to take one's stand on the principle involved.

We must be allowed to think that there is something of a contradiction in wanting to transform an exception into a general norm: exceptional conditions or states cannot become the habitual rule. As for the "exceptional offender," retentionists invoke him, too, from Landru to Eichmann. Thus, people talk of keeping the death penalty at least for social monsters or for crimes against humanity. Society would then act in self-defense and remove these persons as it would dangerous beasts. It is nice to know that those who advocate this theory invoke Saint Thomas Aquinas, Jean-Jacques Rousseau, and Lombroso at the same time.

Here, too, one can join Albert Camus, who frankly raised this very objection, in responding that science has not yet established the existence of such a "social monster." Besides, assuming he did exist, who would decide it? The jury on the basis of an impression? The special judges on the basis of the particular conception they would have of their duties? Experts? Whether or not one wants it, does not the taking of this road mean the admission that some human beings do not have the right to live or may have the right withdrawn from them? Here one approaches some of the worst ideas of totalitarian eugenicism or that presupposed selective racism which the Hitlerian regime propounded. We know to what use it was put. In such a system, an all-powerful state arrogates to itself the ultimate power to decide, under the cover of pseudo-scientific claims, what persons will have the right to live. It is easy to imagine to whom some regimes would be tempted to apply this intolerance and against whom they would employ this right of extermination.

In a world pretending to be humane and to believe in universal human rights, the first right of a person is the right to life that society should guarantee him. Therefore, the first duty of the state is to abstain from killing.

EDITORIAL POSTSCRIPT

Since Justice Ancel wrote his article important changes have occurred. The most significant is the action of the British Parliament in 1965 to abolish the death penalty for murder. Furthermore, the changes in the United States mentioned in later articles in this volume should be recalled here, namely, the abolition laws adopted by Iowa, Oregon, and West Virginia and the nearly total abolition of the death penalty by New York and Vermont. A reasonably complete picture of the present status of the death penalty in the world is found in an article by Clarence H. Patrick, "The Status of Capital Punishment: A World Perspective," published in the Journal of Criminal Law, Criminology and Police Science, *56:397–411, December, 1965. (See also the Selected Bibliography at the end of this book.)*

A Survey of Capital Offenses

ROBERT H. FINKEL

Whether capital punishment exists within a jurisdiction and whether any particular offense is a capital crime, there are, in the first instance, legislative decisions.[1] The current state of the legislative will is contained in statute books. This article reports the results of a survey of the statutes of 54 American jurisdictions[2] as of June 30, 1966—which jurisdictions retain capital punishment, the number and types of offenses so punishable, and some aspects of the execution of the death penalty.

THE ABOLITIONIST JURISDICTIONS

There are eleven jurisdictions in which execution is not an available punishment at all: Alaska, Hawaii, Iowa, Maine, Michigan, Minnesota, Oregon, Puerto Rico, the Virgin Islands, West Virginia, and Wisconsin. There is no apparent common denominator to explain why these particular jurisdictions should be abolitionist. Geographically, an interesting pattern appears: both extra-continental Pacific state jurisdictions are abolitionist; similarly, both extra-continental Atlantic territorial jurisdictions are abolitionist; finally, four abolitionist continental state jurisdictions are contiguously located in the North Central part of the country.[3] The nature of the respective populations and the dates of abolition however, differ widely among these eleven jurisdictions.

New York, North Dakota, Rhode Island, and Vermont are generally considered abolitionist states too, although North Dakota has retained the death penalty for treason and for first-degree murder committed by a prisoner serving a life sentence for first-degree murder, and Rhode Island has kept a mandatory death penalty for a prisoner who commits murder while serving a life sentence for any offense. In 1965, New York abolished capital punishment except for someone convicted of killing a peace officer acting in line of duty and for a life convict who murders a guard or inmate in prison or while attempting to escape.[4] The same year Vermont abandoned the death penalty except for treason, kidnapping for ransom, and for those who have been convicted of murder in the first degree and commit a second "unrelated" murder and for those convicts who murder any employee of the state prison or house of correction or a person known by the offender to be a law-enforcement officer performing the duties of his office.

DESCRIPTION OF OFFENSES

The crimes punishable by death can be divided generally into four categories: (1) crimes against government; (2) crimes against property; (3) crimes against the person; (4) miscellaneous crimes.

A statute may provide that anyone who commits an act shall be deemed guilty of having committed murder in the first degree and shall be punished accordingly. This is a form of "imputed murder," since the statute must be read back through the murder statute for the penalty provision. There are such statutes in almost every capital jurisdiction and for various offenses. In the accompanying table and in the text following, all such statutes will be reported in the category or column, if any, which defines the act and not as murder. If there is no such column, they will be reported as "other offenses."

Crimes Against Government

Only two crimes are in this category: treason and perjury. Treason is the act of levying war against the government of a jurisdiction or of giving aid and comfort to its enemies. Twenty jurisdictions punish treason with death.[5] Twelve of them demand death on conviction—there is no alternative sentence. This places treason third in the rank order of offenses

A short or a long...

...without serving a life sentence for any offense. In 1960, New York abolished capital punishment except in cases of murder committed by a prisoner serving a life sentence and for a person who murders a peace officer who is acting in the line of his duty, in either case while such officer is attempting to make an arrest. The death penalty, in the same way, is without application to those who are guilty of murder by poisoning, and for those who have been convicted of murder in the third degree, and one of a second and later murder; and further, convicts may murder any employee of the state prison, a peace officer, or a prison keeper, by the effort to be held liable for the capital offense.

DISTRIBUTION OF OFFENSES

The crimes punishable by death can be divided naturally into two parts: (1) those against a particular person or crime applied generally, (2) crimes against the state...

A statute may provide that a person who commits murder shall be deemed guilty of murder, whereby... rape in the first degree, and that an unlawful act against... the whole... In a similar manner, kidnapping, rape, and other crimes against the state carry the death penalty...

Central Federal Government

Only two crimes are punishable by death, treason and murder. Treason is the only crime for which the government of the United States... Two crimes... of the third degree... punishable by death... no alternative sentence. If a prisoner found guilty of a crime or offense...

Offenses Punishable by Death—United States, 1966

Jurisdiction	Number offenses	Number mandatory	Murder	Kidnapping	Rape	Dueling	Lifer-assault	Robbery	Explosives	Attempt on executive	Lynching	Assault intent rape	Burglary	Arson	Trainwrecking	Perjury	Treason	Other offenses[b]
Alabama	16	1	1	2	4		1[a]	2	1				1	2			2[a]	
Arizona	7	3	1	1			1[a]	1						1	1	1[a]	1[a]	2
Arkansas	11	1	1	1	2	1			1					1	1	1[a]	1	
California	6	4	1	1[a]	1		1[a]	1	1	1[a]					1[a]		1[a]	4
Colorado	5	2	1	1	1	1	1[a]		2									
Connecticut	6	2	1[a]	1	1				3	1				1	1		1[a]	1
Delaware	3		1	1	1													
District of Columbia	3		1	1	1													
Federal	13	3	1	1	2	1[a]		1		1	1			6	1	1	1	5
Florida	7	3	1	1	1	1		1	2						2		1	
Georgia	21	1	1[a]	1	1	1		1	3			1		6	1	2	1	
Idaho	3	1	1	1	1												1	
Illinois	3	1	1	1	1													
Indiana	7		1	1	2			2							1		1	
Kansas	5	1	1	1	1												1	
Kentucky	12	1	1[a]	1[a]	3		1[a]	2	1		1	1				1	1[a]	2
Louisiana	4	4	1[a]	1[a]	1[a]							1					1[a]	

State														
Mississippi	7	1	1	1	1	1		2		1				1ᵃ
Missouri	6	1	1	1	1	1		1			1	1ᵃ		1
Montana	4	3	1		1						1ᵃ	1ᵃ	1	1ᵃ
Nebraska	4		1	1	1							1		1
Nevada	7	1	1	1	1		1				1	1	1ᵃ	1
New Hampshire	1	1	1											
New Jersey	4	1	1	1			1							1ᵃ
New Mexico	2		1	1										
New York	2	1		1					1					1
North Carolina	5	1	1	1		1				1	1	1ᵃ		
North Dakota	2	1			1ᵃ									1
Ohio	8	2	1	2	1	2ᵃ				1				1
Oklahoma	5	1	1	1		1				1				
Pennsylvania	3		1	1	1					1				
Rhode Island	1	1			1ᵃ									
South Carolina	8	1	1	1		1	1							2
South Dakota	3	1	1	1			1							1
Tennessee	7	1	1	4										1
Texas	14	1	1	1	1	1	1	1	1	3	1ᵃ		1	2
Utah	4	1	1	1	1			1						
Vermont	3	1	1	1									1ᵃ	1
Virginia	13	1	1	1	1	1	1	2		2	2		1ᵃ	1
Washington	3	1	1	1			1			1	1		1ᵃ	1ᵃ
Wyoming	6	1	2	2	2									1

ᵃ Mandatory sentence.
ᵇ See text for enumeration.

punishable by death and first in the rank order of mandatory sentences. There is grave doubt, however, as to whether anyone *can* commit an act of *war* against a state or territorial jurisdiction. The treason statutes of some jurisdictions (e.g., Arizona and Louisiana) on their face apply to acts of war against the United States as well as the legislating jurisdiction. However, this would certainly be an area in which there would be no concurrent jurisdiction but where Federal law would "pre-empt the field."[6]

Capital perjury is generally the act of giving false testimony under oath which causes the conviction and execution of an innocent person. Eleven jurisdictions punish this act, six mandatorily.[7] This places perjury seventh in the rank order of offenses and second in the rank order of mandatory sentences.

Crimes Against Property

Within this category there are three crimes: trainwrecking, arson, and burglary.

Trainwrecking is generally any act, such as tampering with switches or signals or burning trestles, intended to derail a train. In most jurisdictions the offense becomes capital only if someone dies as a result of the derailment. Eighteen jurisdictions provide the death penalty for trainwrecking; three of them make death mandatory.[8] Train wrecking therefore ranks fifth in offenses and fourth in mandatory sentences.

Arson is simply the willful and malicious burning of the building of another, although the crime can be arbitrarily divided into separate offenses by specifying dwelling houses, business properties, farmhouses, etc. Georgia, for example, has six arson statutes—all making arson a capital crime. Four jurisdictions make arson imputed murder if death occurs as a result.[9] Arson is ninth in the rank order of offenses, with nine jurisdictions punishing it.[10] There are no mandatory jurisdictions.

Burglary is a crime with widely varying definitions. The most restrictive is that of the common law: burglary is the act of breaking into and entering the dwelling house of another in the nighttime with intent to commit another felony therein.

The various jurisdictions have omitted this or that element in arriving at a definition.[11] The second felony need not be completed, or even started, so long as it can be proven to have been intended. As a practical matter, where there is no completed act this is proven by inference from the manner of entry and the like. Only three states make burglary a capital crime,[12] and none specifies a mandatory death sentence. This places burglary last in the rank order of offenses punished by more than one state.

Crimes Against the Person

These are the most obvious capital crimes—the crimes of violence. Ten of them will be discussed in this section.

First is murder. Most of the murder statutes in the United States, capital and non-capital, are patterned after the Pennsylvania statute. This statute is divided into three sections: (1) the acts which by their nature must be killings planned in advance, such as "by poison or lying in wait";[13] (2) the general provision against any "willful, deliberate, malicious and premeditated killing"; (3) the so-called "felony murder" provision. On reasoning similar to that used in the first section it is thought that certain crimes are highly likely to result in personal injury and perhaps death, as, for example, when a man goes out armed to rob another. Given the high probability of death, it is felt that when one intends to commit one of these acts and death does occur, no matter how accidentally, he should be held liable for murder. The technical legal explanation is that the intent to commit the original act is "transferred" over to the intent to commit murder. The "high probability" crimes in Pennsylvania are: "arson, rape, robbery, burglary or kidnapping."[14] One might expect that if any crime is to be capital, murder should be, and that all of the 43 capital jurisdictions would so punish it. Actually, only 39 do so generally.[15] On the other hand, only two jurisdictions provide a mandatory sentence.[16] Murder is therefore first in the rank of offenses but only fifth in the rank of mandatories.

Kidnapping involves the carrying away of any person, without color of right, and with intent to detain that person. Capital kidnapping generally involves the additional elements that the detention is for the purpose of extorting a ransom for the return of the victim and that he suffers injury or death while so detained. Thirty-five jurisdictions punish kidnapping with death, two mandatorily.[17] Kidnapping is thus second in the rank of offenses and sixth in the mandatory rank.

Rape is the "forcible carnal knowledge" of a woman above the age of consent and against her will. It is a capital crime in 18 jurisdictions and carries a mandatory death sentence in one of them.[18] Rape is fourth in the rank order of offenses and eighth or last in the mandatory rank.

Dueling as a method of solving personal disputes presumably ceased long ago. As a crime it is capital in 13 jurisdictions,[19] in 12 of them as imputed murder.[20] This anachronistic crime, therefore, stands sixth in the rank of offenses. There are no mandatory jurisdictions. No better example could be found for the proposition that the criminal statutes, orphans of legislation, need review and revision.

Assault by a life prisoner has already been mentioned briefly. Generally, this crime requires either the presence of a dangerous weapon or the result of great bodily injury or death to the person assaulted. Ten jurisdictions punish "life-assault" by death, of which six require a mandatory sentence.[21] It is eighth in the ranking of offenses and third in the ranking of mandatory sentences.

Robbery is the taking of goods from the person or the presence of another by force or fear. Capital robbery generally requires the aggravating circumstance of a dangerous weapon or, in the case of the Federal government, robbery of a bank. Robbery is capital in eight jurisdictions[22] but nowhere exclusively punished by death. It is tenth in the rank order of offenses.

There are a number of statutes whose central core deals with the willful mismanagement of explosives and bombs, causing death or the substantial probability of serious injury. Many of these, for example, deal with bombs placed or carried into public buildings or onto public conveyances. There are eight punishing jurisdictions, none with mandatory provisions.[23] Explosives offenses stand eleventh in the ranking of offenses.

Two types of offenses are listed here as "attempts on an executive." First, two state jurisdictions provide that a mere *attempt* is a capital crime: Connecticut requires a mandatory death sentence for assault on the President of the United States or a foreign ambassador. New Jersey's statute is not mandatory but extends to the presidential line of succession and the governors of the various states. Second, two jurisdictions provide the capital penalty only for *completed* assassinations: Ohio's statute is mandatory and covers the same persons as New Jersey's. The Federal statute is not mandatory; moreover, it does not protect the state governors. With four possible executing jurisdictions for this crime,[24] it comes twelfth in the ranking of offenses. With two mandatory jurisdictions it places seventh in that ranking.

Lynching is punishable by death in four Southern states.[25] It is perhaps appropriate at this point to remind the reader that the mere existence of a statute says nothing about the extent of its utilization or, if used, about the fairness and indiscriminate nature of that use. So far as the statutes can carry us, however, lynching is thirteenth in the rank order of offenses, with no mandatory jurisdictions.

Assault is simply any willful act that places another in fear of a wrongful touching or battery or injury. Simple assault is supplemented in many jurisdictions by the addition of elements of specific intent. This produces crimes such as assault *with intent to rob*, assault *with intent to kill*, etc. Four jurisdictions make assault with intent to ravish or rape a capital crime.[26] This places it fourteenth, or next to last, in the rank order of offenses. No jurisdictions demand a mandatory sentence.

Miscellaneous Crimes

These are crimes which are declared capital in only one jurisdiction. Since any attempt to rank them would have to be purely arbitrary, they have been included in this section, where they are merely listed by the jurisdictions which punish them. In the table they are placed in the column headed "other offenses."

Arkansas: aiding in suicide; causing a boat collision resulting in death (similar to trainwrecking); injury or alarm causing death by night-riders; forced marriage.[27]

Colorado: procuring an abortion resulting in the death of the mother.

Delaware: showing false lights causing a boat collision and death.[28]

Federal: espionage; piracy of an aircraft; violation of specific sections of the Atomic Energy Act (relating to unauthorized dealings with foreign governments, atomic weapons, and licenses for radioactive materials) with intent to injure the United States; communication of restricted data with intent to injure the United States; tampering with restricted data (no intent required).

Georgia: castrating another while fighting or otherwise; possessing or controlling a poisonous snake in a manner endangering public health and safety, if death ensues.

Kentucky: homicide during criminal syndicalism, if the violence *contributes* to the death; homicide from road obstruction (similar to trainwrecking).

Nevada: assault with intent to commit murder, sodomy, mayhem, robbery, grand larceny, or with extreme cruelty and great bodily injury.

Ohio: convict (not necessarily a lifer) killing a guard or officer.

South Carolina: killing by poison; killing by stabbing.[29]

South Dakota: child-molesting resulting in death.

Tennessee: killing an arresting officer.

Texas: abortion resulting in the death of the mother; poisoning (separate statute).

Virginia: throwing stones, shooting, etc., at a vehicle or railroad car, if death results.

Wyoming: conspiracy to kidnap for ransom.

CONCLUSION

We have seen that a great many kinds of criminal conduct are punishable by death in the United States. What the law permits, however, is not always utilized by the courts or the executive authorities. In the last 36 years, executions have occurred mostly for murder or rape, together with a relatively small number of executions for armed robbery, kidnapping, burglary, aggravated assault, and espionage. The law providing death for all other offenses may be regarded as fallen into disuse so far as that penalty is concerned.

Executions in the United States

THORSTEN SELLIN

Accurate national statistics on executions in the United States are available from 1930, when the Bureau of the Census began to compile them from death certificates supplied to its division of vital statistics. Since 1946, the Federal Bureau of Prisons in the Department of Justice has undertaken the task and publishes an annual bulletin devoted entirely to data on executions. The latest of these publications (National Prisoner Statistics, Number 39, June, 1966, *Executions, 1930–1965*) is the source for the information here presented.

At the beginning of the 36-year period, the death penalty existed in Federal law and in all states but Maine, Wisconsin, Minnesota, Kansas, and South Dakota. Michigan and North Dakota had retained it for treason, and North Dakota and Rhode Island for murder committed by a prisoner serving a life sentence. Kansas and South Dakota re-introduced the death penalty in 1935 and 1939, respectively. In 1957, Alaska, Delaware, and Hawaii abolished it, but Delaware restored it in 1961. In 1963, Michigan abolished it for treason. In 1964, capital punishment was stricken from the law of Oregon and in 1965 from the laws of Iowa and West Virginia. Vermont also removed it in 1965 for murder except for a second unrelated murder or the murder of a police officer or prison official on duty. The same year New York joined the abolitionist

Executions Under Civil Authority—United States, by State and Year, 1930–1965

Region and State	Total	1965	1964	1963	1962	1961	1960	1950–59	1940–49	1930–39
United States	3856	7	15	21	47	42	56	717	1284	1667
Federal	33			1				9	13	10
States	3823	7	15	20	47	42	56	708	1271	1657
Northeast	608			3	4	3	7	107	184	300
New Hampshire	1									1
Vermont	4							2	1	1
Massachusetts	27								9	18
Connecticut	21						1	5	10	5
New York	329			2	2		6	52	114	153
New Jersey	74				2	1		17	14	40
Pennsylvania	152			1		2		31	36	82
North Central	403	5	2	3	7	2	2	58	106	155
Ohio	172			2	2	1	2	32	51	82
Indiana	41					1		2	7	31
Illinois	90				2			9	18	61
Iowa	18				2			1	7	8
Missouri	62	1	2	1				7	15	36
South Dakota	4							1	1	2
Nebraska	4							2	2	
Kansas	15	4			1			5		
South	2305	1	12	10	22	26	32	427	832	943
Delaware	12								4	8
Maryland	68					1		6	45	16
Dist. of Columbia	40							4	16	20

State	Total									
Virginia	92				1		1	23	35	28
West Virginia	40					4		9	11	20
North Carolina	263							19	112	131
South Carolina	162			2	2	1	1	26	61	67
Georgia	366		2	1	1	5	6	85	130	137
Florida	170		2		5	3	2	49	65	44
Kentucky	103				1	2		16	34	52
Tennessee	93		1				1	8	37	47
Alabama	135	1	1	2	1	1	1	20	50	60
Mississippi	154		1		1	5	1	36	60	48
Arkansas	118						8	18	38	53
Louisiana	133					1		27	47	58
Oklahoma	59			1	1		3	7	13	34
Texas	297		5	4	9	3	8	74	74	120
West	507	1	1	4	14	11	15	116	149	196
Montana	6								1	5
Idaho	3							3		
Wyoming	7								2	4
Colorado	46				2		1	3	13	25
New Mexico	8						1	3	2	2
Arizona	38			2		1	1	8	9	17
Utah	13						1	6	4	2
Nevada	29						1	9	10	8
Washington	47					1	1	6	16	23
Oregon	19			1			1	4	12	2
California	291	1	1	1	11	8	9	74	80	108

ranks but conserved the penalty for the murder of a policeman on duty or the murder of a prison guard by a prisoner
serving a life sentence for murder. During the period being
surveyed, the number of retentionist states has consequently
been reduced from 40 to 37. Alaska and Hawaii entered
the Union in 1959; therefore, there are now thirteen abolitionist states, compared with eight in 1930. In addition,
Puerto Rico and the Virgin Islands have abandoned the
death penalty.

The number and the trend of executions in the United
States are shown in the table. An annual average of 167 persons was executed in the 1930s. The corresponding figure for
1960–1965 is 32, but an inspection of the table shows a drop
from 56 executions in 1960 to 7 in 1965. Over the years the
most remarkable drop is found in the Southern states. Some
of the general decline is probably due to a considerable reduction in homicide rates, but their downward trend is relatively mild compared with the trend in executions, which
seems largely to be due to an increasing reluctance to employ the death penalty.

In addition to the 33 executions of Federal civil prisoners,
160 executions, not included in the table, were carried out
by the Army (including the Air Force), all but 12 during the
period 1942–1950. Eighty-five of these penalties were for
murder, 21 for rape murders, 53 for rape, and 1 for deser-
tion.[1] The Navy has executed no one since 1849.

The Offenses Involved. Most of the executions—3,332—
were for murder. There were 455 executions for rape and 69
for other crimes. Except for 10 cases in Missouri, all the
executions for rape took place in the Southern states. The
miscellaneous group included 24 cases of armed robbery, 20
of kidnapping, 11 of burglary, 6 of aggravated assault committed by prisoners serving life sentences; there were 8 Federal executions for espionage.

Racial Distribution. Half of those executed for murder, 49
percent, were Negroes, and so were the vast majority of
those executed for rape, 92 percent. A few members of other
races, 42 in all, were American Indians (19), Filipinos (13),
Chinese (8), and Japanese (2).

Women Executed. There were 32 women among those executed. All but two of them had been convicted of murder and 20 of them were white, the rest Negroes. Two Federal prisoners were executed, one for kidnapping and one for espionage.

Method of Execution. Twenty-one states and the District of Columbia used electric chairs in 1930, one used lethal gas (Nevada), one gave the prisoner a choice between hanging or firing squad (Utah), one used electrocution or, if the crime was rape, hanging (Kentucky), and 17 states and the Federal prisons used the gallows.

By 1965, considerable changes had occurred. Twenty-four states had installed electric chairs, eleven had gas chambers, and seven had gallowses. No change had been made by Utah, and since 1937 the Federal government had been using whatever method was applicable in the state in which the sentence was imposed. When Oregon, Iowa, and West Virginia became abolitionist states in 1965, the number of electric chairs, gas chambers, and gallowses was reduced by one each. Only New Hampshire, Kansas, Delaware, Montana, Idaho, and Washington have retained the once universally used method of hanging.

Death Row's Denizens. During the last six years, beginning with 1960, statistics show a steady increase of prisoners awaiting execution, while at the same time executions have become fewer and fewer. At the end of 1960 there were 210 persons on death row; this figure had risen to 331 at the end of 1965. Sixty-seven prisoners under sentence of death were admitted that year. The inference is clear that states with the death penalty may be willing to impose death sentences but are not willing to carry out these sentences. Avoidance is effected not so much by commutations of such sentences, which dropped from 22 in 1960 to 19 in 1965, as by appellate court actions that reverse judgments, vacate sentences, or grant new trials.

PART II

Movements of

Abolition

On the Penalty of Death

CESARE BECCARIA

. . . What can be the right which men claim to slaughter their fellows? Surely not the one from which sovereignty and laws arise. These are but the sum of the tiniest parts of each individual's personal liberty. They represent the common will which is the aggregate of individual wills. But whoever wanted to leave the option of killing him to others? How can the surrender of the smallest fraction of each person's liberty ever involve the greatest good of all, life itself? And were this done, how would such a principle be reconciled with the one that gives no man the right to take his own life? He ought to have that right if he has the power to give the right to kill him to others or to society as a whole.

The death penalty, consequently, is not a right, for I have shown that such it cannot be; it is a war of the nation against a citizen, whose destruction is judged to be necessary and useful. But I shall have won humanity's case if his death can be proved to be neither useful nor necessary.

The death of a citizen cannot be considered necessary except for two reasons. The first when he, although deprived of his freedom, still has such connections and power that the

Translation of Section XVI of the treatise *Dei delitti e delle pene*, originally published in 1764. The translation has been made from the edition reproduced on pp. 381–462 of Cesare Cantù's *Beccaria e il diritto penale*. 466 pp. Florence: Barbéra, 1862.

nation is concerned and his existence could produce a
dangerous revolution in the form of the established government. The death of some citizen may be necessary when
the nation recovers or loses its liberty or in times of anarchy
when disorders replace laws; but during the peaceful reign of
law under a form of government supported by the consensus
of national desires; well defended, internally and externally,
by force and by public opinion, which is perhaps more
potent than such force; when power rests only with the true
sovereign; when wealth buys enjoyment rather than patron-
age, I see no need to destroy a citizen unless his death were
the only real means of deterring others from committing crime.
This is the second reason why the death penalty might be
considered to be just and necessary.

If the experience of all the centuries during which the
ultimate penalty never has discouraged resolute men from
offending against society; if the example of the citizens of
Rome and of the twenty years of the reign of the Empress
Elizabeth of Muscovy—which gave heads of nations illustrious
lessons equivalent, at least, to many conquests bought by the
blood of a nation's sons—would not persuade people to whom
the language of reason is always suspect but the language of
authority persuasive, then an examination of the nature of
man will suffice for realizing the truth of my assertion.

It is not the intensity but the duration of punishment
which has the greatest effect upon man's mind, because our
sensitivity is affected more easily and permanently by small
but repeated impressions than by a strong but momentary
shock. Every sentient being is swayed by habit; by its aid
man speaks, moves, and satisfies his needs. Thus moral ideas
are implanted in his mind only through repeated and pro-
longed impressions. It is not the terrible but fleeting spectacle
of the execution of a scoundrel that is the strongest deterrent
to crime but rather the long and painful example of a man deprived of his freedom and become a beast of burden, repaying
with his toil the society he has offended. Because of its
constant recurrence this has an effect on us (*I myself will
be reduced to the same enduring and miserable state if I
were to commit similar misdeeds*) and a more powerful one

than the idea of death, which men always see in the dim future.

The death penalty makes an impression, the strength of which is promptly obliterated by a process natural to man even in most essential matters and hastened by his passions. Usually, violent passions seize men but not for long and are then apt to induce transformations which turn ordinary men into Persians or Spartans. But, in a free and peaceful nation, impressions should be frequent rather than strong.

For most people the death penalty becomes a spectacle and for some an object of compassion mixed with abhorrence. Both of these sentiments dominate the minds of the spectators more than the salutary terror which the law wants to inspire. But in moderate but continuous punishments the latter sentiment dominates because it is the only one. The limit which the legislator should set to the rigor of punishments seems to lie in the sentiment of compassion, at the point when this begins to prevail over other sentiments in the minds of the spectators of a punishment which is designed more for their profit than for the criminal.

In order that a punishment be just it should have only the degree of intensity sufficient to keep men from committing crimes. No one today, in contemplating it, would choose total and perpetual loss of his own freedom, no matter how profitable a crime might be. Therefore the intensity of the punishment of perpetual servitude as substitute for the death penalty possesses that which suffices to deter any determined soul. I say that it has more. Many look on death with a firm and calm regard—some from fanaticism, some from vanity which always accompanies man beyond the tomb, some in a last desperate attempt either to live no longer or to escape misery —but neither fanaticism nor vanity dwells among fetters and chains, under the rod, under the yoke or in an iron cage, when the evil-doer begins his sufferings instead of terminating them.

A mind is more resistant to violence and extreme but momentary pains than to time and incessant vexation because it can, so to speak, compress the former into a moment and instantly repel them, but the power of its elasticity does not suffice to resist the long and repeated effect of the latter. In the case of an execution a crime can furnish only one example to the nation, but in the case of perpetual penal servitude a single crime can provide numerous and lasting warnings. Were one to say that perpetual servitude is as painful as death and therefore equally cruel I would reply that, adding all the unhappy moments of servitude together, the former would be even worse, but these moments are scattered over a lifetime, while the death penalty expends its total influence in a single moment. That is the advantage of penal servitude; it frightens the one who observes it more than the one who undergoes it; the former thinks of the sum total of miserable moments, but the latter is distracted from thoughts of the future by his unhappiness in the present. All evils grow larger in the imagination; he who suffers them finds aid and consolation not known or imagined by the spectators, who substitute their own sensitivity for the calloused soul of the wretched prisoner.

A thief or a murderer who has nothing to weigh against the breaking of the law except the gallows or the wheel, reasons something like this (I know that putting one's own thought into words is an art taught by education, but though a thief might not know how to express his own principles well, they are no less forceful): "What are these laws that I should respect and that leave so great a gap between me and the rich man? He denies me the penny I beg of him and justifies himself by offering me work to which he is a stranger. Who has made these laws? Rich and powerful men who have always disdained to visit the squalid hovels of the poor and who have never sliced a moldy loaf amidst the innocent cries of famished children and the tears of a wife. Let us break these bonds, fatal to most people but useful to a few lazy tyrants; let us attack injustice at its source. I will return to my natural state of independence and live free and happy for a while on the fruits of my courage and my loot. If, by chance, the day of pain and reckoning arrives, it will be brief and I shall pay with one day of suffering for many years of freedom and pleasure. As head of a small gang I shall correct the errors of fortune and see these tyrants grow pale and tremble before me, whom they with insulting arrogance rated lower than their horses and dogs." Then the criminal, who abuses everything, remembers religion, which, by presenting him with easy repentence and an almost certain eternal bliss, greatly lessens the horror of the final tragedy.

But he who sees before him a great many years or even a lifetime passed in servitude and suffering before his fellow citizens with whom he is living free and sociably, subject to laws which protect him, makes a salutary comparison between all this and the uncertain success of his crimes and the brevity of the time during which he might enjoy their fruits. The constant example of those whom he actually sees to be victims of their own imprudence makes a much stronger impression on him than the spectacle of an execution which hardens rather than corrects him.

The example of atrocity that the death penalty presents to man does not make it useful. If passion or the necessity of war has taught the spilling of human blood, laws designed to temper human conduct should not enhance a savage example which is all the more baneful when the legally sanctioned death is inflicted deliberately and ceremoniously. To me it is an absurdity that the law which expresses the common will and detests and punishes homicide should itself commit one and, in order to keep citizens from committing murder, order a public one committed. What are the true and most useful laws? The covenants and conditions which all would wish observed and proposed, while the insistent voice of private interests is silent or merged with that of the public. What are people's ideas on the death penalty? We note them in the acts of indignation or scorn with which people look on the executioner, who is merely the innocent performer of the common will, a good citizen who contributes to the common welfare, a necessary instrument for public security at home just as brave soldiers are elsewhere. What is the origin of this contradiction? And why is this feeling, contrary to reason, indelible in man? Because in the most hidden recesses of his mind, that part of which more than every other still preserves the original character of his primitive nature, man has always believed that his own life was at nobody else's disposal save in the case of necessity which rules the universe with its iron scepter.

What might people think when they see learned magistrates and solemn ministers of justice, who with indifferent calm cause a criminal to be dragged to his death in a slow ceremony and while the poor wretch, in the convulsions of his last agony, awaits the fatal blow, with insensitive coldness and taking, perhaps, even a secret pleasure in their own authority, leave the scene to enjoy the comforts and pleasures of life? They will say: "These laws are only the cover for force and the studied and cruel ceremonials of justice are only a conventional language used in order to kill us in greater safety like victims marked for sacrifice to the insatiable idol of despotism. We see murder, which is preached to us as being a terrible misdeed, employed without repugnance and anger. Let us profit from the example. From the descriptions given us, violent death seemed to be a terrible event, but we see that it is just a moment's business. How much less terrible must it be for one who is not expecting it and is spared almost all of what it has of pain?"

Such are the fateful arguments which men disposed to commit crime make, if not clearly at least vaguely, men in whom, as we have noted, the abuse of religion, rather than religion proper, dominates.

If I were confronted with the argument that almost all centuries and almost all nations have provided the death penalty for some crimes, my reply would be that the argument fails when faced with truth which knows no statute of limitation. The history of man appears to us as an immense ocean of errors among which there float a few scattered truths far apart from each other. Human sacrifice was common in almost all nations, but who dares to defend it for that reason? That a few rare societies have abstained, if only briefly, from executions rather favors my argument than otherwise, because this agrees with the fate of all great truths, the duration of which is but a flash compared with the long dark night which envelops mankind. That happy era has not yet arrived in which truth will belong to the majority, as error has hitherto done universally, save only those truths which an infinite wisdom has wished by revelation to set apart from the rest. . . .

Beccaria made no mention of the irreparable nature of capital punishment when he presented his arguments for its abolition. This omission was corrected later. In 1790 he was appointed member of a commission to revise the penal code of Austrian Lombardy, and in a minority report signed by him and two other members we find the following statement:

"Finally, we claim that in view of the inevitable imperfection of human proof the death penalty is inappropriate because it is irreparable. Even if it were just, even if it were the most effective of all penalties, it would, in order to be justly applied to a criminal, have to be proved to be so in a way that would exclude the contrary. This is manifestly due to the irreparable nature of the punishment. If that proof were now required for sentencing a criminal, there would never be a case in which this penalty would be executed. Nor can it be said that it might be expedient to leave it in the law as a threat to inspire terror, for if it is not in fact executed it loses the great effect of an example, which consists in the inevitability of the punishment; thus it also weakens the force of other penal laws. This fact and the study of legislations therefore show that adequate proof for imposing a death sentence on a criminal has never been such as to exclude this contrary possibility: hence, neither testimony, even by two witnesses, nor circumstantial evidence, even when accompanied by the criminal's confession, can establish complete moral certainty, for such evidence, upon examination, presents only high probability and nothing more. In almost all nations there are known cases of presumed criminals, who were sentenced to die on evidence supposed to be incontrovertible. We do not accuse their judges of arrogance, negligence or evil intent but rather the imperfection of the laws. Every time these practically inevitable errors

of the courts have come to public notice, time having brought to light the innocence of the defendants, the event has been regarded as a public scandal and the judges have become the victims of public execration due to no fault of their own. Faced, then, with the necessity of imposing sentence while guided by the often dim light of moral certainty, there is no comparison between a punishment which can be in some measure modified during the criminal's life and the penalty of death, which is irreparable once inflicted."[1]

An Ancient Debate on
Capital Punishment

WILLIAM McALLEN GREEN

An interesting feature of the later period of the Roman Republic is the practical discontinuance of the death penalty. Proscriptions might be carried out in a wholesale fashion or political offenders executed under such extraordinary grants of powers as Cicero exercised in dealing with the accomplices of Catiline, but of executions in the regular course of judicial procedure we have no record after that of Manlius, 384 B.C.[1] Polybius declares of the Romans of his day that "whenever those on trial for their lives are convicted, their custom gives them the right to depart openly as long as a single tribe of those that are confirming the verdict is still left to vote."

Reprinted, by permission, from *The Classical Journal*, 24:267–275, January, 1929. A few passages in Latin in the original article have, with the author's permission, been rendered in English. The translations are from the Loeb Classical Library editions, *Sallust* (by J. C. Rolfe) and *The Speeches of Cicero* (by Louis E. Lord), Cambridge: Harvard University Press, 1921 and 1959, respectively.

This practical abandonment of the death penalty seems to have been confirmed by the *lex Porcia* and other laws which specifically forbade the execution of Roman citizens, at least without special authorization of the people.[2]

The causes of such an important change in the penal practice of the Romans must be of interest to us today, especially in view of the fact that many modern states have already abolished, or are considering the abolition of, the death penalty.

Some of the leading modern writers on Roman law have been inclined to view the disappearance of capital punishment in Rome as a mere accident in the development of their legal procedure. Maine says:

The disappearance of the punishment of death from the penal system of Republican Rome used to be a favorite topic with the writers of the last [*i.e.*, eighteenth] century, who were perpetually using it to point some theory of Roman character, or of modern social economy. The reason which can be confidently assigned for it stamps it as purely fortuitous.

He then argues that the *quaestiones perpetuae*, which came to be the regular criminal courts, derived their authority from the *comitia tributa*, which could not punish a criminal with death nor delegate that power to the courts. Hence the death penalty simply lapsed by non-use.[3]

Mommsen's comment on the abolition of capital punishment is that "two institutions chiefly brought this about—self-banishment or exile, and the procedure of the *quaestiones*."[4]

Strachan-Davidson would have the outcome an equally undesigned result of the machinery of appeal. He dismisses the "fanciful explanations" of Maine and others and continues:

The true solution is to be found, I am convinced, simply in the reason alleged for the arrest of Kaeso Quinctius, namely, that, unless he were arrested, there was nothing to prevent the accused from running away; and that previous arrest became by the abuse of the tribunician *auxilium* so difficult, that the obstacle to departure was practically never interposed. With a people like the Romans it is only a step from this practice to the doctrine that the criminal has a right to evasion, and so the result of the *leges Porciae* and the other laws . . . is, as Sallust says, *condemnatis civibus non animam eripi sed auxilium permitti.*[5]

That a people like the Romans—or any other practical people—should have abandoned capital punishment by pure accident and then afterwards have passed laws simply to confirm the outcome, would seem to imply a surprising lack of attention or control in the development of their system of law. But, on the contrary, the Romans are distinguished for their careful attention to the organization and improvement of the law. Cicero, in fact, points to this very matter of the abolition of the death penalty as an intentional and praiseworthy achievement:

> What could I more desire than that in my consulship I had removed the executioner from the Forum, the cross from the Campus? But that praise, Quirites, belongs first to our ancestors, who, when they drove out the kings, kept no trace of royal cruelty among a free people; then to the many brave men who willed that your liberty should not be menaced by harshness of punishments but protected by the mildness of the laws.[6]

The record preserved of the debate as to the punishment of the Catilinarian conspirators shows that the question of the death penalty was fully discussed in ancient Rome, as it is in modern America.

Lentulus and a few others of Catiline's agents had been arrested and confronted with evidence of their conspiracy to overthrow the government, organize slave insurrections, summon barbarian aid, seize the property of the rich, and give the city to flames. They had confessed, and Cicero had proposed the death penalty, whose abolition he had so warmly paised a short time before in the defense of Rabirius.[7]

In the debate which followed, the principal speakers were Caesar and Cato. Though in the course of the discussion Cicero delivered the *Fourth Catiline*, that speech is chiefly noteworthy for its straddling of the question and its failure to influence the action of the senate. Shorthand reporters were present, and their record of Cato's speech was extant till the time of Plutarch. It is Sallust who gives us the fullest account of the argument of Caesar and Cato. Though the speeches are written in his own rhetorical style, we may be sure by a comparison with other accounts that he has faithfully reported their substance.[8]

The question to be decided was, of course, the fate of the arrested conspirators; but as so often happens in popular discussion of capital offenses, the wisdom of the death penalty itself pressed forward for consideration. Leaving out those portions of the argument which applied only to the particular case, one is struck by the resemblance of the debate to our modern debates on capital punishment. At least five issues may be noted for which modern parallels are to be found. These we shall take up singly.

1. *Innocent men are sometimes punished.*

Caesar declares that a reason for the substitution of exile for the death penalty was the fact that the innocent were being punished:

> Afterwards, when the state reached maturity, and because of its large population, factions prevailed; when the blameless began to be oppressed and other wrongs of that kind were perpetrated; then they devised the Porcian law and other laws, which allowed the condemned the alternative of exile.[9]

Caesar is thinking of the execution of political offenders in times of civil strife and revolutionary disturbance. Since many were unjustly condemned, exile was allowed as a protection. Our modern discussions are concerned not so much with the rash execution of political offenders as with erroneous convictions in our ordinary court procedure. No argument is more regularly introduced by the opponents of capital punishment. Says Wendell Phillips:

> The number of persons sent to execution by the courts, and afterwards proved to be innocent, has been counted by hundreds in Great Britain, and must probably be counted by thousands, taking in even only the civilized states.[10]

Another writer argues:

> How many innocent men undergo the death penalty will never be known. . . . Sir James Mackintosh declared that at least one innocent man was hanged by the High Court in England every three

years. How many do you suppose our five hundred American criminal courts, with their less exact procedure, execute every year?[11]

Lafayette's words are so often quoted as to have become a
classic:

I shall continue to demand the abolition of the death penalty
until I have the infallibility of human judgments demonstrated to
me.[12]

2. *If the extreme penalty is required, why not add torture?*
Sallust quotes Caesar: "But, by the immortal gods! why
did you not add the recommendation that they first be
scourged?"[13]

Clarence Darrow can put the question in a most picturesque way:

But why not do a good job of it? If you want to get rid of killings
by hanging people or electrocuting them, because these are so
terrible, why not make a punishment that is terrible? . . . Why not
boil them in oil, as they used to do? Why not burn them at the
stake? Why not sew them in a bag with serpents and throw them
out to sea? . . . Why not break every bone in their body on the
rack, as has often been done for such serious offenses as heresy
and witchcraft?[14]

3. *Does not severe punishment win sympathy for the
criminal?*
Caesar declares that people will forget the crimes of the
prisoners and remember only what happens last, the execution of the death penalty.

But most mortals remember only that which happens last, and
in the case of godless men forget their guilt and descant upon the
punishment they have received, if it is a little more severe than
common. . . . But, you may say, who will complain of a decree
which is passed against traitors to their country? Time, I answer,
the lapse of years, and Fortune, whose caprice rules the nations.[15]

So the most casual reader of the daily press cannot fail
to note the tendency to picture as a hero the condemned man
or woman when facing execution. Says an English writer:

This state of morbid public interest in murder trials and morbid
sympathy for the murderer is, I think, very largely the effect of

the death penalty. . . . The accused man becomes to some extent a hero, his photograph is in every illustrated paper, and his most trivial utterances are recorded by the halfpenny papers with a minuteness otherwise reserved for those of royal personages alone. Once his days have been numbered by his sentence, he becomes an object rather of sympathy than of the general reprobation which he often deserves.[16]

4. *Is death, in fact, a punishment?*

Thus does Caesar answer in the negative:

So far as the penalty is concerned, I can say with truth that amid grief and wretchedness death is a relief from woes, not a punishment; that it puts an end to all mortal ills and leaves no room either for sorrow or for joy.

Cicero reports Caesar's thought in a very similar way:

[Caesar] is convinced that death has been ordained by the immortal gods not as a punishment but as a necessity of nature or a relief from toil or trouble. And so philosophers have never accepted it unwillingly, brave men often gladly.[17]

The following quotation from a modern writer would almost pass for a paraphrase of Caesar's words:

Is an execution any punishment at all? I deny it. To kill is not to punish, but it simply puts him out of the way and beyond all human punishment. . . . If by death we cut off his joys and happiness, in the same measure we cut off his sorrow and humiliation. . . . Death is an asylum, impregnable against punishment. Death is nature's haven and refuge from unbearable conditions. Death comes to the rescue the instant pain and suffering reaches its limit, and still we call nature's great and final balm for all extreme suffering a punishment—. . . the very reverse of its design by nature.[18]

Cato thought it worthwhile to answer this argument by suggesting that, in spite of the fineness of Caesar's language, death might not be the end of everything, but that there were rewards and punishments in the lower world:

In fine and finished phrases did Gaius Caesar a moment ago before this body speak of life and death, regarding as false, I presume, the tales which are told of the Lower World, where they say that the wicked take a different path from the good, and dwell in regions that are gloomy, desolate, unsightly, and full of fears.[19]

Evidently there was just such a clash of views in ancient Rome as is disclosed by the comment of a modern writer:

> I do not think it can be denied that the literal belief in the fires and tortures of hell is gradually on the wane, and when the criminal is freed from this . . . the death penalty will be robbed of a very considerable part of its terrors.[20]

5. *Is the death penalty necessary to protect society from criminals?*

After all the other issues have been discussed, the final decision as to the use of capital punishment must rest on the question, Is it necessary, in order to overawe criminals and prevent crime? Compared with this issue, all other arguments, in fact, appear trivial. It might even be urged that in the four arguments quoted above Caesar was only clouding the debate with rhetoric. The only point of these arguments was to justify the laws which made the death penalty illegal, and thus to persuade the senate that the laws ought not to be disregarded.

There are two phases of this question of preventing crime by the punishment of criminals: first, the deterrent effect of the punishment on other prospective offenders; second, the prevention of further criminal activity on the part of those once arrested. In the case under discussion there was a widespread conspiracy to be checked, as well as the few arrested leaders to be disposed of.

As for the need of severe measures to meet the widespread danger, Caesar would relieve his hearers of fear by pointing to the ample forces which Cicero had collected to defend the state.[21]

As for the four whose fate the senate was to settle, Caesar would by no means propose their dismissal to join Catiline and continue their bloody designs against the state. Instead, he proposed an irrevocable sentence of life imprisonment:

> But imprisonment and that too for life certainly was devised as a notable punishment for foul crimes. . . . [Caesar] surrounds them with grim guards such as the crime of these disgraceful men deserves. He ordains that it may be impossible for anyone, by vote of

either the senate or the people, to lighten the penalty of those whom he condemns. He takes away every hope, which alone can console men in their miseries.[22]

The opponents of capital punishment today offer the same substitute as did Caesar:

The deprivation of liberty for the natural duration of the criminal's life is equally efficacious. . . . At the present time a sentence of penal servitude for life does not necessarily imply a life-detention. . . . A very brief action on the part of the legislature would remedy this, if desirable, and a life sentence might be rendered an unconditional one and irrevocable. From the date of admission into the convict prison, the life would be forever closed to the world . . . for inside the prison walls he would die, and the intra-mural cemetery would hold the coffin.[23]

But Cato believed that swift and exemplary punishment was necessary, and on this issue his fiery speech turned the day against Caesar. He scarcely noticed the fine arguments of his opponent, except to make a vicious intimation that Caesar was himself involved in the conspiracy. He declared that the life of the state was at stake, that "gentleness and pity" would be paid for by the blood of the citizens. Vigorous action would weaken the courage of the enemies in the field, while the least weakness would fill them with daring:

The more vigorous your action, the less will be their courage; but if they detect the slightest weakness on your part, they will all be here immediately, filled with reckless daring.

In words which sound strangely modern he extols the diligence, justice, courage, and purity of their forefathers, denouncing the extravagance, greed, and idleness of his own day. Distinctions between right and wrong were breaking down. When each one takes counsel only for self, enslaved to pleasure, wealth, or influence, one can only expect an attack on the defenseless state!

We extol wealth and foster idleness. We make no distinction between good men and bad, and ambition appropriates all the prizes of merit. And no wonder! When each of you schemes for his own private interests, when you are slaves to pleasure in your homes and to money or influence here, the natural result is an attack upon the defenseless republic.[24]

So Judge Talley concludes his appeal for the retention and rigorous enforcement of capital punishment:

We, in this country today, are being swept by a fire that has for its basis and origin an unprecedented challenge of authority. We are swept by a fire that represents a desire, upon the part of too many of our people, for inordinate pleasure as the only object worthy of effort. We are swept by a fire of inordinate pursuit, not only of pleasure, but of wealth. We are swept by a fire of unprecedented lawlessness, disrespect for law, disregard of authority.

This is no time to advocate mitigating the rigors of punishment of the criminal. This is the time to get back to common sense in the treatment of the willful violator of the law, the steady desecrators of the Temple of Justice. And unless, ladies and gentlemen, we come to a realization of that necessity in these our own days, the institutions that we boast of as American . . . would be swept away.[25]

From a comparison of ancient and modern discussion of the question one would be led to conclude that the problem itself and the attitudes of the people toward the problem must be very similar, even if separated by two millenia. As to the observation that the death penalty simply fell into disuse in Rome because of the privilege of exile, the procedure of the courts, or the tribunician *auxilium,* it may be noted that similar tendencies operate today. Juries refuse to convict of capital crimes or, where allowed a choice, determine on a punishment of imprisonment instead of death. Executives grant pardons or commutations of sentence. The net result is that comparatively few offenders are executed, until in many states the end is finally reached of abolishing capital punishment. But neither in our own states nor in ancient Rome is the result "purely fortuitous." It is merely the crystallization of a public sentiment that is reluctant to take the life of a criminal and that looks to other means for the protection of society.

Two Debates:
France, 1791; England, 1956

FINN HORNUM

The main arguments for or against the death penalty have remained remarkably unchanged in the course of the centuries. This can best be seen by a comparative study of two debates separated in time by 165 years. The first took place in the French Constituent Assembly in 1791 and is notable because it was also the first parliamentary debate on a proposal to abolish the death penalty by substituting other punishments for it in the penal code project then under discussion. The second occurred in the British House of Commons in 1956 when an abolition bill introduced by Sidney Silverman was debated.

THE FRENCH DEBATE

The Assembly had before it the project of a penal code, which was presented by the reporter of the drafting commission, Lepelletier de Saint-Fargeau. In his opening address he reviewed the history of criminal legislation in France and the modern ideas on punishment as voiced by contemporary philosophers and systematized by Beccaria. He summarized them by saying that

it is necessary that punishments be humane, justly graduated, corresponding exactly to the nature of the crime, equal for all citizens, free from judicial arbitrariness; that they be repressive, principally by privations and restraints, by publicity, by their proximity to the place of the crime; that they reform the moral sentiments of the

The sources drawn on for this article are the *Archives parlementaires de 1787 à 1860*, Ser. I (1787–1799) Tome XXVI; and *Parliamentary Debates*, Commons, 5th Series, Vols. 548, 550, and 555.

convict by habituating him to labor; that they decrease in severity as they approach the final date of their duration and, finally, that they be temporary.

In speaking of the death penalty, Lepelletier said:

Should the death penalty remain in our criminal law? In discussing this important and frightful theory, we shall not dwell on the question of whether or not society has a legitimate right to employ this penalty. This is not the nub of the problem. That right seems incontestable, but should society exercise it? It is on this point that powerful considerations balance and divide opinions. . . . Though the basis of the right is unquestionable, it is only from its necessity that the legitimacy of the use of the penalty is derived. Just as a private individual cannot kill in self-defense except when this is the sole means of saving his own life, society cannot legitimately exercise its right over life and death unless it is clearly proved that no other punishment suffices to repress crime. If we can use punishments equally deterrent, we must reject the death penalty.

The first major speaker to address himself to the capital punishment issue was Louis-Pierre-Joseph Prugnon. Like Lepelletier he had a background in law and was extremely active throughout the Constituent Assembly's discussion of judicial organization and penal law. He had been a deputy of the Third Estate to the States-General and represented the interests of his class in the Assembly. Prugnon argued in favor of retention. He insisted upon the right of the state to take the life of a citizen. He held that the death penalty was the only effective deterrent to those who would commit murder. The alternative of imprisonment he heatedly rejected. It has no deterrent effect, he argued, since people forget about the sentence as soon as the convicted murderer is put out of sight. There are chances for escape and little chance for rehabilitation. Inmates are likely to become worse rather than better in prison, due to their association with other criminals and, furthermore, the professional criminal, who appears the best adjusted in prison, simply knows how to adapt and is in reality unchanged. The final part of his speech consisted of a strong plea to the Assembly to abolish all torture and cruel methods of inflicting death. Such measures, he said, do not deter but have a brutalizing effect upon the spectators. He concluded, "I ask, then, that the death penalty be retained for traitors, murderers, poisoners, incendiaries, and those who invent false accusations, without it ever being possible to pronounce any other punishment than simple death."

The next speaker was Maximilien François Marie Isidore de Robespierre. Thirty-three years old at the time, Robespierre had just begun to court that public favor with the Parisian masses which eventually would bring him to the pinnacle of political power and to his death. A glance at his career before 1791, however, makes it obvious that his position on the issue would be that of an abolitionist. Before the start of his political career as a deputy of the Third Estate to the States-General, he had resigned his post as criminal court judge in Arras because he wanted to avoid pronouncing the death sentence.

Retorting to Prugnon's insistence on society's right to impose the death penalty, Robespierre responded that the great power that society exercises over man should not be utilized in this manner. Only the law of natural defense should be allowed. The state's execution of the death penalty is legalized murder. The death penalty, he continued, is the weapon of tyrants against their slaves. It is not a deterrent to would-be murderers and its use diminishes man's respect for the authority of the law. Punishment should be meted out in response to the emotions which produced the act and not blindly to all crimes of a particular type. Furthermore, the experience of other countries such as Japan, Greece, Rome, and Russia shows that it is possible to do without it. Finally, the risk of error is very great. Human judgments are not infallible and an innocent man may be condemned to death and executed. Most important, however, is the denial to the accused of a chance to repent his acts.

Robespierre's short, but magnificent, oratory ended the capital punishment debate for that day. On the following day, May 31, 1791, four more speakers added their arguments to the discussion. The opening remarks were by a retentionist, Antoine-Boniface Mougins de Roquefort, secretary of the As-

sembly. He had been curate in Grasse before being elected
deputy for the clergy to the States-General. The oldest of
the debaters, 59, he died in 1793. The experience of other
countries, he said, society's right to impose the death penalty,
the truly deterrent effect of this punishment, the support of
such famous writers as Montesquieu, Rousseau, Mably,
Filangieri, and d'Etand, and the inadequacy of imprisonment, both as a deterrent and for security reasons—all prove
that the death penalty should be retained.

The next speaker, an abolitionist, was during this phase
of the Revolution as famous and as popular as Robespierre
and Mirabeau. Jérôme Pétion de Villeneuve had practiced
law in his native town of Chartres before the start of his
political career. He was made a deputy of the Third Estate
to the States-General and was elected president of the Constituent Assembly in 1790. Like Robespierre, he courted the
favor of the Parisian masses and was crowned, with him,
with a civic crown by the populace after the last meeting
of the Assembly. In November, 1791, he was elected mayor
or Paris and also became the first president of the National
Convention. His jealousy of Robespierre allied him with the
Girondin party and when he was elected to the first Committee of Public Safety, in 1793, he lost no time in attacking
his former "royal" colleague. When the wind turned he
escaped to Caen and led the provincial insurrection against
the Convention. He committed suicide in 1794.

The future mayor's arguments for abolition are not very
different from those of his rival for public favor. Society's
lack of right to punish is rejected; rehabilitation is advocated
as the real purpose of punishment; retentionists have failed
to show that imprisonment, as it would be practiced under
the new penal code, is not a deterrent; the death penalty
is no deterrent and the spectacle of its execution corrupts
public morals; all these arguments were presented in considerable detail and with great zeal and fervor. Pétion de
Villeneuve used American experience to support his abolition argument:

It is true that the Americans . . . have not erased this act from
their criminal law, but . . . [in] no other country in the world are

crimes more rare, in no country is the guilty man treated with more kindness, with more humanity; it is here that one sees the erring scoundrel return to virtue; it is here that one sees the virtuous Quakers devote their entire lives to the consolation of the unfortunate imprisoned in the houses of correction, providing them with the most touching and the most fraternal care.

Another well-known Frenchman, Anthèlme Brillat-Savarin, took his place on the podium. The "physiology of taste" of this famous gourmet did not include abolition of capital punishment. Brillat-Savarin had been deputy of the Third Estate to the States-General and was an avid speaker during the meetings of the Constituent Assembly. His political career was interrupted during the Terror when he fled to Switzerland and the United States, but upon his return to France in 1796 he became a judge of the Court of Cassation during the Consulate. His retentionist arguments contained little that was new. His impressions of the contemporary penal system, based on personal experience, showed the consciousness of its inadequacies among legislators. "But do not men become better in these prisons? On the contrary, they hold between them a kind of school of crime; they instruct each other how to combine the tricks of the most highly skilled with the means of escaping from confinement. . . ."

Adrien Duport, the final speaker in the debate, summed up the case for abolition. Duport was 32 years old and like Lepelletier he had been advocate at the Paris *parlement,* had been appointed deputy for the nobility to the States-General, and had put his eloquence at the service of the popular cause. He had been very active in the debate of the penal code from the beginning and had argued strongly in favor of the use of juries in both civil and criminal cases. Later, he was a member of the commission which interrogated Louis XVI after his flight to Varennes. Subsequently, however, he broke with the Jacobins, was arrested, but managed to escape to Switzerland through Danton's personal intervention. He died there in 1798.

Duport advanced the usual argument for eliminating the death penalty completely. Society does not have the right to take the life of a citizen. Death is no real deterrent to crime since it is bound to happen anyway and thus cannot produce the necessary fear. The risk of error is too great and the spectacles of public executions destroy the nation's morality. What, then, are the measures which can repress crime?

1. Justice, the mildness of the laws and the probity of the government.
2. Local institutions established to prevent that desperation and extreme poverty among men which are the usual sources of crime.

Furnish men with work and give help to those who cannot work and you will have destroyed the principal causes, the most usual occasions, I could almost say the excuse, for crimes.

It is difficult to summarize briefly the impression of the debate. The most lasting impression one receives is perhaps the flavor of the oratory. The skill in public speaking exercised by these men, the mixture of strong emotional appeals and references to social and political theories, and their zeal in defending the rightness of their cause, stand out. Another lasting impression is the intellectual prowess of the orators. Their constant references to Montesquieu, Rousseau, Beccaria, Mably, Filangieri and others, and their knowledge of other countries' experiences with the death penalty showed them to be well-read students of political and social classics.

THE ENGLISH DEBATE

We have discussed the French debate in some detail because of the intrinsic historical interest attached to its content and the characteristics of its participants. The English debate is of such recent origin and has been so extensively discussed by Elizabeth Tuttle in *The Crusade Against Capital Punishment in Great Britain* (London, 1961) that a few comments should suffice.

Thirty-three major speakers participated in the three days of debate on the Silverman Bill. While the division on the issue was not along political lines, it is apparent that the Labour members of Parliament generally favored abolition while Conservatives favored retention. Of the 16 abolitionist speakers, ten were Labourites, five were Conservatives, and one belonged to an Irish political party. Thirteen Conservatives, three Labourites, and one Irish representative spoke in favor of retention.

Though the historical frame of these men has not yet been assured, a great many distinguished Members of Parliament took part in the debate. Two Cabinet members presented the government's case for retention of the death penalty and extensive changes in the law of murder. The Home Secretary, Major Gwilym Lloyd George, opened the debate. The Lord Privy-Seal, R. A. Butler, well-known as one of the leaders of the Conservative Party, wound up the first day's debate. Other prominent retentionists included a former Chief Justice of India, Sir Patrick Spens, and a former Attorney-General, Sir Lionel Heald.

On the side of abolition were several prominent participants known both for their governmental activities and their position on capital punishment. Two former Labour Home Secretaries, Chuter Ede and Herbert Morrison, spoke the first day. Other party leaders favoring abolition included the opposition whip, G. H. R. Rogers, and Anthony Greenwood, one of the most active Labour parliamentarians. Among the "professional" abolitionsts, one must mention Sidney Silverman, the sponsor of the abolition bill, and George Benson. Silverman had dominated the crusade against capital punishment in Parliament since the end of World War II. A dedicated pacifist since World War I, when he was jailed for his views, he had been suspended from the Labour Party several times and was perhaps the best-known gadfly in the House of Commons. George Benson was best known for his chairmanship of the Howard League for Penal Reform.

COMPARISON OF THE TWO DEBATES

In order to contrast the actual arguments used in the two debates, it seems desirable to juxtapose the actual words used by the participants, structuring the presentation by considering each major argument from both points of view.

Deterrence

FRANCE, 1791   ENGLAND, 1956

The Retentionists:

The prospect of punishment even seen in the distance, frightens criminals and stops them. . . . There is a class of people with whom the horror of crime counts a great deal less than the fear of punishment; their imagination needs to be shaken, that necessitates something which will resound in their soul, which will move it profoundly, so that the idea of punishment is inseparable from that of crime. . . . The wicked does not fear God, but he does have fear, i.e., the sentiment which the scoundrel feels at the sight of the scaffold. . . .

PRUGNON

Remove . . . from someone who is considering the death of a human being, the most attractive satisfaction for a vindictive heart, I should say the enjoyment of triumph, and you will observe that the fear of losing life, will stop his arm and calm his furor.

ROQUEFORT

I thus suppose, gentlemen, that . . . those who contemplate a penal code should act as if society were composed of three classes of men: the first of these consisting of those who were born good and virtuous; the second of those who were born

What of the . . . aspect of deterrence, that is, the operation of the fear of being hanged if one commits murder? . . . To common sense it appears, I should have thought obvious, that death is more feared than practically any other punishment. . . . The effect of hanging as a deterrent is to be seen not in those who commit murder but in those who do not. . . . The professional criminal is prepared, apparently, to accept imprisonment as an occupational risk, but not hanging. . . . The man who lives by large-scale crime is accustomed to assessing his risks. Suppose that the risk of hanging . . . is removed. . . . What, then, is to deter him from shooting to avoid capture and to silence the only witness?

LLOYD GEORGE

Everyone of us knows—knows inside himself—whether death is a deterrent to us. . . . I am absolutely convinced—I know—that fear of violent death is a deterrent, and no statistics, no arguments whatever will convince me that it is not.

SPENS

[Capital punishment] is particularly applicable in the case of the older criminal whose expectation of life may not be

villains; the third, and most numerous, of those who at birth carry ambiguous dispositions, and for whom circumstances or upbringing determine either vice or virtue. Punishments are not for the first two classes of men; one of them has no use for it; the other has the ferocious courage to disregard it. They are thus truly applicable to the third class. . . . Remove from them the death penalty, and even the most feeble imagination would accept without horror, I would even say, with tranquility, the purpose of the punishment taking its place. . . . Watch what calculation goes on in the mind of the man who contemplates becoming a criminal; he soon gets accustomed, and when he has acknowledged the maximum term which crime can lead him to, he has already committed the act in his soul and lacks merely the opportunity.

BRILLAT-SAVARIN

more than 14 or 15 years in the natural course. . . . If he commits a crime which may land him in jail for the rest of his natural life, that is one thing. If he takes a gun and commits murder, as the law is now, he will be hanged; but if the Bill is passed he can commit a crime and for committing murder get a sentence no greater than his natural expectation of life. I refuse to believe, especially in the case of the professional criminal . . . that hanging is not a deterrent. That is a common-sense view, bearing in mind [that the] Royal Commission said: "Capital punishment has obviously failed as a deterrent when a murder is committed." We can number its failures. But we cannot number its successes. No one can ever know how many people have refrained from murder because of the fear of being hanged.

SIR ROBERT GRIMSTON

The Abolitionists:

The death penalty is necessary, say the partisans of this antiquated and barbaric routine; there is no fear so powerful against crime. Who has told them this? Have you taken count of all the resources by which penal laws can act upon human feeling? Alas! how many physical and moral sorrows may man not endure before death. . . . When the legislator can

I am less convinced that the death penalty is a decisive deterrent in cases of murder. . . . In the bulk of murder cases, when the person commits the murder he probably is not thinking a great deal about the penalty. . . . It is the fact that abolition of the death penalty has increasingly occurred. . . .

MORRISON

strike citizens in so many different sensitive spots, how can he believe it necessary to employ the death penalty? Punishments are not designed to torment the guilty, but to prevent crime by the fear of incurring them.

ROBESPIERRE

It is not the fear of punishment which stops the sacrilegious hand of the assassin. The expectation of impunity reassures him against the danger that he courts. The scoundrel always flatters himself that he will escape the law's surveillance and bury his crimes in forgetfulness. . . . Also, one cannot believe that the man who is so barbaric that he can soak his hand in the blood of his fellow man will be held back by the distant appearance of a cruel fate.

VILLENEUVE

I ask of the most zealous partisans of the death penalty, that they answer the following dilemma: if the scoundrel is affected by the idea of infamy attached to his crime, then it is much more useful to join it to a punishment which is living and durable; because he will certainly be more sensitive when he personally is the object, than when it, after him, should be affixed to his memory; if he will not be affected by the idea of infamy, then you are forced to conclude that death

Before the case for capital punishment can be established, it has to be proved that capital punishment acts as a deterrent. We have had capital punishment as part of our penal code in this country for hundreds of years. It has not prevented murders. . . . The Royal Commission . . . has had numerous witnesses from abolitionist countries before it to give evidence. The evidence of the witnesses . . . was that abolition did not result in any increase in murders.

WILLIAM REID

It seems to me that when capital punishment is abolished and the rate of murders does not go up, that is substantial proof that the supposed deterrent was not in fact a unique deterrent. If a motor car runs at exactly the same speed whether the brakes are on or off, surely it is an indication that the brakes are not working.

NIGEL NICHOLSON

is no more to him than an accident common to all men.

DUPORT

Society's Right
The Retentionists:

In the state of nature, I have the right to repulse force with force. . . . In society, I have given up this power . . . to the law or to the magistrate who is its spokesman. It neither can nor should use it, except as I would have used it myself. It is obliged to watch out for the preservation of my existence; and the man who has interrupted that course . . . should be condemned to die. . . .

ROQUEFORT

The death penalty . . . is nothing other in the social contract, than the compromise clause by which every individual assures, with his life, the life of his fellow citizens; and in this point of view, the death penalty is . . . the fundamental basis for all political aggregates, and when the death penalty has been used, it is as if [society] had said to every man: if your life is precious to you, respect that of your fellow man, because you are responsible for it with your own life. . . .

BRILLAT-SAVARIN

The first function of capital punishment is to give emphatic expression to society's peculiar abhorrence of murder. . . . It is important that murder should be regarded with peculiar horror. . . . I believe that capital punishment does, in the present state of society, both express and sustain the sense of moral revulsion for murder.

LLOYD GEORGE

. . . The first duty of any Government is to defend the lives and property of the people. . . . For that purpose it is necessary to do two things. It is necessary to provide properly armed and equipped forces. It is equally necessary to provide properly equipped civil power. . . . I would like to know how it can be suggested that one can logically depart from that principle in regard to the death penalty. Can we, as Members of Parliament, deny to the State the ultimate sanction of life and death?

SIR LIONEL HEALD

The Abolitionists:

. . . In society where the force of all is mobilized against one, what principle of justice author-

I now believe that capital punishment is wrong because it is against the basic Christian prin-

izes it to impose death? . . . A victor who would kill his captured enemies is called barbaric! A man who butchers a child whom he can disarm and punish seems like a monster! An accused condemned by society is like a conquered and powerless enemy; he is weaker before it than a child is before a man. . . . In the eyes of truth and justice, the scenes of death which society orders . . . are nothing other than cowardly assassinations, formalized crimes committed, not by individuals, but by entire nations. . . .

ROBESPIERRE

ciples on which our civilization is supposed to rest. . . . I affirm that no Christian can say that the gentle teacher from Nazareth would have supported capital punishment had He been in this world today.

G. H. R. ROGERS

The Alternative

The Retentionists:

What do you pretend to establish in its place? A mild punishment, a punishment for life? What will you respond if any of these criminals, whom you would condemn to perpetual slavery, broke their fetters and came to frighten society with new crimes? . . . What inequality do you not insert between the poor and the rich! A jailer, of all beings, is not the most incorruptible. . . . Suppose that they complete their 12 or 24 years; how many cannot corrupt, between them, men who have communicated vices during 24 years? . . . There are some who do not escape from Brest or Toulon so as not to be

If capital punishment were abolished, there would be a number of prisoners who would have to be detained for the rest of their lives, or until they were so enfeebled as no longer to present a risk. . . . The absence of hope is a terrible thing. . . . That is the position which—I put it no higher—if it is a question of cruelty, the people who advocate abolition ought carefully to consider. I ask those who oppose capital punishment on humanitarian grounds to weigh the possible suffering of the alternative.

LLOYD GEORGE

. . . I believe we are about to

executed. . . . If you force our judges to respect the life of these beings [the habitual criminals] who regard punishment as their natural fate, what will become of public safety? . . .

PRUGNON

Hard labor, which one would substitute for the death penalty, will everywhere be the fate of poverty; and one would confuse the criminal with the poor, the assassin, the parricide, with the man pursued by misfortune, or overwhelmed by bad luck.

ROQUEFORT

take a backward step, returning to just the same state of affairs where there is not marked and clear differentiation between the criminal who has taken human life and the criminal who commits an ordinary offence. . . . In my view, it is quite wrong that there should be no clear differentiation to set apart the crime of murder . . . as something which the community as a whole condemns above all other crime.

JOHN EDEN

The Abolitionists:

Certainly, I abhor with you the barbaric and perverted man who spills the blood of his fellow man. Like you I want him to be punished, not by abridging his life by a murder, but by prolonging his punishment, by applying it to him through all the moments of his existence, by imposing deprivations of all kinds upon him, by rendering him useful to the society that he has offended, and by making his long suffering a formidable example to those who would attempt to imitate him.

VILLENEUVE

. . . The alternative to capital punishment. . . . Quantitatively, it is a small problem, involving probably a dozen or so murderers hanged per year. . . . Qualitatively, compared with other criminal offenses . . . murderers are less likely . . . to revert to crimes of violence. . . . The Report of the Royal Commission tells us . . . that we should not shrink from contemplating the occasional sentence of 15–20 years imprisonment. That is a grim thing to contemplate. I thought the Home Secretary painted such a grim picture of what it would be like . . . that it ought to have led him to the conclusion that the difference was so striking as to make the long sentence an adequate deterrent.

KENNETH YOUNGER

The Experience of Other Countries

The Retentionists:

. . . In Egypt homicide and perjury were struck down with death. In Judea, capital punishments were common. In Athens, in Rome, the death penalty was pronounced against the murderer. It it permitted among all nations today, particularly in England; and the criminal laws adopted by that nation cannot be suspect among us, as it is from that [nation] that we have borrowed our institution of justice. . . .

ROQUEFORT

Sweden is a country which enjoys living standards and standards of education that compare very favorably to our own, and Sweden abolished the death penalty in 1910. If the argument that the death penalty is no deterrent is a valid one, then we would expect that the murder rate per million of the population in England and Wales would be roughly comparable to that in Sweden. . . . Instead in the three decades that followed the abolition of the death penalty in Sweden, had the murder rate in England and Wales been the same as the rate in Sweden, there would have been 3,500 more murders in England and Wales. There would have been double the number of murders that took place.

S. N. EVANS

The Abolitionists:

The death penalty is necessary you say? If so, why have several people decided to pass it by? . . . Look at Japan, no kind of death penalty and the crimes are no more prodigious, no types of crimes are either as frequent or as atrocious. . . . The republics of Greece, where punishments were moderate, where the death penalty was either infinitely rare, or absolutely unknown, did they offer

After all, the Dutch, the Scandinavians, and even the Swiss are not so very different from ourselves. . . . Yet they have managed to get on quite well without the death penalty for many years and when the death penalty was abolished in those countries, there was no startling rise in the murder rate and it was not necessary to arm the police.

MONTGOMERY HYDE

more crime and less virtue than the countries governed by the law of blood? Has Russia been wrecked while the despot who governed it completely suppressed the death penalty, as if by this act of humanity and philosophy, the crime of keeping millions of men under the yoke of absolute power had been expiated?

ROBESPIERRE

Timing

The Retentionists:

Alas, at what moment do you abolish the death penalty? In a time of anarchy, when you do not have enough force against masses, of which one has learned that they can do anything; when it would be necessary to increase their fears and raise barriers against them instead of reducing them; at a time, finally, when the sentiment of religion is close to becoming extinguished in most of society's classes, and when morals in general are not very pure?

PRUGNON

I am not asking the House to conclude that because crimes of violence have apparently increased more than murders, the death penalty is a more effective deterrent than imprisonment. What the figures lead me to say is that, prima facie, a time when there are so many crimes against the person, when these crimes are apparently on the increase, is not a time when capital punishment can safely be abolished.

LLOYD GEORGE

The Risk of Error

The Retentionists:

No human institution is infallible—a mistake may be made. This as an abstract proposition is no doubt true, but let us consider how many institutions, before an innocent man is hanged,

must make not only a mistake,
but the same mistake. The police, the judge, the Court of
Criminal Appeal, the Home
Secretary—all, though anxiously
searching for the truth, have to
fall into error. . . . I go further
—I do not believe that in recent
times there is any case in which
an innocent man has been
hanged.

LLOYD GEORGE

The Abolitionists:

. . . Human judgments are
never so certain that society
can allow the death of a man
condemned by other men, without being subject to error. Even
if you imagine the most perfect
judicial order, with judges of
the highest integrity and en-
lightenment, there will always
be some place for error and for
prejudice. Why do you ban the
way to rectify them?

ROBESPIERRE

I feel sure that many votes in
1948 were swayed by the as-
surances of Sir John Anderson
and of Sir David Maxwell Fyfe
that there was no reasonable
practicality of an innocent man
being hanged. Then, within two
years, Timothy John Evans was
hanged. The worst thing about
the death penalty is that it can
persuade a highly intelligent, responsible, conscientious humane
man like the present Home
Secretary to convince himself—
because he dare not believe the
contrary—that Timothy John
Evans was guilty, as charged,
of the crime for which he was
executed. Does the right honourable and gallant Gentleman
really believe now, that there is
no scintilla of doubt?

SILVERMAN

The Demoralizing Effect of Capital Punishment
The Abolitionists:

It is thus necessary for laws to
present the purest model of

All of us read with a good deal
of distress the enormous public-

justice and reason to the people. If, in the place of powerful, calm and moderate severity which ought to characterize them, they cause anger and revenge; if they make human blood, which they could save, run, and which they do not have the right to spill; if they flaunt cruel scenes and cadavers murdered by torture before the eyes of the people, then they alter the idea of justice and injustice in the hearts of citizens. . . . Man no longer appears a sacred object to man; there is a lesser idea of his dignity when public authority itself plays with life.

ROBESPIERRE

ity given, not necessarily to murders, but to executions. That is a revolting, sordid and disgraceful practice. . . . We shall not stop that sort of publicity in this country until we abolish the death penalty. I ask those people who wish to retain the death penalty to consider the effect of newspaper publicity on members of the public. . . . I believe it to have a very deleterious effect indeed on certain sections of the public. . . .

D. M. KEEGAN

Public Opinion
The Abolitionists:

Do not fear to shock a remnant of popular prejudice against the suppression of the death penalty. . . . Rest assured, Gentlemen, that the law which abolishes the death penalty will be respected and be more respectable than a great number of those which you have passed . . . it is not always by a servile obedience to the demand of public opinion, that legislators pass the most useful laws for their countries.

DUPORT

I am very conscious of the fact that a majority of my constituents were they in the same position would speak and vote in the opposite sense. I only go against a majority wish . . . because I believe that this is truly a matter of individual conscience and of judgment.

NIGEL NICHOLSON

Eight arguments for and against the death penalty have been compared in some detail above. The first thing one notices is the remarkable similarity in these comments, 165 years apart. There is hardly a single idea in either one of the debates that cannot be found in the other. Selecting arguments for juxtaposition involves a great deal of subjective judgment, of course, but it is believed that the statements quoted above contain the core of the arguments presented.

The favored argument for the retention of the death penalty was that the fear of death prevents people from committing capital crimes—the deterrence argument. In both debates this was the most widely discussed issue by both retentionists and abolitionists. The retentionists usually supported their case with an appeal to "common sense." The speeches by Prugnon, Mougins de Roquefort, Lloyd George, and Sir Patrick Spens all reflected this view. Professional and older criminals were said to be particularly deterred by the fear of the death penalty. Interestingly enough, the retentionist argument by Brillat-Savarin contradicted the latter contention. The "born villains," he argued, have courage to disregard the consequences.

The abolitionists countered the deterrence argument primarily with the failure of homicide rates to increase in countries and states where the death penalty had been eliminated. This argument was apparent in the speeches by Nigel Nicholson and William Reid in the English debate and will be considered later. Another retort by the abolitionists was that there was little evidence that individuals who commit murder consider the penalty before and during the act and that what evidence there is points, in fact, in the opposite direction. Though there were no criminological studies to this effect before the French debate, this argument was indicated in Pétion de Villeneuve's statement. Herbert Morrison also mentioned it in his speech. Not even in the British debate, however, was reference made to the high incidence among those executed of felony murderers whose criminal motivation was hardly a desire to kill. Neither did the British abolitionists point to the frequently close relationship between the offender and his victim in homicide cases, lending support to the notion that murders are impulsive crimes and crimes of passion. They might also have mentioned the fact that a number

of murderers commit suicide after the act, pointing to the un-
likelihood that these men, at least, feared death!

Society's, or the state's, right to impose the death penalty
upon its citizens was an argument which recurred often in the
French debate and it was even brought up in the British
debate, though only tangentially. The argument, which in the
18th century was primarily used by abolitionists, apparently
grew out of the strong commitment of intellectuals to the
social contract theory. Beccaria, especially, questioned society's right to take life on the grounds that, since society had
been originated by men ceding to a higher authority a part
of the freedom they possessed in the "state of nature" and,
since man did not have the right to take his own life, he could
not delegate it to the state. This was the argument countered
by Brillat-Savarin in his speech about the compromise clause
in the social contract. Robespierre, however, took a different
approach. His speech questioned the moral right of an all-
powerful state to confront its weak members with its power
and concluded that this was pure tyranny. His argument was
much the same as that advanced by G. H. R. Rogers on religious grounds. There were also strong moral overtones in
Lloyd George's formulation, and Sir Lionel Heald reacted to
Robespierre by reversing the roles of society and the individual.

Just as the abolitionists were put on the defensive when
confronted with the argument that the death penalty was a
deterrent to murder, the retentionists had to make a case to
show that imprisonment, the usual alternative to capital punishment, was unsuitable as a punishment for murder. While
the abolitionists stressed the beneficial effects of institution-
alization and the possibility for rehabilitation in prison, the
retentionists argued that the risk of escape was too great, that
corruption, rather than rehabilitation, was likely to be the
result of incarceration, and that long imprisonment could be
more cruel than a swift death penalty. The six statements on
this issue, quoted previously, present some interesting observations. The exchange between Lloyd George and Kenneth
Younger is a marvelous example of how the stressing of a
point may almost defeat its purpose. Even more curious is

Villeneuve's statement which, in part, agrees with Lloyd George but comes to the opposite conclusion. John Eden's comment, finally, urged a clear differentiation between homicide and other "ordinary" offenses, while Roquefort warned not to confuse the criminal with the poor.

Using the experiences of other countries with the death penalty as evidence for its retention or abolition was equally and eagerly pursued in both debates. The search for statistical proof occurred even in the French Constituent Assembly. Lloyd George attempted to prevent the use of this argument in the British debate by referring to the conclusion of the Royal Commission on Capital Punishment that there was no clear evidence from these countries that the abolition of capital punishment had led to an increase in the homicide rate nor that its re-establishment had led to a decrease, but he was not even successful with his retentionist colleagues who, just as frequently as the abolitionists, used comparisons with other countries when the evidence pointed in the right direction. Incidentally, S. N. Evans' argument was an amusing example of the misapplication of rates. As one of his opponents was quick to point out, the comparison between Sweden and England hardly held unless the Swedish figures were interpreted relative to the figures before abolition.

The argument on the inappropriateness of abolishing capital punishment at that particular time seems to indicate that, at least to the retentionist, the right time will never come.

The risk of executing an innocent person has always been a strong abolitionist argument. There is not much difference between Silverman's and Robespierre's arguments with the exception of Silverman's reference to the Evans-Christie case. Much of the British debate was a discussion of the guilt or innocence of Timothy John Evans and indicates the public furor which this case produced. It is noteworthy that the French retentionists apparently had a difficult time finding a retort to this argument; no one raised the point on that side of the aisle.

The emphasis in the French debate on the demoralizing and brutalizing effect of capital punishment upon the population is not surprising. Public executions and the frequent use of torture and cruel methods of inflicting death were common in France before the Revolution, and no member of the Constituent Assembly argued against the abolition of these barbaric measures. What is interesting, however, is the switch in the English debate. It is no longer the actual witnessing of executions which corrupts public morals but "sordid" newspaper accounts. This point was raised by several speakers in the English debate.

It is perhaps with regard to the references to public opinion that one finds the clearest indication of the influence of social science upon public policy. Duport's statement was the only direct reference to public feelings on the issue in the French debate. Attitude surveys and public opinion polls had of course not yet made their appearance. In the British debate, however, there were constant references to public opinion polls, and it was indeed fortunate for the debaters that the polls conflicted enough to provide evidence for both sides.

Two major arguments that were not used in the debates are those of the cost of executions relative to the cost of life imprisonment and the discriminatory selection of those murderers who do receive the death penalty. Brillat-Savarin briefly mentioned cost toward the end of his speech but only to state that he was not going to discuss it, and Prugnon's reference to the inequality between the poor and the rich in relation to imprisonment showed at least an awareness of differential treatment by the correctional system.

What may we conclude from a comparison of these two debates? First, that capital punishment apparently is one of those issues where attitudes change very slowly. Second, that social science research has had little, if any, influence upon the molding of the opinions of public policymakers, except in the area of public opinion polling, which is hardly the most noteworthy of social science endeavors. We conclude with Silverman:

I do not think anyone would commend [the debate] in the first place for its originality, because the truth of the matter is that there are very few arguments either way on this issue, that most of us know them all, and that we have made our own individual assessments where in the end the balance of the argument lies, and are unlikely at the end of this debate, after all the debates we have so far had, to be shaken by arguments now.

A Canadian Debate, 1966

In March and April, 1966, the Canadian House of Commons debated a motion, introduced by three members, which read as follows: "Resolved that it is expedient to introduce a measure to amend the Criminal Code for the purpose of (a) abolishing the death penalty in respect of all offenses under that act; (b) substituting a mandatory sentence of life imprisonment in those cases where the death penalty is now mandatory; and (c) providing that no person upon whom a mandatory sentence of life imprisonment is imposed shall be released from imprisonment without the prior approval of the governor in council."

The motion was extensively debated and was finally defeated. Had it passed, the government would have been expected to introduce a bill abolishing the death penalty and incorporating other provisions of the motion.

Numerous speakers, for or against the motion, participated in the debate. A few selections from their addresses are reproduced here. They present some of the major arguments on both sides.

THE RETENTIONISTS

The question of capital punishment is one which arouses emotion in each of us. I am grateful for this non-partisan debate on the basis of personal conviction. I believe it has been of a very high standard and a credit to the house. Abolitionists and retentionists both claim evidence to support their arguments. Conflicting evidence confuses the picture. In my opinion the reason there is no convincing evidence on the subject is that it is difficult to measure man's mind. Therefore what we say is basically for the record as we explain the reason for our personal votes. . . .

I cannot support the motion before us because I am convinced that it would be wrong to abolish the death penalty completely. . . . I cannot accept the statement . . . that to retain the death penalty is to cling to a hangover from the barbaric past. In my Christian faith I believe that human life is most sacred. Man was created in the image of God. In the commandments of Moses I am told by God not to kill. When others in my society accept this command with me, then I have personal safety of life as do my family and neighbours.

The sanctity of human life cannot be questioned. Christ has told us to love our neighbours. Murder, the taking of life, is not to be condoned. It is therefore the continuing responsibility of the Christian to interpret to those about us that every human being must have as his basic right not only justice before the law but also our personal understanding, respect and concern because he, like me, is a human being and our brother under one God, Creator of us all.

However, in determining my own stand on the question of abolition versus retention I cannot rely entirely on my own judgment. There are still those old-fashioned enough, and I am one of them, who believe that God has provided in His Word guidance to meet every problem which may confront us. In *James* 1:5 we read:

If any of you lack wisdom, let him ask of God, that giveth to all men liberally, and upbraideth not; and it shall be given him.

To me, at the root of every question the Scriptures must be our final authority, not my opinion or someone else's. It is not the reasoning of one who differs with me which must be my final guide. It is not the norm of what is considered the lowest common denominator of custom or current practice. It is not even what the church itself teaches, for again it is the Bible, not the church, which is the final authority. In my understanding of Scripture I find that capital punishment was intended by God as a penalty for those who take law and justice into their own hands or who for personal gain willfully take the life of another person.

Prior to the days of Noah there was no death penalty. When Cain killed his brother Abel there was no such law and no such sentence was passed. He was banished from the Garden for life. Following this the descendants of Cain became part of a society which was grossly corrupt, rotten with sin and violence, and God sent death universally upon all but one family. Following the flood God says in *Genesis* 9:6:

Whoso sheddeth man's blood, by man shall his blood be shed; for in the image of God made he man.

Exodus 21:12 says the same thing:

He that smiteth a man, so that he die, shall be surely put to death.

Significantly this passage in many Bibles falls on the same page as the Ten Commandments which are the basis of our Canadian law and fundamental to the moral conduct of the individual. Some argue that the New Testament has changed this Old Testament teaching. They say the New Testament has replaced the "eye for an eye" philosophy with an ethic of love. However, the ethic of love theme of the New Testament applies only on a person to person basis, as do the Ten Commandments. The command to turn the other cheek cannot apply to law enforcement by the state; otherwise lawlessness would be encouraged. The right of the state to punish with death is more expressly established in chapter 13 of *Romans,* verses 1 to 5. Here the apostle Paul describes the law enforcement officials as "ministers of God" who "bear not the sword in vain."

Many Bible commentators, much more wise in their understanding of the Scriptures than myself, interpret this passage as supporting capital punishment. Among them are such men as Luther, Calvin, Hodge, Clarke, Moule, Meyer and Studd. Capital punishment is the traditional Christian position. It was also held by the Roman Catholic theologian, Thomas Aquinas. According to the Romans' passage, God gave the state the power of death for two reasons, first, to satisfy the demands of God's justice and, second, to serve as a protection to society by deterring crime in the future.

When the state takes the life of a capital offender it does so as God's agent, having received express authority from God. In the performance of law enforcement law officials are likewise responsible. Therefore it is as much a dereliction of duty for law officials to execute men who do not deserve death as it is to fail to execute criminals who deserve it. That does not mean that every capital offender must be executed. Far from it. The Bible permits and encourages justice to be tempered by mercy at times but not all the time. . . .

I respect the appeal the abolitionists have made in this debate. However, I believe their suggested solution is one which will have far greater and more serious consequences than those which the specific problem presents to us now. There are a few comments I should like to make regarding some of the arguments presented by those who support abolition.

First, it is said that capital punishment is not a deterrent. If capital punishment appears to be not much of a deterrent the reason is that a lot of the sting has been taken out of it. Although crime has steadily increased the use of the death penalty has steadily decreased. Practice in Canada during recent years is equivalent to the abolition of capital punishment. It is for this reason that I believe the resolution before us must be permitted to come to a vote. I had intended at first to move an amendment but as the debate has progressed I have become convinced that the question has been well put. This debate, therefore, should be terminated without undue extension by a specific vote.

It is argued also that society should be concerned about the redemption of the criminal, a redemption that might be prevented by an execution. However, by the same argument society should be concerned for the safety and welfare of potential murder and rape victims. One of Caryl Chessman's targets, a 17-year-old girl, was subjected to brutal depravity for four hours. Twelve years later she was still in a trance with little hope of recovery. Jack Graham blew up an airliner containing his mother and 43 innocent victims. How much opportunity did these victims have to prepare for eternity, for eternal redemption?

On the other hand, there needs to be more concern for crime prevention. Is it reasonable to campaign strongly for the possibility of the redemption of murderers, most of whom have a long record of violent crime, while millions of pliable minds watch men and women being stabbed, shot, strangled, drowned, poisoned, and maltreated in almost every possible way as often as 20 times a day on television? If those who lead the movements for abolition are really concerned for the sacredness of life they should do something about the disrespect shown for life on television programs and in movies, which do so much to influence pliable minds.

It appears that with a decrease in the severity of punishment for criminals comes a corresponding increase in crime and the suffering of the innocent. In recent years, for example, the number of policemen murdered by felons has been larger than the number of felons executed by the state. It is argued that the administration of capital punishment is attended by many abuses. This may be so. The same can be said of the administration of Christian churches. Do we, therefore, eliminate the Christian churches? No, we try to eliminate the abuse. The same approach applies to the abuses of capital punishment.

Abolitionists make much of the loss of innocent lives through the death penalty. They overlook the fact, however, that more innocent lives have been lost through non-executed criminals who remained alive to commit more crimes than through executed non-criminals.

It has been said that the science of penology as well as the improvements in standards of social work and law enforcement have advanced to the point where society is protected to a greater extent than by the imposition of capital punishment. It is true that we have more effective police forces and more thorough rehabilitation of criminals. However, of the 14 states in the United States which abolished capital punishment prior to 1962, 8 have reinstituted it. Penology does give more protection now than formerly against criminals committing crimes in the future, but it cannot protect against persons committing crime in the first instance.

Every one of us still reflects the image of God. To murder a man is still an outrage, an outrage against God, the Creator, against man, the victim, against the victim's loved ones, against society and against the institution of government. Because life is sacred, life must be protected against maltreatment and murder. Policemen charged with the enforcing of the laws of the state must have the right to kill in self-defence or in the interest of law enforcement. The state must punish severely, at times with death, those who willfully disregard the sacredness of the lives of others. I believe this is necessary for the general good of society.[1]

                                                    R. N. THOMPSON

Capital punishment is . . . a gruesome thing, no doubt. But there are many things in life which are necessary and which are unpleasant. Today, especially, when contract murder is being carried out as part of organized crime throughout North America we must be very careful where we go. The fact that capital punishment is not a pleasant thing is no reason for rejecting it. It is hard to find a suitable comparison to make, but the abolition of capital punishment would, in the thinking of many people, be similar to our passing a law prohibiting surgeons from carrying out extensive and gruesome operations on persons suffering from particularly bad diseases. It is the only choice. It is not a pleasant one, but in my judgment it is the least of a number of evils in a given situation.

Capital punishment has been referred to by some as just legalized murder. To me this is a shamefully irresponsible statement. I think the main difference between capital punishment and murder, legalized or otherwise, is the effect on the citizens of this country. No citizen who has even a minimum of respect for the law or for the rights of his fellow men need have any fear that he will be the victim of capital punishment. A citizen can even commit murder—as a crime of passion— and not suffer capital punishment. Yet what about the victims of murderers? The most upright citizen in the land may be slaughtered in cold blood, or his children may be abducted and murdered on their way from Sunday school, as has happened many times in the past. To call capital punishment legalized murder is a complete distortion of anything which is logical. It is, I suppose, an attempt to play on the emotions of those who must deal with the fact that we do have murderers in our society.

What we are all interested in, I believe, in the fairly enlightened society in which we live, is the achievement of a net saving of human life, because we respect human life and recognize that the right to live is the primary right of all individuals. However I think there has been a great deal of misplaced sympathy for the murderer. I suppose this is understandable. The murderer is fairly tried in public in a court of law. He is the subject of news broadcasts and newspaper stories. He is probably photographed daily and his story is given on television every day.

But what about his victim? Nobody hears anything about the victim, though he, or she, may have been killed in cold blood. The public achieves some affinity with the murderer but none with the victim, because the victim is already dead and buried before the trial takes place. There is no word said about the orphans and widows. There is no concern about them, because their story has not been publicized. . . .

I have great sympathy for the position of law enforcement officers. After all, society depends a great deal on law enforcement officers so that we can walk in safety on our streets, and sleep at night knowing that our houses will not be broken into. Only today I received a telegram, as I am sure did most honourable members, from the annual meeting of the Federation of Quebec Municipal Policemen, representing more than 6,000 municipal policemen, conveying the text of a resolution saying it had been unanimously resolved (a) to oppose the abolition of the death penalty, and (b) to establish a national fund of indemnification concerning dependents of murder victims. I cannot help but support their point of view.

There has been a great deal of argument about whether the death penalty is a deterrent, how much of a deterrent, and whether it is a greater or lesser deterrent than life imprisonment. This is an argument that cannot be proven on either side but I would not like to have to try to convince any-one that capital punishment is not a deterrent. Statistically this cannot be proven because the deterrent effect on both capital punishment and life imprisonment is obscured by the fact that most criminals plan a crime on the basis that they are going to avoid any penalty, and that is the basis on which cold-blooded murders are committed.

To say that you can judge the deterrent effect of capital punishment or life imprisonment by interviewing the criminals who have been caught, tried and convicted, is not logical, because there you are dealing with cases where the deterrent did not work. I say the deterrent value is with respect to people who did not commit crimes, who were deterred from becoming murderers by the fact that capital punishment or some other heavy penalty would be meted out to them if caught. . . .[2]

J. J. MACLEAN

An outstanding justice of the Ontario appeal court said a few years ago, and I quote:

The irrevocable character of the death penalty is a reason why all possible measures should be taken against injustice—not for its abolition. Nowadays, with the advent of armed criminals and the substantial increase in armed robberies, criminals of long standing if arrested, must expect long sentences. However, if they run no risk of hanging, when found guilty of murder, they will kill policemen and witnesses with the prospect of a future no more unhappy, as one of them put it, than being fed, lodged, and clothed for the rest of their lives. In addition, once in prison, such people who are capable of anything could kill their guards and their fellow inmates with relative impunity.

It is clear that those words are as timely as ever. Nobody will deny that the execution of a murderer and everything that surrounds it is a terrible thing, but the murder itself is even more so.

Capital punishment must be retained to prove the sanctity of that most precious thing which is the gift of life; it embodies the repulsion and horror that we feel for the greatest of crimes.

Society has the right to protect the integrity of the human

being and the life of its members against what threatens them. That is why it exists. Because the government of a country has the duty to protect and defend the common good, it has the right to take the necessary legal steps to protect the physical, moral, emotional and intellectual welfare of the community as a whole.

If the state has the right and the duty to defend the community against outside aggression, such as in time of war, and within the country, for instance, in case of treason, crimes against the state, etc., and that to the extent of taking the life of the aggressors and guilty parties, if the citizen wants to protect his own life by killing whoever attacks him without any reason, the state can do the same when a criminal attacks and endangers the life of the community by deciding to eliminate summarily another human being. I think that society represented by the government can use capital punishment to eliminate a person who, willfully, does not follow the laws of society and endangers the life of a member of the community, if it is proven that such a punishment, by its nature, is a good protection for that same society, particularly against the repetition of this odious crime by protecting people who otherwise would be future victims.

Would life imprisonment, which often is nothing of the kind, advocated by the abolitionists, have that effect to the same extent as capital punishment?

Personally, I am morally convinced that the death penalty alone constitutes a measure with enough deterrent power to prevent such crimes and that is the main reason why I intend to vote for retaining the death penalty. That does not mean that I am in favour of retaining hanging as the only method of execution; I would like to see it replaced by the electric chair or even the gas chamber. . . .

Capital punishment certainly acts as a deterrent.

For most people, life is priceless and they will do anything and suffer the worst privations to preserve it, even when life itself does not hold many consolations or bright prospects for the future. According to an old proverb, fear is the beginning of wisdom, and undoubtedly capital punishment is an effective deterrent. This fear protects criminal organizations against indiscretions and blunders of their accomplices. What holds back professional criminals should all the more hold back potential criminals. . . .

As a deterrent, the death penalty is playing its part for which there is no substitute. To this, abolitionists answer mainly that statistics, in countries and states where the death penalty was abolished, compared with those where it was retained or re-established, would show that the homicide rates do not increase in the first case. I suggest that statistics do not prove much, either on one side or the other, as far as the efficiency or non-efficiency of capital punishment is concerned. There are too many variations, too many changes as regards circumstances, conditions, between one period and the other, to enable us to make worthy comparisons. To those who rely upon statistics, we could say that according to the press, in Great Britain, during the first year of abolition of capital punishment, namely in 1965, the number of murders is reported to have increased by one third, from 182 in 1964 to 249 in 1965. . . . It will never be possible to appreciate adequately the deterrent effect of capital punishment, but I am sure it exists and to a greater extent perhaps in our society than in others. Prison guards and other people have referred to the beneficial effect a hanging has on inmates of a jail where it takes place. You can feel then an atmosphere of meditation which reflects a general feeling of disapproval for this most odious of all crimes.

One of the chief arguments used by those who advocate abolition is the possibility of a miscarriage of justice taking place where an innocent person would be executed instead of the actual murderer. . . . I believe no case can be quoted where, in Canada, it has been found that an innocent person has been executed. Under our judiciary system, the accused is deemed to be innocent, and the Crown has to prove beyond every doubt that he is guilty. Theoretically, there is room for an error, but in practice it is almost impossible. The accused is judged by 12 jurors whose verdict must be unanimous; if he is found guilty, the decision is reviewed by the Court of appeal and, normally, it is then brought before the Supreme Court. Finally, the case is submitted to the Cabinet with a view to commutation. The execution of an innocent person is almost impossible, and the chances of a miscarriage of justice are reduced to a minimum. . . .[3]

YVES FOREST

There are two sorts of arguments in favour of the retention of capital punishment. First, so to speak, there is the doctrinal or philosophical point of view, which may be summarized as follows: "Human life is so sacred that every means must be used to protect it. He who takes away life deserves death." There is also the argument of deterrence: "If, in taking away life, a man knows he is risking his own, he will not kill."

On the other hand, there are also two sorts of arguments put forward by the enemies of capital punishment. The first is also based on the sacred character of human life: "If life is sacred, we have no right to take it away from anyone." The second concerns the deterrent aspect of capital punishment. It may be summarized as follows: Apart from any moral consideration, we might be in favour of the death penalty if only there was evidence that it reduces the number of murders. Such is not the case. Statistics prove nothing, either in favour or against. Therefore, capital punishment must be abolished.

I shall not attempt to develop the first argument based on the sacred nature of human life. I readily realize that from the same premises can be drawn diametrically opposed conclusions and that such an abstruse reasoning will convince nobody. The second argument, as well as the second objection, is more valid and deserves more consideration. However, before dealing with capital punishment as a repressive measure, I should like to attempt to answer an argument often put forward by those who oppose it.

For these people, capital punishment would simply be, basically, some sort of a community revenge complex; a modern form of the old *lex talionis:* an eye for an eye, a tooth for a tooth. What formerly held for relatively primitive communities, for some eras infinitely remote from ours, no longer holds for our infinitely more progressive and modern society. To this I would reply that what is contemptuously referred to as the *lex talionis* is no more than a perfectly legitimate attempt to make the punishment fit the crime. To serious crime, serious punishment. But it will be objected that this is an obsolete notion and that in this day there can be no question of making punishment fit the crime when what we need, on the contrary, is to make the punishment fit the criminal.

Modern penal science no longer seeks to suppress or punish, but to rehabilitate, and capital punishment, because it is past recall—by its very definition, if I may say—has obviously no corrective value.

While this argument makes some sense, it should not, I feel, be developed to its utter limit, because it is ridiculous to claim that in deciding upon penalties, the seriousness of the crime should never be taken into account and that the criminal should be the only consideration.

Besides, those who are not forcibly against severity, the most inclined to leniency towards criminals, are not always logical with themselves. They want to protect society; yet, in their concept of individual protection, they want us to believe that criminals are rather victims of this society, instead of guilty people; they forget that murder and homicide are direct infringements on the freedom of individuals, and hence are crimes against society.

In my opinion, society is the association of all individuals making up the society; and when I say that it must be protected, I think, for instance, of my right to stroll quietly about the streets without being attacked. And this is the right of millions of law-abiding Canadians who have the right to insist on the protection of public powers.

Someone will say that I go a little too far, that my freedom is not threatened that much, neither my life, and what proves that they would be better protected by the retention of the death penalty?

That the freedom of individuals to attend quietly to their business, without fear of evil-doers, is nowadays more threatened than it was before the Second World War, is a truth unanimously admitted and confirmed by statistics. The present debate deals with the death penalty; otherwise, I could dwell at great length on the continual increase of the number of crimes with violence, which often end in murder. I am con-

vinced that this state of things is due to lack of vigorous reactions of society in the face of this threat. But instead of
imputing this phenomenon, as they should, to the fact that
public opinion does not support energetically enough the
police forces or the courts in their fight against criminals, some
people prefer to blame our penal system.

It is not to a member in whose riding is located one of the
largest penitentiaries of the country, that of St. Vincent de
Paul, that you have to prove that our present system is not
perfect. But there is one consideration that is never kept in
mind. The more we pity the criminal, the more we criticize the
courts for being too severe, the more we condemn our prison
system in general, the more the number of crime increases.
Why not try an experiment for once? Why not stop our
criticism? From now on, why do we not encourage our courts
to be more severe, instead of feeling sorry, as we do, for the
criminals? How do we know that the figures on crime would
not diminish?

It is said that statistics on the number of murderers, as compared with those on the number of executions, do not prove
any deterrent value at all to the death penalty. It is concluded
therefrom that fear of the gallows never caused any murderer
to hesitate. But there seems to be one thing forgotten, that is
in our times, in this country—and the present debate is evidence of this—the death penalty is rejected by a good part of
public opinion. Those who stand against it, surely in good
faith, are often influenced in their great devotion for what they
believe is a good cause. In the end, they have created so much
confusion in the minds of the people that every time the question of an execution comes up, thousands of citizens immediately have pity on that poor criminal. There is so much
criticism against capital punishment that people are trying to
find all sorts of excuses for the offender. In this way, an atmosphere which is almost favourable to murder is created.
Young people who grow up in a society where they are sure
to find defenders everywhere, whatever they do, in the end
have a complete disregard for the law. Laws do not so much
prevent crime as the moral climate of society. We can retain
capital punishment but as long as there are people who dis-

parage it, who cry injustice and inhumanity every time there is talk of its application, there will be less and less hesitation before killing. But if it were certain that society as a whole abhors murder, do you really think one would so easily risk being an accessory? Those who know criminals will tell you that a great many of them have a great capacity for self-pity and for finding all sorts of excuses for themselves.

As long as people here and elsewhere find them more deserving of mercy than strictness, as long as people, every time a criminal is executed, rise and say, along with I forget which movie director: "We are all murderers," murderers will find themselves interesting. What is more, they will feel all the more innocent if they find here and there people ready to weep over their sad plight.

I do not want to be cynical or merciless towards the unfortunate people who must be removed for the benefit of society, but I want us to consider not only the murderers but the victims also. If the death penalty could prevent only one murder, it should be maintained.

I am convinced that if the critics of capital punishment were silenced and if, for once, we were to think of the fate of the victims instead of that of the murderers, we would go a long way toward cleaning up the moral atmosphere of our community. . . .[4]

JEAN-L. ROCHON

THE ABOLITIONISTS

I am in favour of the motion to abolish capital punishment and I am also supporting the amendment to put it on a five-year trial basis. I doubt that there is much new that can be said in this debate. The entire field has been well covered but I should like to put very briefly four reasons for my opposition to capital punishment. The first is that capital punishment is contrary to the highest concepts of the Judaic Christian ethic. I do not propose to go into theological arguments, but both in this debate and in the discussions which have taken place outside the house many people have been quoting Scripture in support of retaining the death penalty.

It is always a dangerous practice to quote isolated passages of Scripture. The Bible has been quoted in times past to support slavery, child labour, polygamy, the burning of witches, and subservience to dictators. The Scriptures have to be viewed as a whole. The Bible is not one book, it is many books. It does not have a static concept. It represents man's emerging moral concepts as they have grown through the centuries.

It is true that the Mosaic law provided the death penalty for murder. It is equally true, if one looks particularly at the 20th chapter of the book of Leviticus, that the Mosaic law provided the death penalty for 33 crimes including such things as adultery, bestiality, homosexuality, witchcraft and sacrificing to other gods than Jehovah. It seems to me that those who want to pick out isolated texts from the Bible in support of retaining the death penalty for murder have to be equally consistent and ask that the death penalty be retained for all the other crimes listed in the Mosaic law.

Of course, those who take this position overlook several facts. They overlook, first of all, the fact that the Mosaic law was an advanced law for the primitive times in which it was formulated. It was later succeeded by the Hebrew prophets who introduced the idea of justice superseded by mercy, the possible redemption and re-establishment of the individual. They overlook the fact that if any nation in the world ought to feel itself bound by Mosaic law it should be the state of Israel. The state of Israel abolished the death penalty many years ago except for Nazi war criminals and for treason committed in times of war. The religious hierarchy of the state of Israel enthusiastically supported the Knesset in abolishing the death penalty in that country.

But for those of us who belong to the Christian religion it seems to me we have to remember also that the Christian religion went far beyond the Mosaic law. In the days of the founder of Christianity the Mosaic law still obtained. This law decreed that a woman taken in adultery could be stoned to death. We should remember the statement of Jesus of Nazareth when he came upon a group of poeple preparing to stone such a woman to death. He said, "Let him who is without sin among you cast the first stone."

When the crowd had dwindled away so that only the woman was left he said to the woman, "Go and sin no more." It seems to me that this is the ultimate culmination of the Christian concept of the application of mercy and the possible redemption of the individual.

My second reason for opposing capital punishment is that I believe capital punishment brutalizes the society that uses it without providing any effective deterrent that cannot be provided equally well by life imprisonment. I believe that any society that practices capital punishment brutalizes itself. It has an effect upon that society and I do not believe that society can rid itself of murderers by itself becoming a murderer. Surely if brutality would deter the committing of a crime Great Britain should have been a place of law-abiding citizens because a little over 150 years ago there were over 200 crimes for which an individual could be put to death. Instead of making Britain a nation of law-abiders it was a country where crime abounded, where human sensibilities were dulled by the public execution of criminals. It is rather significant that in that day, as in this, it was often the juries who were more humane than the lawmakers. It was only because juries refused to convict, knowing the terrible punishment which would follow, that the lawmakers were forced 150 years ago to remove the death penalty from a great many of the crimes for which it had been prescribed.

All of the evidence which can be gathered seems to indicate that the death penalty is not a unique deterrent and that life imprisonment can be equally effective. Most honourable members are familiar with the works of Thorsten Sellin, a professor at Pennsylvania University, and his book *The Death Penalty Relative to Deterrence and Police Safety.* Many figures have been quoted and I do not think there is any need for me to quote them again. Certainly his study in the United States, which compared states which have abolished the death penalty with states which have retained it, led him to the conclusion that "abolition had no visible effect on homicide rates."

Marc Ancel, who did the United Nations study which looked into the experience of the many countries which have abolished capital punishment, some of them as long as 50 years ago, and states which have retained it, came to this conclusion:

Removal of the death penalty has never been followed by a notable rise in the incidence of crime no longer punishable with death.

I readily agree that quoting endless statistics is not going to to prove either the case for abolition or the case for retention, but there certainly seems to be no convincing volume of evidence which would satisfy any unbiased individual that abolishing the death penalty has resulted in an upsurge of homicide or that those states which have retained the death penalty are any freer of capital crimes than those which have not.

After all, who is it that the death penalty deters? It has certainly not deterred the man who commits murder. Will it deter him in the future? Surely he can be deterred in the future by being incarcerated for the remainder of his life. Who is deterred if this man is hanged? Is he to be hanged as an example to the rest of the community? I can conceive of nothing more immoral than to break a man's neck as an example to other people, but if that is the argument . . . we ought to have public executions. . . .

The fear of death will deter normal men but when a man commits murder, is he normal? Can we understand the motivation that causes a man to take a human life? When a man commits homicide, does he sit down and assess whether he is committing it in a state that has capital punishment or in a state that has abolished capital punishment? I think not. In the main the man who commits homicide is the man who is mentally ill, the man who kills does not make the common, rational judgments, that are made by the average individual.[5]

T. C. DOUGLAS

Hanging to me is a symbol of the imperfections and hypocrisy of our affluent society. I say this because I know too many people who find security and salve for their conscience in the mistaken belief that hanging produces for them at least a degree of protection against what they seem to think is a segment of society with which they have nothing in common, and will never come into contact.

I suggest that the conscience of this country must be awakened to the fact that no one is born to be a murderer. Murderers, with very few exceptions, are victims of certain circumstances such as mental illness or, to our shame, are the products of man's inhumanity to man. I hope when hanging is abolished public opinion will demand that the pockets of poverty in this country be eradicated, that the slum areas in our big cities be demolished, because society will then realize, in their search for some other form of protection, that the areas of poverty and slums in big cities create strong forces that breed crime and criminals. I fully believe that as long as we resort to periodic hangings to convince ourselves that law and order reigns and that crime is under control, people will continue to resist providing moneys that are needed for new penal institutions, new forms of rehabilitation and new universities to train the psychiatrists and psychologists that are needed in such vast numbers if rehabilitation is to have any effect. . . .

I am an avowed abolitionist and I approached this debate expecting that some speakers would speak in a clinical manner while others would approach it emotionally. That has been the case, but frankly I am surprised to find that in general it is the retentionists who fall back on emotional arguments, and those who support abolition who have attempted to bring a certain degree of science to their arguments. . . .

I do not intend to be emotional in this connection. I should like to do what others more learned than I have done, and try to apply statistics to the problem at hand. There is an old saying that there are liars and statistics. But of course I believe all of us realize that statistics do play a very important part in Canadian life. Statistics are the basis of much of the legislation on Canada's statute books; statistics provide information figures on unemployment in this country; statistics are the basis of the insurance industry. There is nothing wrong with statistics—unless there are those who, including myself, would use them without a thorough knowledge—because this is a science. But that does not prevent me or anyone else in this house relying upon the findings of those who are trained in the use of statistics. There are statisticians, social scientists, criminologists, men capable and trained to interpret figures accurately and objectively. Such a man is Professor Sellin, a professor of sociology, President of the International Society of Criminology and a pioneer in the field of criminology and the prevention of crime. Statistics coming from him would be those of a man trained for a very long time in the field of criminology and should carry some weight in a debate such as this, particularly among people who are trying to be objective in forming a conclusion.

Time does not permit a review of all the remarks of this learned professor, but some statistics are very relevant and I think should be read into the record. I do this because a subject of some misgivings in this debate has been the danger or so-called danger to prison guards and policemen from a man convicted of murder and serving time. In this instance the figures relate to American penitentiaries. Professor Sellin in reviewing the incidence of murder in United States penitentiaries in the year 1964 found that in 30 states there were 26 murders. But significantly, of the 26 murders all but two took place in states which have the death penalty, and those two took place in the state of Michigan which is an abolition state.

The policemen in this country have my sympathy but, as the honourable member for York South (Mr. Lewis) mentioned today, there are occupational hazards in all lines of endeavour. In reviewing statistics concerning the danger of policemen being murdered, Professor Sellin considered the statistics made available to him by the Federal Bureau of Investigation in the years 1961, 1962 and 1963. The professor found that 140 policemen were killed by suspects or offenders in that period, or an average of 47 policemen a year. Of these 47 policemen killed, 9 were killed in abolition states: 2 in Michigan, 4 in Wisconsin, 2 in Minnesota and 1 in North Dakota. In the 9 states bordering these 9 abolition states, 21 were killed, 4 in Massachusetts, 4 in Indiana, 4 in Illinois, 5 in Ohio, 1 in Iowa and 1 in Montana; there were 2 killed in Michigan, an abolition state, but 5 killed in Ohio and 4 in Indiana which border Michigan and are retention states.

I should like to refer to statistics a little closer to home. One of the arguments advanced by the Minister of Justice of the

province of Quebec is that since it has become the policy of
this government, and was that of the previous government, to
hand out commutations on a rather generous basis, this has
had a tremendous effect on the crime rate, particularly in the
case of capital murder, in the province of Quebec. I went to
what I thought was the most reliable source of statistics in this
regard, namely, the Dominion Bureau of Statistics. I had
hoped to draw a pattern or draft of the incidence of murder in
my province. I found that before 1960 murders were not reported to Ottawa by the province of Quebec, at least not
through the provincial police department, although they were
gathered haphazardly from different communities.

Therefore, much as I would have liked to take in the period
1960 to 1964 and compare it with 1956 to 1960, those figures
were not available from the Dominion Bureau of Statistics.
They are available, of course, from 1961 to 1964. In the year
1961 there were 39 incidents of murder in the province of
Quebec; in 1962 there were 42; in 1963 it jumped to 50, giving
some credence to the theory that criminals were taking advantage of the policy of commutation. Then in 1964, the last
year for which statistics are available, the number of murders
decreased from 50 to 45. The number of victims follows a
similar pattern. In 1961 there were 42; in 1962, 44; in 1963, 57.
But in 1964 it dropped to 46.

Whether we are abolitionists or retentionists, all of us, I am
happy to say, realize that relatively few murderers fall into the
category of cold, callous killers. Most people in justifying their
argument for retention, and I respect this argument, emphasize
the role that syndicated crime takes right now. I agree with
them to the extent that I would not particularly care if one of
these particular murderers was captured and hanged, because
I suppose they must be called the dregs of society.

That is the emotional answer I would give; but the cold,
clinical answer is that statistically, at least on the information
available in the United States, where some states are abolition
and some retention, this type of professional killer does not
expect to be captured. They are so cynical of the death penalty
that they continue to operate in the main from those states
that retain the death penalty when they could quite easily have

their base of operations in what is known as an abolition state. I believe that the greatest deterrent the Canadian people can put at the disposal of law and order is not a continuation of the death penalty but an increase in the number of people captured.

The greatest deterrent, I suggest, is the fear of capture, not the fear of penalty insofar as hardened criminals are concerned. If we want to do something about murder, and I presume that is what this debate is all about, we have to hire more policemen. Most of the police forces of the large cities are badly understaffed, as the police chiefs will tell you.

In conclusion, most of the retentionists have advanced but two good arguments. The first one has been that the death penalty is a deterrent. I hope I have proven to someone's satisfaction, as I have proven to my own, that according to statistics retention does not prevent crime. Secondly, of course, there are those who, like the honourable member for Red Deer (Mr. Thompson), quote the Bible so profusely. I can appreciate and understand those who want to retain the death penalty as a form of punishment. A man is entitled to his religious convictions, but quoting the Bible almost indiscriminately as justification for retention of capital punishment does not hold water when one realizes that the state of Israel has abolished the death penalty. . . .[6]

B. S. MACKASEY

I have noticed from the speeches to which I have listened and the comments of my colleagues in the House of Commons that everybody has been giving the subject deep and earnest consideration. Personally, I have tried to weigh the relative merits of the arguments which have been made on both sides, arguments which seemed to be so well balanced that one appeared to offset the other, to the extent that it took me some time before I was able to come to a firm decision.

Finally, I did come to a decision. The decision to which I came was that I would have to support the abolition of capital punishment. Granted, there are many factors involved and there are some intangibles for which there is no yardstick. Men of good faith and high principles support both sides;

and there is no doubt that the sincerity of the one side, regardless which side it is, is equally matched by the sincerity of the other side.

I reached my conclusion for two particular reasons, among many others, and I should like to deal with them very briefly in a few moments. I do not wish to cover ground that has already been well covered by speakers before me, but I should like to say that it is to be expected that the general character of the people of Canada will be reflected in their laws.

These laws are designed not only to protect society but also to encourage the continuance of the principles which have been an abiding source of strength to all people in our nation.

In the present debate arguments are made both for and against retaining capital punishment. Those who support retaining capital punishment and those who support its abolition are both endeavouring to bring in legislation which will be for the betterment of Canada. I think there is no doubt about their intentions. However I believe that capital punishment ought to be abolished, if for no other reason than that to some extent it is unenforceable. It seems that it is becoming more and more difficult to enforce laws on the statute books that prescribe capital punishment. Where hangings are concerned juries seem to be unwilling to bring in verdicts of guilty. Quite often when a man is sentenced to hang, the verdict is changed to one involving penal servitude.

As things are today a man knows when he commits murder that he has an excellent chance, if caught, of not being executed. Therefore what are the advantages of retaining capital punishment? Under circumstances such as these, any deterrent effect capital punishment has is negated by the fact that the sentence to hang is seldom carried out.

I believe that the value of a deterrent depends largely upon the certainty and swiftness with which justice is dispensed. As things are there can be no certainty that capital punishment will be carried out. It is almost certain that when a man is sentenced to hang there will be interminable delays. As I said, juries seem hesitant to bring in verdicts finding accused persons guilty of capital murder, when they know that the convicted man very likely will hang. As a result there are laws on the statute books which are not enforced. That being the case, I maintain that it is better to rewrite the laws than to have them ignored.

On the other hand if the sentence for capital murder were life imprisonment, in my view juries would not be reluctant to bring in verdicts of guilty. There would be a far greater certainty that a murderer would be found guilty and punished if it were realized that the consequences of murder were certain penal servitude for life. I submit that the real deterrent would be the realization by would-be murderers that the law would be enforced, and enforced swiftly.

Another reason why I think hanging should be abolished is the effect that I think legalized killings or executions have upon the public character. When I talk of this I realize that I am talking of something about which it is impossible to quote statistics. It must be a matter of opinion, and it must be something for which there can be only a belief. It cannot be substantiated by fact. I agree with the man who said that whenever a criminal dies on the gallows a little part of the nation dies with him. I believe that an execution by the state has a detrimental effect upon the character of the people. I believe it has a detrimental effect on both the state and the people. Also, I believe every time a man is hanged, the dragon's teeth for future crime are sown. I believe by the very means by which we seek to abolish crime we are in fact sowing the seeds of future crime. I believe it is wrong for the state to take upon itself the prerogative to say that it is permissible to kill in the face of the divine command: Thou shalt not kill.

I believe, too, that it is wrong in this modern age, in a country known for its humanities, for its forward looking social thought and conscience, that we should have today as part of our system of justice an instrument of medieval murder which is comparable with the rack and the thumbscrew. I believe it is time that the people of Canada should banish from this land the shadow of the gibbet.[7]

C. R. GRANGER

I wish to say right now that I am in favour of abolition. As a matter of fact I have been in favour of abolition for a

good many years now. What I have heard in this debate has
convinced me this is the proper stand to take, the correct
stand at this time. I am going to adduce just a few of the
facts which have impressed me in this debate, and the facts
about which I shall tell my constituents when I go back
home. I have no idea what a poll would show in my riding.
I believe the majority of the people there, given access to the
facts which we have had, would be in favour of abolition,
because they are reasonable and sensible people who I think
will approach this matter without emotion and look straight
at the facts?

What are the facts? Here are some of them. First of all, . . .
we have seen from the facts that whether or not a country
or a state has seen fit to retain or abolish capital punishment the rate of murder has remained practically unchanged,
has remained virtually the same. All right then; I would say
. . . the rate of murder is virtually the same whether you retain or do away with capital punishment, we have the right
and the obligation to say to our constituents that capital
punishment does not protect them any better than a method of
keeping the criminal in custody safely away from society.
We have the right and the obligation to take away from our
constituents a false view; that is, that capital punishment
somehow protects them just because we always have believed
that. We should give them the facts and figures to support this.

I believe we have the right to let them know in respect
of the policemen and the prison guards who have been killed,
that in no overwhelming number of cases has that killing
of policemen and prison guards been done by murderers. It
has been done by a hard core of criminals, just as many of
whom were non-murderers as were murderers. I think we
have the obligation to tell that to Canadians. I believe that
once the people realize these are the facts, we do not need to
fear their reaction. I am not afraid of any feeling on the part
of Canadians. I believe they would want to have the truth in
front of them and would want to know what it is. . . .

Hanging does not bring the dead back to life, nor does it
help the survivors. In my view—and I think I am saying
something which nobody else has said yet in this debate,

and this is hard to do—I cannot see why it would not be an excellent thing, while the murderer is retained in prison, to employ him at some useful work, the result of such work being directed to helping the family of his victim. In that way his rehabilitation can be a useful way of making a measure of restitution, though there never could be complete restitution. However, I think he should be given an opportunity to make up to the family and relatives of the victim as much as he can. I believe this is in line with the thinking of modern penology.

In my view when a murderer commits a crime, if the state snuffs out his life the state compounds the crime and commits a second one. What happens when a boy kicks his younger brother and the father turns around and kicks the bigger boy. This does not help the little fellow and it implants in the bigger boy a feeling that he wants to get a little older so that he can get back at the fellow who kicks him. That is the type of thing we want to get away from.

We have been struggling through all this miasma of fear; I have seen this in the house. Of course we are afraid, because we are on the frontier of evolution in this matter. This is the reason in many ways it is a thrilling debate—because it is new for Canadians. But it is not new for other people. The whole trend in the world today is towards the abolition of the death penalty. This has been brought out by one or two other members, but I wish to bring it out again, because I think it is important. The fact is that country after country —and Europe is the place where one finds it most frequently —has reached a point today where capital punishment has been done away with. Luxembourg began the process in 1822, Belgium in 1863, Portugal in 1867—100 years ago when we were beginning as a country—the Netherlands in 1870, Italy in 1890, Norway in 1905, Sweden in 1921, Denmark in 1930, Switzerland in 1942, and Great Britain in 1965. All the enlightened, forward looking countries, when at last they reached the stage where they got it through their minds that capital punishment was barbarism which belonged in the middle ages, did away with the death penalty.

It is interesting to note that during the Mussolini regime

Italy again brought in the death penalty and that during Hitler's regime Germany also brought back the death penalty. When Hitler and Mussolini brought barbarism back to these two countries the death penalty also returned. Italy and West Germany have subsequently abolished the death penalty. East Germany does not belong to that part of the world that we consider advanced in these matters.

Britain, as honourable members realize, has abolished the death penalty for a five-year trial period. The veteran Labour member who has led the fight in Britain for the abolition of capital punishment for years is Sidney Silverman. Last year he enjoyed the fruition of his campaign and capital punishment was abolished for a trial period of five years. It is interesting that during the recent election campaign Sidney Silverman was opposed by a close relative of a little girl who had been the victim of a horrible sex slaying. He rattled all the chains he could during the campaign but to the eternal credit of the British people they elected Silverman with a greatly increased majority.

That is the kind of thing that happens when people are prepared to make decisions with their eyes open on the basis of facts rather than emotion. Emotions should be considered and then put out of the way so that the facts can be deliberated and decisions made.

Over and over again during this debate honourable members have referred to the fact that in Canada we have in effect had no capital punishment, de facto, since December of 1962. Even before that time Canada's position on capital punishment had been weakening. When the former government divided the categories of murder into capital and non-capital it took a step in the direction of manifesting Canada's maturity in civilization and its ability to do away with capital punishment.

That was the first step toward the abolition of capital punishment. The second step has been the attitude of the government in not carrying out the sentence of death since the latter part of 1962. I suggest these steps are indications that this country has been readying itself for complete abolition of the death sentence. There would be a tremendous outcry by the people of Canada if pending executions were carried out as a result of a vote in this house to retain capital punishment. The people of this country in increasing numbers have become aware that capital punishment is not consonant with these times. In ever increasing numbers they are becoming prepared to do away with this form of barbarism.

Not long ago I received a letter, as did every British Columbia member, from the B. C. Corrections Association. This letter is dated March 18, 1966, and it states in part:

> We felt that you, as a British Columbia member, might be interested to see an expression of opinion on this issue from the present membership of our association. We represent all facets of correction, probation officers, parole officers, prison personnel, social workers, welfare workers and others.

In other words, this is representative of all types of people involved in criminal correction and rehabilitation in British Columbia. This association sent out a questionnaire in which they asked the recipients of the questionnaire to indicate whether they were in favour of complete abolition of capital punishment, abolition except in respect of capital murder of prison personnel and law enforcement officers, or retention of capital punishment. There were 64.3 per cent in favour of complete abolition, 25.7 per cent in favor of abolition except for the capital murder of prison personnel and law enforcement officers, and only 10 per cent in favour of retention.

It is my opinion that if 64.3 per cent of a representative group of people working closely with criminals are in favour of the complete abolition of capital punishment, the majority of Canadian people are ready for its abolition. . . .[8]

GRACE MACINNIS

As the members who favour abolition present their case, I notice that a recurring theme in their argument is that capital punishment does not effectively deter homicide. This theory is immediately challenged by the retentionist, and the argument goes on with each side summoning impressive documentation for their respective positions. In my own studies, and I have tried to consider this matter objectively, I have become convinced that there is no proof that capital punishment is an effective deterrent or the only deterrent force.

I believe that many statements and much evidence supporting this fact are typified by the rather concise statement, which might be considered a ready or available reference for the average Canadian, as found in the latest edition of the *Encyclopedia Britannica*. It is as follows:

Regarding deterrence, it is well established by statistical studies that (1) when comparisons are made between contiguous states with similar populations and similar social, economic and political conditions—some of these states lacking and others retaining capital punishment—homicide rates are the same and follow the same trend over a long period of time regardless of the use or nonuse of capital punishment; (2) the abolition, introduction or reintroduction of this penalty is not accompanied by the effect on homicide rates that is postulated by the advocates of capital punishment; (3) even in communities where the deterrent effect should be greatest because the offender and his victim lived there and trial and execution were well publicized, homicide rates are not affected by the execution; (4) the rate of policemen killed by criminals is no higher in abolition states than in comparable death-penalty states. Capital punishment, then, does not appear to have a specific influence on the amount or trend of the kind of crime it is supposed to deter people from committing.

The point is certainly not that the *Encyclopedia Britannica* is a particular or ultimate authority in this matter, although I have been in touch with their editorial board who inform me that their statement is the result of many hours of study and research the world over. The point is rather that a reasonable doubt exists as to the basic value of capital punishment. There is reasonable doubt that this nation gains any great benefit from the use of the gallows. It is my understanding that in their wisdom the courts of this great land caution the many Canadians who are asked as jurors to judge their peers to remember that, if a reasonable doubt exists, that doubt must free the accused. . . . In this case, that doubt is present, and as a member of the jury judging capital punishment, I must, in all human conscience, cast my vote for abolition.

I have mentioned reasonable doubt as to the effective value of the ultimate penalty. There is another area of reasonable doubt which is in my opinion of prior importance and could well be the prime consideration in regard to the whole issue before us.

In this twentieth century, in spite of all the knowledge and experience at our disposal, there is possibility of error whereby an innocent person has been, and under our present Criminal Code can be, put to death for a crime which he or she did not commit. In this debate actual cases have already been mentioned in this connection. I am sure that there are and must be many more. . . .[9]

KEITH HYMMEN

Movements to Abolish the Death Penalty in the United States

LOUIS FILLER

The struggle against the death penalty has been carried on parallel to, though not necessarily hand in hand with, that for better treatment of prisoners. There were no early movements, in the organized sense, to reduce the number of capital offenses. The abolition of death for witchcraft, for example, resulted from a general revulsion against the witchcraft frenzy and its abettors. In the eighteenth century the American colonies averaged about a dozen crimes for which death could be asked. This was very few when compared

Reprinted, by permission, from *The Annals of the American Academy of Political and Social Science*, 284:124–136, November, 1952.

with England, the common law of which they had taken over, where more than two hundred crimes carried the death penalty. The relatively low number of such crimes in America was due to the scarcity of labor; that there were a dozen was due to a lack of prisons for keeping convicted criminals. With county jails inadequate and insecure, the criminal population seemed best controlled by death, mutilation, and fines.[1]

The "Great Act" of William Penn (1682) showed some concern for prison conditions, and broke with precedents by prescribing death for premeditated murder only. Such extreme mildness offended official sensibilities. In 1718, as a by-product of a serious clash between colony and crown representatives, the harsher penal code of England was adopted in Pennsylvania, and included thirteen capital offenses. As William Bradford was to observe, there was no evidence that the earlier, milder regime had resulted in more frequent or more "flagitious" offenses in that state than had occurred elsewhere.[2]

In 1764 Cesare Beccaria published his *Essay on Crimes and Punishments,* translations of which profoundly impressed American readers. They were also influenced by the writings and example of John Howard, the English prison reformer, as well as by the writings of Montesquieu, Voltaire, and Bentham, among others. In 1776 the Philadelphia Society for Relieving Distressed Prisoners was organized, but in that year of revolution it was not able to get under way. Largely spurred by Quaker interest, however, the Philadelphia Society for Alleviating the Miseries of Public Prisons began its work in 1787, with a membership including Dr. Benjamin Rush, Caleb Lownes, Tench Coxe, Thomas Wistar, and other notables of state and nation, some of whom furnished descendants to carry their work in prison reform down to modern times, with the same organization, since 1833 named the Pennsylvania Prison Society.

Benjamin Rush

As early as 1787, Dr. Rush read a paper at the home of Benjamin Franklin entitled *An Enquiry into the Effects of*

Public Punishments upon Criminals and upon Society. His paper expressed, in part, the dissatisfaction of Pennsylvania reformers with the penal law of 1786, which had been expected to reform the 1718 law mentioned above, but had embodied evils of its own, including provisions for "infamous" prison clothes, shaved heads, degrading work and conditions, and public humiliation.

Rush's paper, moreover, contained the first reasoned argument in America favoring the abolition of capital punishment. For this reason it drew criticism and rebuttal. Rush was engaged in open controversy which he summed up in his *Considerations on the Injustice and Impolity of Punishing Murder by Death* (1792). Here he cited (as he had earlier) the arguments of Beccaria, joined issue on what constituted the Christian view of the death penalty, and referred to the experiences of Russia, Germany, Sweden, and Tuscany with abolition. Here were arguments which were repeated, with additions, numerous times in the next hundred years and beyond.

William Bradford

More moderate, yet one of the most influential pamphlets in the entire abolitionist literature, was that prepared by William Bradford, attorney general of Pennsylvania and later of the United States, at the request of the governor of Pennsylvania. As expanded and published in 1793, it contained the valuable addition of Caleb Lownes's "Account of the Gaol and Penitentiary House of Philadelphia, and of the Interior Management Thereof."

Turning to the constitutions of the several states, Bradford observed that New Hampshire's warned against too sanguinary punishments, that Vermont's enjoined hard labor to lessen the necessity for capital punishment, and that the 1776 Pennsylvania constitution had asked for a revision of the penal laws so that penalties would be in proportion to offenses. Maryland's constitution explicitly stated that capital punishment ought to be avoided as much as possible.

Bradford was satisfied that capital punishment, as such,

did not stop crime: for example, horse stealing, though capital in Virginia, was the most frequent crime in that state. Nor was it easy to obtain a conviction in such a case: the severity of the penalty was its own undoing. If a law could not be enforced, it was worse than useless. Bradford concluded, with Beccaria: "A mitigation of punishment ought, therefore, to be accompanied, as far as possible, *by a diffusion of knowledge and a strict execution of the law.*"[3]

Bradford was not for abolishing the death penalty, necessarily, and thought it would be rash to abolish it entirely. In analyzing such capital crimes as counterfeiting, rape, arson, manslaughter, and petit treason, he considered each on its own merits. In 1794 he was instrumental in persuading the Pennsylvania legislature to make legal the distinction between first and second degree murder: thereafter only premeditated murder would occasion capital punishment.[4]

Influential, too, was the account by Caleb Lownes of the work of the Philadelphia Society to provide sufficient prison facilities and conditions encouraging criminal reform. As Lownes wrote: "It is a strange kind of oeconomy, to hang our fellow-creatures to avoid the expence [*sic*] of preparing a proper place of confinement."[5] Because of the Society's efforts in both respects, it received inquiries from other states concerning its work and ideas—the most famous and controversial being its system of solitary confinement—and, in turn, made efforts to secure information about experiences in other parts of the country, by corresponding with prison wardens.[6]

REFORMERS IN EARLY
NINETEENTH CENTURY

During the early decades of the nineteenth century, individual reformers made efforts to advance the cause of abolition. In New York, Governors George and De Witt Clinton and Daniel D. Tompkins at various times urged the New York legislature to modify or end capital punishment.[7] Nevertheless, popular understanding of the subject did not advance markedly. A New York beam-maker, of Quaker persuasion, perched his views precariously on Biblical texts, his practical cure for murderous impulses being an "enormous duty" on all kinds of strong liquor. A New York clergyman linked his pacifist convictions with those opposing capital punishment.[8]

Reflections Occasioned by a Public Execution, at Boston, April 25, 1822, anonymously issued, was filled with confused sentiments about the awfulness of the spectacle and a strong concern with the hereafter, which cannot be classed as favorable or unfavorable to the death penalty. Perhaps the most influential of all prison reformers of the time, Thomas Eddy, a Philadelphia Friend whose major work is identified with New York, does not appear to have given deep thought to the problem, though he did to all other problems in penology. The first decades of the century, to be sure, did see progress in prison organization and a general reduction in the number of death penalties.[9]

Edward Livingston

Perhaps the most distinguished of all American reports involving capital punishment was issued in 1821. In 1803, Edward Livingston, at a turning point in his extraordinary career, had emigrated from New York to Louisiana. In 1821, the future Secretary of State and Minister to France under Jackson was appointed a commissioner by the legislature of Louisiana to revise its criminal code. Influenced by the *Code Napoléon,* he set out to compile the penal law of Louisiana, which he prepared with introductory reports on codes of crimes and punishments, procedure, evidence, and reform and prison discipline. He dealt at length with the death penalty (a subject which had long and actively interested him) as a deterrent to crime and an instrument of justice.

A great part of my task [Livingston believed] is rendered unnecessary, by the general acknowledgment, universal, I may say, in the United States, that this punishment ought to be abolished in all cases, excepting those of treason, murder and rape. In some states arson is included; and lately, since so large a portion of our influential citizens have become bankers, brokers, and dealers in exchange, a strong inclination has been discovered to extend it to forgery, and uttering false bills of exchange.[10]

Livingston developed a systematic rebuttal of all arguments favoring capital punishment. The official nature of his report, its breadth of argument and illustration, and its well-constructed character gave it great prestige, influenced penal legislation in some South American countries, and inspired the legend in America and abroad that it had been adopted in Louisiana. Its wide influence cannot be questioned, and it inspired abolitionists for generations after, who circulated it with enthusiasm. It was, however, too far advanced for acceptance in Louisiana proper, and Livingston's many concerns left him no time to press for its acceptance by that state.[11]

THE ERA OF REFORM

The 1830's were a time of rising reform, politically, socially, intellectually, and for abolitionists, as well as others. Pennsylvania led the way in 1834 by abolishing public executions.[12] Petitions asking for the termination of the death penalty were now regularly received by the legislatures of the several states. In 1832 a report to the New York legislature citing Beccaria, Franklin, and Livingston, as well as the standard Bible arguments, and the usual appeals to precedence, in this case Russia, Tuscany, and periods in Egyptian and Roman history, introduced a bill to end capital punishment.[13]

In 1835, Robert Rantoul, Jr.—worthy son of a pioneer abolitionist destined to outlive him—an antislavery Democrat and a vigorous leader in Massachusetts reform, reported to the state House of Representatives the first of his abolitionist bills. The next year saw a lengthier report by Rantoul, the most famous, which excited partisan attention and called forth a third from him—the most eloquent and varied of the three.[14]

Thus, Rantoul exhibited what seemed to him the best defense of capital punishment which he had seen, one prepared in 1831 by a Frenchman, Urtis, whose *Necessité du Maintien de la Peine de Mort* defended suicide and concluded that the state ought to be atheistic. Ingenious arguments and illustrations strengthened the propaganda value of Rantoul's work and aided the movement which he led to force modifications in Massachusetts law.[15]

THE "MAINE LAW"

The *Report on Capital Punishment Made to the Maine Legislature* (1836) capped a long period of agitation in that state, accompanied by the usual petitions and memorials. Leaders in the Maine movement included the author of the *Report,* Tobias Purrington, of Cumberland, a senator in the Maine legislature, and chairman of the investigating committee. A bulwark of the movement, too, was Professor Thomas C. Upham, since 1824 in charge of Mental and Moral Philosophy at Bowdoin College, a pioneer in psychology, and author of *The Manual of Peace* (1836).

As a result of the controversy in Maine, where there had not actually been an execution for some years (the execution of one Joseph Sager in Augusta, in 1835, bringing the matter to a head), a law was framed which in effect abolished capital punishment, or was thought to do so. Governor Dana, in his annual message to the legislature in 1849, referred to the "general impression" that capital punishment had been practically abolished in Maine, and "to the impropriety of enforcing the death penalty while such an impression exists."[16] The "Maine Law" did not permit the executive to issue his warrant for an execution within one year after the criminal had been sentenced by the court; and its discretionary character, so opposed to the imperative of former laws, was responsible for the interpretation given it.

The influence of the "Maine Law" was considerable, extending into all New England, though with various results,[17] and being held responsible for the impulse which made Michigan the first state to abolish capital punishment officially.

THE HIGH POINT OF REFORM

The rising sentiment against the death penalty, the fact that juries were prone to acquit and governors to override convictions, gave new incentive to abolitionists and a new urgency to those who favored the retention of capital punishment. The 1840's were the high point for reform in the pre-Civil War decades, and were filled with effort and debate. As with the antislavery movement, reformist ranks were filled with clergymen; as one defender of the death penalty bitterly charged:

Who are its [capital punishment's] most fierce antagonists? . . . On the Sabbath, in edifices built to imitate the temples of Jehovah, they reiterate the doctrine preached to our first parents in Paradise—"Ye shall not surely die." The law of God is the great castle at which all their weapons are aimed.[18]

But if the Rev. Charles C. Burleigh, famous among antislavery partisans, issued his dissident *Thoughts on the Death Penalty* (1845), the Rev. George B. Cheever, also firm in opposition to slavery, and even more famous, was the author of two works defending capital punishment which Burleigh himself thought "written with an ability worthy of a better cause."[19] As with other reforms of the time, not a little of the controversy was based on interpretations of Biblical passages presumed to be directives to mankind. Debates were earnestly attended and were influential in organizational campaigns. Thus, a sermon preached in Philadelphia in 1842 favoring capital punishment resulted in a town meeting of dissenters who appointed a committee of twenty-five to examine and report upon it. The abolitionist committee was still extant three years later.[20]

ABOLITIONIST SOCIETIES

In 1844 antigallows societies were formed in Massachusetts and New York, with formidable sponsors. In Massachusetts, among many others were Rantoul, Wendell Phillips, John G. Whittier, and John A. Andrew, who was to become wartime governor of the state. The society's indefatigable secretary was the Rev. Charles Spear, one of its founders and author of *Essays on the Punishment of Death* (1844), dedicated to Professor Upham, a large-scale work which was in its fourth

edition eight weeks after publication. Spear also founded, in
1845, *The Hangman,* which the next year became *The Prisoner's Friend.* It continued until 1859. Spear was also favorable to pacifism, a movement which provided a quota of
active abolitionists; though some pacifists, like William Ladd,
did not feel it necessary to "attach" other causes to their
major one.[21]

The New York Society for the Abolition of Capital Punishment claimed so influential a figure as Horace Greeley, such
dedicated reformers as the Rev. William S. Balch and the
Rev. Samuel J. May, and a host of sympathizers, among whom
were John Quincy Adams, William H. Seward, and former Vice Presidents of the United States Richard M. Johnson of Kentucky and George M. Dallas of Pennsylvania.
John L. O'Sullivan, talented young editor of the *United States
Magazine and Democratic Review,* coiner of the phrase "Manifest Destiny," and author of a highly esteemed report to
the New York legislature asking for the abolition of the
death penalty,[22] was corresponding secretary.

The meeting in May 1845 of the New York abolitionists
resulted in the formation of a national society, which met in
the fall of that year in Philadelphia. But before it convened,
a Pennsylvania Society for Promoting the Abolition of the
Death Penalty had been born. By 1850, state societies existed
also in Tennessee, Ohio, Alabama, Louisiana, Indiana, and
Iowa.[23]

FEDERAL LAW AND THE DEATH PENALTY

Of distinctive importance was the agitation, in 1852, for
commutation of the death sentence upon a marine, under
United States law, for a murder which was asserted to have
been unpremeditated. Basing his appeal on an opinion of
Attorney General William Wirt in 1820 and another by Attorney General John Y. Mason in 1845, that the President was
empowered to commute sentences, Purrington, of Maine, peti-
tioned Millard Fillmore to prevent the execution. With officers
of the Marine Corps, as well as clergymen, adding their pleas
to Purrington's, Fillmore acceded to their requests and
changed the sentence to life imprisonment.[24]

Abolition and Marvin H. Bovee

In 1847 Michigan distinguished herself by becoming the first state legally to abolish capital punishment. Early liberal in her penal enactments, with capital punishment limited to murder as far back as 1820, and the death penalty actually a dead letter since 1830, she had proponents of abolition who were active and persistent, and skillful in parliamentary procedure.[25] Two other states joined Michigan in abolishing the death penalty in the pre-Civil War era: Rhode Island in 1852 and Wisconsin in 1853.

The latter fight brought to the fore one of the most vigorous of all fighters for abolition, whose work has been inadequately appreciated. Marvin H. Bovee, born in New York in 1827, removed with his family in 1843 to Wisconsin, and later, as a state senator, was chairman of the select committee which reported the abolition bill of 1853. Working without pay, and at personal expense, he traveled through half the states lecturing on capital punishment and co-operating with anti-capital-punishment societies. About 1860 he established a state reformatory which aimed to surround youthful criminals with wholesome influences.[26]

Bovee's efforts took him to New York where ardent campaigns in 1860 won an equivalent of the "Maine Law." This prevented executions for two years, but was then overthrown. Bovee first visited Illinois for reform purposes in 1859. In 1867 he and his co-workers were able to abolish public executions in that state and give juries discretionary powers in sentencing murderers to death or prison. He then turned his attention to Minnesota, where a similar victory was won.

In 1869 Bovee published a major work: *Christ and the Gallows; or, Reasons for the Abolition of Capital Punishment.*[27] In this he collected a vast number of arguments, endorsements, and new illustrations of the inadequate operations of the death penalty (which included the hanging of a ten-year-old child for murder), and summed up the "Progress of Penal Legislation in the United States" in a fashion which reflected the accomplishments of the time, as well as the too-sanguine hopes of crusaders like himself.

POST-CIVIL WAR TRENDS

In fact, the period of the Civil War and, even more, the temper of the post-Civil War era did seem, at first glance, encouraging to reformist enterprises in abolition. Governor Andrew of Massachusetts in 1861 addressed the legislature on the subject, strongly urging it to do away with the death penalty. Three years later, the governor of Maine made vain efforts to pass a law instituting the death penalty and thus to end the state's abolitionist tradition.[28] Fugitive arguments for and against capital punishment continued to appear, and legislatures to be memorialized on the subject.

Maine added the letter to the spirit of her long experience with abolition, making it legal in 1872. Restored in 1878 following the attack of an insane convict on a keeper, capital punishment was again abolished in 1887. Iowa abolished the death penalty from 1872 to 1878, and Colorado in that same year of 1872 began an erratic career of abolition and restoral. Kansas, too, in 1872 began a long tradition on the abolitionist road,[29] which was only to be stopped, at least temporarily, in the 1940's.

In addition, the subject was debated elsewhere, and gains were recorded in connection with first and second degree sentences, public executions, the shortening of the list of capital crimes, and other aspects of the question. But positive accomplishments appear more as end products of earlier eloquence and seasoned agitators. New progress and interest centered in the larger area of prison reform and administration. As Frederick Howard Wines, himself one of the outstanding reformers of the post-Civil War decades, observed in 1895, the state of American prisons twenty-five years before had been far from satisfactory.[30]

PRISON REFORM AND THE DEATH PENALTY

It was due to the energy and vision of Frederick Wines's father, the Rev. Dr. Enoch C. Wines, that a congress of reformers actively interested in prison work convened in Cincinnati in 1870 and formed the National Prison Association. They were interested in the novel aim of influencing the criminal for the better. Many of them knew of the experience of Sir Walter Crofton with the Irish "convict prisons," where notable progress had been achieved; and the creation of the New York State Reformatory at Elmira gave them their opportunity to try out humane approaches to the prisoner.

At this and subsequent meetings they heard of the "indeterminate sentence," developed in this country by Zebulon R. Brockway as early as 1860. This stipulated a minimum and maximum sentence upon a convicted person, and left for future determination how long he would actually serve. And though Massachusetts was not in the forefront of abolition, she did pioneer the system of probation which spread through the other states.[31]

The significant fact for abolitionists was that the new approach emphasized a more scientific view of crime and criminals, and thus seemed to prepare the way for a more reasonable consideration of the value of the death penalty. As Colonel Brockway—who was no gentle hand as a prison administrator—himself concluded by 1890:

> My experience with prisoners and their disciplinary governing has effected in my mind a depreciated estimate of the value of deterrents. Punishments applied to deter . . . are, usually, pernicious. . . . The strongest argument against capital punishment is not either the uncertainty of convictions, the cruelty of it or the sacredness of life; but rather the injury of it to the public tone. . . .[32]

Prison discipline, then, seemed increasingly to provide an opportunity to abolitionists to move in step with other reformers. At the 1870 meeting in Cincinnati, William Tallack, secretary of the abolitionist Howard Society of England, spoke vigorously in favor of humanitarian treatment of criminals, with many a hint that capital punishment was undesirable. The milestone 1878 meeting of the International Penitentiary Congress in Stockholm was heartily supported by abolitionists. And in 1883 a reorganized National Prison Association heard Alfred H. Love, of the Pennsylvania Prison Society, a pacifist and opponent of the death penalty, who in that period made earnest and unsuccessful efforts to turn his organization to active support of abolition.[33]

Early in the 1880's the impending execution of Guiteau for the assassination of President Garfield provided a point of public controversy, permitting the intransigent Cheever and Wendell Phillips, among others, to speak their opposing minds. Late in the decade the advent of the electric chair offered a novelty and renewed debate on the relative merits of the several modes of execution.[34]

FEDERAL REFORM

One of the strongest arguments of the abolitionists had always been that the conscience of mankind revolted against the death penalty, and that therefore it could not be enforced; in other words, that the death penalty assured the complete freedom of most murderers. In the post-Civil War era, with the high incidence of unpunished killing in the cattle country of the West and with the rise of lynch law in the South, to say nothing of the actions of susceptible juries in the North, the situation came close to being scandalous. As William Tallack pointed out, for the year 1894, in the United States, there were 9,800 murders, which were followed by only 132 legal and 190 "illegal" executions; that is, 29 out of 30 murderers escaped capital punishment.[35]

This, too, was the burden of what was the most important of all abolition crusades of the 1890's. The Hon. Newton M. Curtis, a Civil War general and New York reformer, who had written and spoken against capital punishment for years, now, as a member of the House of Representatives, undertook to persuade Congress to define, in the words of his proposed bill, "the crimes of murder in the first and second degree, and manslaughter, and providing punishment therefor, and to abolish the punishment of death."[36]

In the material which he prepared for the consideration of

the Committee on the Judiciary of the House of Representatives, Curtis attempted to show that "in the first thirty-seven years of the Republic the letter and spirit of the criminal laws were supported by public sentiment, which is essential to the successful enforcement of criminal statutes," but that a great change had taken place. In the earlier years of the Republic, about 85 percent of those tried had been convicted, as compared with more recent figures of less than 20 percent in the federal courts and a still lower percentage in the state courts.

Other statistics were calculated to show that those states having the greatest number of offenses carrying the death penalty suffered the greatest number of homicides, and that lynchings had increased at the expense of legal executions. Curtis brought up to date facts concerning laws of the then forty-one states, and the increasing experiences abroad.

By 1897 Curtis had modified his bill "to reduce the cases in which the penalty of death may be inflicted," and this became law that year. The sixty federal offenses previously punishable by death were reduced to treason, murder, rape, and capital offenses enumerated in the articles of war for the Army and Navy. In addition, in instances of murder and rape, juries might qualify their verdicts by adding "without capital punishment," and the penalty would be changed to life imprisonment at hard labor.[37]

THE PRE-WORLD WAR I ERA

The reformers of the 1900–1914 period, who concerned themselves so sensationally with all aspects of local and national affairs, did not forget the problem of crime. Organizationally, however, the abolition movement lagged behind that of penal reform. Charles Edward Russell, a leader of the muckrakers, wrote effectively on the question, and maintained an interest in abolition to the year of his death. Maynard Shipley, a California penologist, prepared learned articles on aspects of the subject.

One of the most active of all the reformers was Brand

Whitlock, whose interest in abolition dated back to 1893, when he met Clarence Darrow in connection with an effort to save from execution a youth who had assassinated Carter Harrison.[38] As Mayor of Toledo, Whitlock worked earnestly to end the death penalty in Ohio. He wrote in a letter in 1906: "I have been, as perhaps you know, conducting a sort of guerrilla warfare against capital punishment." However, a bill which he engineered through the Ohio legislature failed of passage. His novel, *The Turn of the Balance* (1907), a powerful indictment of backward prison practices and capital punishment, was harshly criticized, and his unsuccessful efforts appear to have exhausted him.[39]

Yet the 1910's began as a period of brilliant promise. Minnesota abolished the death penalty in 1911. In 1913 the state of Washington followed suit, and after her Oregon, North Dakota, South Dakota, Arizona, and Missouri. Tennessee abolished the death penalty for murder (retaining it for rape) in 1915, but restored it in 1917.[40] As instruments of reform and agitation, a number of organizations and agencies were created during that period.[41] Typical of developments which seemed about to carry abolitionists to a broad victory was the fact that the Pennsylvania Prison Society, without flagging in its zeal for prison reform, and after having avoided the issue of the death penalty for over a hundred years, finally took its stand directly against it.[42]

THE YEAR 1917

The year 1917 promised to be the wonder year of abolition. True, the *Survey* thought that legislators did not "seem to be as favorable to the abolition of the death penalty as the recent spread of humanitarian ideas in the prison field might indicate." In Colorado, Utah, and Vermont measures had been killed outright. A bill had been lost in Massachusetts.[43] But twelve states were already in the abolitionist column, and only twelve states still made the death penalty mandatory for convicted murderers. West Virginia, Indiana, North Carolina, Pennsylvania, New York, New Hampshire, Illinois, and Nebraska were considering the subject, and, in addition, many other bills relating to prison reform as such were under debate.

Nevertheless, 1917 was destined to be catastrophic for the abolitionist cause. Under the nervous tensions created by American entrance into World War I, four of the abolitionist states returned to capital punishment. Promising movements in other states were repulsed.

Typical of the spirit which set back abolition was that which prevailed in Pennsylvania, where the Prison Society, aided by the Prison Reform League, worked to pass an abolition law. It passed the Senate, and was expected to pass the House "with votes to spare." Unfortunately, "A day or two before the vote was taken, there was an explosion in a munition factory near Chester, which was at first thought to have been caused by spies or alien enemies."[44] As a result of this misadventure, members of the Assembly changed their minds and the bill was lost.

FOLLOWING WORLD WAR I

Although there were distinguished advocates of abolition as America entered the 1920's, conditions did not appear promising for them. Governor Harry L. Davis, of Ohio, showed himself as earnest and energetic as Whitlock before him.[45] Dean George W. Kirchwey, Clarence Darrow, Thomas Mott Osborne, and other opponents of capital punishment wrote or presented their views before such influential bodies as they could reach. It was the Loeb-Leopold case that revitalized the movement and gave it direction. The arguments of Clarence Darrow and the prosecutor were both largely based on those deriving from the question of abolition. The new interest in the subject was indicated by the preparation of a bibliography specifically to satisfy demands.[46]

In August 1925 the League for the Abolition of Capital Punishment opened its offices in New York under the active working leadership of Miss Vivian Pierce, and prepared to start a nationwide campaign. The following February it opened its campaign in Wallack's Theater in New York, its speakers including Warden Lewis E. Lawes, of Sing Sing, a convert to abolition, Darrow, Dudley Field Malone, and Kathleen Norris. The following day, Darrow spoke before Congress on the subject.[47]

In 1927 the Sacco-Vanzetti case, or rather its climax, resulted in the formation of the Massachusetts Council for the Abolition of the Death Penalty, and in that year, Mrs. Herbert B. Ehrmann, wife of one of the counsel for the condemned anarchists, began her long services in behalf of abolition.[48]

RECENT TRENDS

Since then, the movement, through organizations more or less vigorous, more or less adequately staffed and supported, has continued to press for reform measures, including abolition, has kept alert to possible reversals in states already free of the death penalty, has prepared bills, distributed educational materials, and directed its crusade through such channels as have been available to it. In the 1930's it gave up its appeal to sentiment and religious opinion, and presented its arguments in more practical and pertinent form.[49] It printed leaflets, brochures by such stalwarts as Lawes and Darrow, and reprinted the arguments of widely known sympathizers. A major campaign aimed to abolish the mandatory death penalty, and today it prevails only in Vermont and the District of Columbia.

To those concerned with the pro and con of the subject, developments in the states have been neither encouraging nor dismaying. World conditions have undoubtedly confused the picture. In 1939 South Dakota re-enacted capital punishment, but authorized no funds for the purchase of an electric chair. In 1942 an appropriation for the purpose was made, but there appeared to be no materials available for the construction of such a chair! In 1944, after Kansas had re-enacted the death penalty, three executions took place at the State Penitentiary. Feeling was high, and the warden of the institution resigned, refusing to enforce the penalty.

A promising token to one protagonist of abolition lay in the fact that capital punishment was no longer a major means for dispensing justice. Only in New York, North Carolina, and Georgia did it play an important role. In 1943 there were 135 executions in the United States, one-third of which took place in these three states. Of these executions, 118 followed instances of murder, 17 of rape. There were no executions for any other offenses.[50]

WHERE WE STAND

"There is reason to believe," thought one expert on capital punishment in 1926, "that in the course of the present century the use of the death penalty will finally pass away."[51] However, the partisans of capital punishment have not retreated from their position, and those who advocate abolition have been required to take into account two levels of opposition. First, there is the intellectual defense of capital punishment: the argument that there is a moral and legal right to kill, and that capital punishment is a deterrent to crime.[52]

Much more challenging, in some ways, is the spontaneous reaction to murder on the part of emotion-stirred people. Much of the essence of the controversy may be found in such responses as the following to the recent murder in New York of a young girl by a psychopathic stranger, who had obviously been released prematurely from hospital care. Her parents were quoted as having taken a "Christian attitude" toward the killer: "They were glad he had been caught and hoped he would be 'put away' so that no one else might be harmed. Some of the neighbors . . . were less resigned and called for vengeance."[53]

EDITORIAL POSTSCRIPT

In recent years, numerous church bodies have adopted resolutions favoring the abolition of capital punishment, the most recent being the Lutheran Church in America

*(June, 1966). Previously the following bodies had done so:
American Baptist Convention (1960), Church of the Brethren
(1957), Disciples of Christ (1957), Protestant Episcopal
Church in the United States (1958), American Ethical Union
(1960), Union of American Hebrew Congregations (1959),
General Conference of the Methodist Church (1960), United
Presbyterian Church in the United States (1959), American
Unitarian Association (1956), Universalist Church of America
(1957), and numerous state and local church organizations.
The Anglican Church of Canada's Executive Council (1958)
and the United Church of Canada (1960) have passed
similar resolutions.*

Experiments with Abolition

THORSTEN SELLIN

In debates on capital punishment the states which have
abolished and later re-introduced the penalty are often cited
as affording proof of the dire effects of abolition. It would,
therefore, be useful to examine the evidence on which this
"proof" rests. If it is claimed that such evidence often has
a shaky foundation, the fact remains that both abolitionists
and retentionists exploit it for their own purposes.

Eleven American states have experimented with abolition
for periods of time varying in duration—the death penalty
has temporarily been removed by the statutes and not merely
by practice. These states are Arizona, Colorado, Delaware,
Iowa, Kansas, Maine, Missouri, Tennessee, Oregon, South
Dakota, and Washington. The quality of the pertinent data
from these states on the effect of abolition on the murder
rates is admittedly poor in many instances, but we shall
present what is known.

Arizona had no death penalty for murder from December,
1916, to December, 1918. The governor of the state reported

to the British Select Committee on Capital Punishment in 1931 that 41 murderers were convicted in the two years before abolition, 46 during the abolition years, and 45 during the following two years.

Colorado abolished capital punishment in 1897 and returned to it in 1901. The average annual numbers of convictions for murder during the five years before abolition, the abolition years, and the five years following were, respectively, 15.4, 18, and 19. The corresponding figures on convictions for manslaughter were 2.6, 4, and 1.5.

Delaware abolished the death penalty in April, 1958, and reinstated it in December, 1961. The average annual number of murders and non-negligent manslaughters was 22.3 during 1956–1958 and 14.3 during 1959–1961.

Iowa had no death penalty from 1872 to 1878. During the seven years before abolition the average annual number of convictions for murder was 2.6. This figure rose to 8.8 during abolition and to 13.1 during the following seven years. The death penalty was again abolished in 1965.

Kansas lacked a death penalty between 1907 and 1935. The five years before 1935 showed an annual average homicide death rate of 6.5; the next five years, this rate was 3.8.

Maine first tried abolition during 1876–1882, but the lack of data make any useful comparisons fruitless. Final abolition came in 1887.

Missouri abandoned the death penalty in 1917 and brought it back in 1919. The homicide death rate per 100,000 population during 1911–1916 averaged 9.2 a year and during abolition 10.7; during 1920–1924, it was 11.

Tennessee abolished capital punishment for murder in 1915 but retained it for rape. Reinstatement of the punishment came in 1919. Homicide death rates are available beginning with the year 1918, when the rate was 6.9 for whites and 29.2 for the colored population. Except for a slight drop in 1920 in the white race, both rose steadily after the introduction of the death penalty to 10.8 for the whites and 52.5 for the colored population in 1924.

Oregon had no death penalty during 1915–1920. Information supplied to the British Select Committee on Capital Punishment in 1931 indicated that 59 "murderers" were committed to the state penitentiary during the five years before abolition and 36 during the abolition years.

South Dakota re-introduced the death penalty in 1939, having abolished it in 1915. Identical average annual homicide death rates were reported during the five years before and the five years after the restoration.

Washington was without the death penalty during 1913–1919. The average annual rate of deaths due to homicide was 6.5 during 1908–1912. "In 1913 it was 6.5, but it rose in 1914 to 10 and then gradually fell to 8.9, 5.5, 5.5, and 4.2 (1918). The year the death penalty was again introduced, the rate rose to 7.5 but during the next five years, 1920–1924, it was 5.1, 5.9, 5.2, 4.7, and 6.2. The average annual rate was 6.8 during the period of abolition and 5.8 during the first six years after the re-introduction of the death penalty."[1]

If any conclusion can be drawn from all the above data, it is that there is no evidence that the abolition of the death penalty generally causes an increase in criminal homicides or that its re-introduction is followed by a decline. The explanation of changes in homicide rates must be sought elsewhere.

Abolition and Restoration of the Death Penalty in Missouri

ELLEN ELIZABETH GUILLOT

Throughout the nineteenth century and up to the present time, there has been in the state of Missouri a more or less academic interest in the subject of capital punishment. Various articles

Reprinted, by permission, from *The Annals of the American Academy of Political and Social Science*, 284:105–109, November, 1952.

for or against the practice have made their appearance in the press from time to time. The matter was, however, of crucial importance in the spring of 1917, when the legislature abolished the death penalty, and again in 1919, when it was restored. As far as Missouri is concerned, the most significant interest in this subject is confined neatly within this period. It is possible, therefore, to present a fairly comprehensive account of the history of capital punishment in Missouri within the limitations of those two years.

THE MOVEMENT FOR ABOLITION

In connection with the act abolishing capital punishment passed by the Missouri Legislature in 1917, it is to be remembered that the movement for the reform of prison life and the reformation of individual criminals was at that time nation-wide. It is therefore natural to believe that the Missouri act was a part of this greater movement.

The basic idea was that capital punishment forestalled the possibility of reformation. In addition, it had become increasingly difficult to get properly qualified jurors to serve in cases of capital crime, because of their conscientious scruples against the infliction of the death penalty. For example, Judge Nick T. Cave,[1] now of the Kansas City Court of Appeals, told the writer that in 1914, while he was Prosecuting Attorney for Callaway County, he prosecuted, for first-degree murder, a colored man who was accused of shooting and killing a white boy. The case was opened on Monday and went to the jury on Wednesday afternoon. The jury did not report until Saturday afternoon, when it was called into court by the presiding judge. It was learned later that on the first ballot the jury was unanimous in its verdict of first-degree murder, but on the question of inflicting capital punishment the jurors failed to agree; seven were for hanging and five for life imprisonment. A decision by the jury regarding punishment was therefore impossible.

The movement for the abolition of capital punishment is described as gradual and as characterized by a sensible approach. A good many reforms in the treatment of prisoners had already been carried out, such as establishment of night classes at the penitentiary, exercises out of doors, dedication of a new playground for prisoners with facilities for playing baseball, elimination of the contract labor system, and the purchase of a prison farm along the rich Missouri River bottoms where quantities of fruits and vegetables were raised and the prisoners given opportunity for work in the out-of-doors; severe punishments (such as hanging up by the thumbs) had been done away with, and the parole system had been rewritten.[2]

THE ACT OF 1917

The bill for the abolishment of capital punishment in Missouri was introduced in the Forty-ninth General Assembly in 1917 by Representative O. B. Whitaker of Hickory County. Whitaker was a man of importance in the state; he had been president of three small colleges, and had written a number of books on Christian fellowship and social problems.[3] The revised statute as adopted read as follows:

An Act to Abolish Capital Punishment in the State of Missouri. From and after the taking effect of this act it shall be unlawful in this state to take human life as a punishment for crime, and no court shall enforce capital punishment as a penalty for crime. All acts and parts of acts inconsistent or in conflict with this act are hereby repealed.

The act was approved on April 13, 1917. It never appeared in the Revised Statutes of Missouri, since it was repealed before the codification of 1919.

It will be noticed that this important enactment was made just when this country was entering the First World War. There was probably little opposition to the law; so occupied were the people and the newspapers with the war that the enactment was hardly noticed in the press. There were, however, some brief comments expressing satisfaction that the spectacle of public execution, with its attendant debauchery, would no longer take place.[4]

The matter was perhaps exaggerated, since the number of

criminals put to death was certainly not large. The *Kansas City Star* reported that there were in Jackson County nine victims in twenty-six years,[5] and the *St. Louis Post-Dispatch* noted that not a single execution had taken place in St. Louis County during the fourteen years previous to the passage of the act.[6]

Opinion For and Against

There were certain serious misgivings and difference of opinion as to what would result from the repeal of the law inflicting the death penalty. Hunt C. Moore, then prosecuting attorney of Jackson County, declared that the new statute was a humane law and that the abolition of capital punishment would have no effect on the spread of crime. It would also, he thought, make it possible to secure better juries in first-degree crime cases.

Judge Ralph S. Latshaw of the same county, however, was bitterly opposed to the new enactment. He thought it had been made by softhearted legislators who allowed their sympathies to overpower their reason. He believed that the penitentiary held no terror for the rapist, the robber, or the murderer, and that life sentences were a joke. He said that there was but one man in the State Penitentiary at that time who had been there over ten years, and that he was a poor, unknown, friendless Hawaiian who would also have been free if he had had a single friend. Judge Latshaw also said that kidnapping and train robbery were so rare since they had been punishable by death that not a single instance had come to his attention. He quoted the Bible as his authority: "Whosoever sheddeth the blood of man by man shall his blood be shed."[7]

Dissatisfaction among law enforcement agencies with the new law abolishing capital punishment seems to have grown during the two years following its enactment, for we find that Prosecuting Attorney McDaniels of St. Louis County issued early in January 1919 an appeal for the re-enactment of the older statute.[8]

This was possibly in some measure provoked by a situation described by Judge Cave, who records the commission of a serious crime shortly before the abolition act was repealed. Men from St. Louis came to Fulton, in Callaway County, where copper wire was stored preparatory to the construction of certain electrical installations. Copper wire was very valuable at that time. The robbers cut the wire into short lengths and loaded it into their truck. They carried it to St. Louis, and it was reported to the police that the truck was to be stored in a garage behind an apartment building. Police officers were stationed at the garage to await the arrival of the robbers. The men drove the truck into the alley leading to the garage, and when officers attempted to put them under arrest, a battle followed. Two policemen were killed. Later the men were caught and came to trial. They were sentenced to the penitentiary for life.

There was a hysterical reaction to these murders. People who had previously been opposed to capital punishment were outraged, and newspapers that had supported its abolition now advocated the restoration of the death penalty for murder. It was argued that the criminal element had no fear of the law and that criminals could "shoot their way out." If they surrendered to the police, they would be sent to the penitentiary; if they murdered the police, they would also merely be sent to the penitentiary. The law thus gave no protection to the police. Law enforcement officers throughout the state urged the restoration of capital punishment.

THE ACT OF 1919

The consequence of McDaniels' appeal and of the situation just described was the introduction in the Missouri Senate, Fiftieth General Assembly, by Senator Mayes of Penobscot County, on January 20, 1919, of Senate Bill 84, entitled

An Act to Repeal an Act of the Forty-ninth General Assembly, approved April 13, 1917, entitled "An Act to Abolish Capital Punishment in the State of Missouri" and to enact a section reviving all former laws providing for capital punishment.

The bill went through the ordinary routine of legislative procedure in the Senate and, on April 3, 1919, was passed by a vote of 26 yeas, 8 nays, absent 3. However, when the bill came up in the House, at a time when it was next to impossible to keep more than a bare quorum in their seats, it lacked three votes to pass that body.[9]

One does not know how long the bill abolishing capital punishment in Missouri might have remained on the statute books had it not been for a series of crimes that greatly disturbed the public mind. In the jail at Lamar, in Barton County, there was confined a man ominously named Jay Lynch. It is believed that his wife or mother or both of them delivered to him a package containing a pistol. Lynch, so equipped, made his dash for liberty and in so doing killed the sheriff and the sheriff's son. He seems to have been tried and sentenced to life imprisonment. A mob broke into the jail and seized and lynched him early in June, 1919.[10] Representative Chancellor of Barton County told his fellow legislators that this lynching would not have occurred had it not been for the law of two years earlier abolishing capital punishment.[11] Also at the same time, peace officers of Lafayette County were murdered.[12]

But the most disturbing event of this kind was in connection with the robbery of the Meramec Trust Company in St. Louis County, June 12, 1919, on which occasion one patrolman was killed and another wounded. A number of "Letters from the People" appeared in the *Post-Dispatch*, some of which are extremely interesting in their reflection of public sentiment. On June 17 one correspondent quotes from a recent editorial in the *Post-Dispatch*, "the stolen money was speedily recovered, and two desperate principals were by arrest permanently removed from the class of those who prey on the community." He then goes on:

The *Post-Dispatch* is slightly mistaken. First, they were not desperate. Desperate men fight to the last. Secondly, they will not be permanently removed, at least so long as there is a workable parole board. They will probably be at liberty in three or four years, as is usual in such cases. A short time ago I read in your esteemed paper where five hundred or so murderers were let loose in society. All paroled by the board. Will they commit murder again? . . . It it truly marvelous that we do not have more lynching than we do. The people of Missouri deserve credit for it. If the law don't protect, who will? Shall we have to go back to the day when every man carried his own legislature and his justice strapped to his belt.

Another letter writer on June 28, however, declaring himself opposed to capital punishment, quotes *Genesis* 9:6, as given above, and adds, "This would exterminate the race."

Action by Special Legislative Session

Significant action connected with the settlement of the issue came from the Tenth Ward Improvement Association of St. Louis.[13] It happened that a special session of the Missouri Legislature had just been called by Governor Frederick G. Gardner to convene July 2 to consider and ratify the amendment to the federal Constitution granting suffrage to women. The Tenth Ward Improvement Association joined in the current demand on the governor to issue a supplemental message to the legislature calling upon it to consider a bill restoring capital punishment in Missouri. The association complained that St. Louis had been overrun with crime during the past year and said that crime had been violent because criminals knew that capital punishment was no longer law in Missouri.

Governor Gardner, in his reply to the Tenth Ward Improvement Association, stated that he had not included the question of the restoration of capital punishment in his call because the legislature meeting in regular session had opposed restoration. A new legislature would be chosen in eighteen months, and it might view the matter differently. He added that he had been in communication with the governors of eleven states in which capital punishment had been abolished, and they had been asked if crime had increased. "None said that it had increased, and eight declared that it had not." The governor was thus reluctant to have the matter of the restoration of capital punishment considered at the special session of the legislature.[14]

A petition was circulated by Representative Chancellor of Barton County that requested the governor to send a special message to the legislature submitting the question of restoring capital punishment. This petition was quickly signed by 78 members of the House, six more than a constitutional majority.

The governor was anxious to hold down the expenses of the special session and to confine the members to action on the issue they had been summoned to consider. However, he met with four or five petitioners, discussed the matter with them, and demanded of them statistics. In spite of the fact that none of them had any statistics, he yielded to their argument that public sentiment among their constituents was most decidedly in favor of restoring the capital punishment law for the purpose of discouraging highway robberies, bank robberies, and attendant murders.

The governor thus gave his consent, but the session that restored capital punishment in Missouri was a stormy one. The friends of the governor resorted to obstructive tactics to prevent the matter from coming to a vote, and the debate was complicated by the proposal of an amendment to substitute the electric chair for the noose.[15]

The legislature at this special session repealed the act of 1917 and re-enacted sections of the revised statutes of 1909, so that treason, rape, kidnapping for ransom, perjury committed in the trial of any indictment for a capital offense, train robbery of certain sorts, and murder in the first degree remained punishable by death at the discretion of the jury.

CONCLUSION

The abolishment of capital punishment in Missouri thus came about as part of a general movement for the amelioration of the lives of the condemned that was nation-wide, and capital punishment was restored by an urgent public sentiment of fear and indignation brought about by crimes following the First World War.

It has been said that the race question entered into the matter of the reenactment, but this seems not to be true. Indeed, Judge Cave assures the writer—and his assurance is supported by examination of the press of the state—that the race question did not enter into the issue of capital punishment in Missouri, since the crimes were those of whites against whites and were not reflective of race prejudice. . . .

PART III

The Problem of

Deterrence

Homicides in Retentionist and Abolitionist States

THORSTEN SELLIN

It is generally claimed that the states that have abolished the death penalty have lower homicide rates than those that have retained it. This is true, in general, but only if one ignores the great differences among states in the nature of their populations and their economic, social, and political conditions. It does not appear to be true if we compare retentionist and abolitionist states that are contiguous and, therefore, more nearly alike in these respects. This can be illustrated in two ways. To make a comparison, we can take (1) the rates of murders and non-negligent manslaughters known to the police or (2) mortality rates due to willful homicides, as recorded in our vital statistics. Neither is a perfect measure of the amount or trend of capital murder, a special form of homicide that no one has succeeded in counting accurately. Capital murders are hidden in the statistics just mentioned, and we have to assume that their proportion remains fairly constant from year to year within the statistics of known murders and manslaughters or the statistics of deaths due to homicide.

There is good reason to believe that the two series of data mentioned are highly correlated, but the data on homicidal deaths are considerably older and are also more complete for all but relatively recent years than the police statistics reported

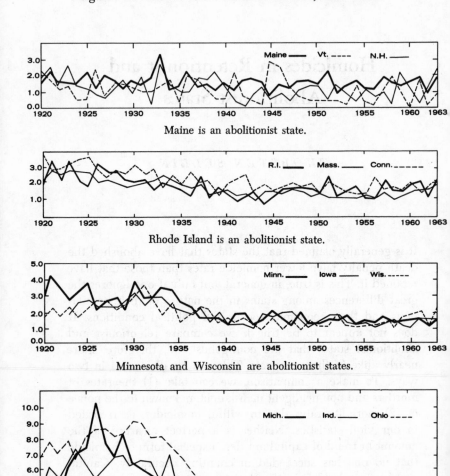

Homicide Death Rates (per 100,000 Population) in Contiguous Abolitionist and Retentionist States, 1920–1963.

Maine is an abolitionist state.

Rhode Island is an abolitionist state.

Minnesota and Wisconsin are abolitionist states.

Michigan is an abolitionist state.

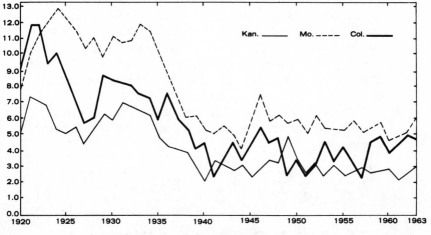

Kansas was an abolitionist state until 1935.

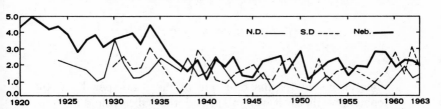

North Dakota is considered an abolitionist state.
South Dakota was abolitionist until 1939.

in *Uniform Crime Reports*, published by the Federal Bureau of Investigation.

The preceding figures are self-explanatory. Homicide death rates have been so grouped that one of the states in each figure is an abolitionist state bordering upon retentionist states, whose homicide rates serve for comparison. An inspection of the figures shows (1) that the level of the rates is not the same in all regions; (2) that within each group of contiguous states it would be impossible to identify the abolitionist state, were it not designated as such; and (3) that the trends of the rates of the states compared are similar.

The conclusion is inevitable that the presence of the death penalty—in law or practice—does not influence homicide death rates.

The Death Penalty and Police Safety

THORSTEN SELLIN

One argument for the retention of the death penalty is the contention that if it were abolished, the police would be more likely to be killed or injured by criminals or suspects when they are encountered. It is assumed that the presence of the threat of possible execution deters persons from carrying lethal weapons when they engage in crime or from using them against the police when they are in danger of arrest. These opinions have been voiced on many occasions. . . .

There are great obstacles in the way of making a conclusive study of this problem. From a *theoretical point of view* what

Reprinted by permission of the Queen's Printer and Controller of Stationery, Ottawa, from Second Session, Twenty-second Parliament, 1955; *Appendix "F" of the Minutes of Proceedings and Evidence, No. 20, of the Joint Committee of the Senate and the House of Commons on Capital and Corporal Punishment and Lotteries*, pp. 718–728.

one should like to know is first of all whether or not a larger proportion of criminals actually *carry* lethal weapons in abolition states. This is probably impossible to discover with any degree of accuracy. Failing this, one would like to know if criminals in these states *use* such weapons in encounters with the police more frequently than in the death penalty states, whether or not a wounding or killing of a policeman occurs. In reading police reports one sometimes finds a notice that a policeman has been commended for bravery because after an exchange of shots he succeeded in wounding the criminal or disarming him, although he himself was not injured. To secure reliable statistics of such attacks would, however, be virtually impossible. One is, therefore, compelled to seek data on the number of police killed or wounded. There is an a priori likelihood that records of such occurrences are kept in police departments. Although in discussions of the relationship of the death penalty to police safety references are generally made only to policemen killed, it is obvious that woundings are equally important, for every wounding can be regarded as a killing that was avoided merely by chance, because the bullet or the knife failed to strike a vital spot or medical aid was so promptly given that an otherwise possible death did not occur.

In brief, one should have data on the number of attacks on the police by criminals or suspects, whether the police are hurt or not, since the use of a lethal weapon (gun or knife) indicates a disregard for the consequences and since such a weapon is potentially fatal to life. If such data cannot be secured, we should have data on actual woundings and killings resulting from such attacks or encounters. *At the very least* we should have data on police killed by lethal weapons.

There are not only theoretical but also practical difficulties in making a comparative study of police safety in states with and those without the death penalty. These difficulties arise from the fact that many police departments possess unsatisfactory record systems and have, in some instances, evidently failed to keep information on the events here under discussion. Another problem is that of securing the cooperation of the police even when they undoubtedly possess records. This particular problem will become quite clear when in later pages we note the extent of cooperation in the study which will be reported on presently.

In the author's seminar in criminology at the University of Pennsylvania during the academic year 1954–1955, several studies were carried on relating to various aspects of capital punishment. One of these studies was specifically designed to secure data on the comparative risk of a policeman's being injured or killed by a criminal or suspect using a lethal weapon. It was hoped that by securing data of this nature from cities in capital punishment states and in abolition states, some idea might be gained of the extent to which the police might be better protected in states with the death penalty. . . .

During the middle of December, 1954, a letter was mailed to police departments in all cities with more than 10,000 population, according to the census of 1950. This letter asked for data to be supplied on two schedules. One of these requested information, year by year beginning with 1919 and ending with 1954, on each case of a wounding or a killing of a member of the police department by a lethal weapon in the hands of a criminal or a suspect. A brief description of each incident was requested indicating, if possible, the nature of the offence involved. Furthermore, in each case information was asked about the kind of weapon used and whether or not the offender was insane. . . .

Seventeen states were selected for the study. All the six states which have no death penalty and had abolished it before 1919 were included and eleven states bordering on the abolition states. Knowing the great variations in the homicide rate in the United States, . . . it was assumed that states from about the same culture areas would afford the best basis for comparison.

Altogether 593 letters were sent out in the first mailing and after two months a follow-up letter was sent to departments that had not responded. As a result of this procedure 274 schedules were returned. Of these 265 proved to be adequate; those that were not used offered data for only a few years or reported that the data could not be compiled. The distribution of the schedules mailed out is found in Table 1, as follows:

TABLE 1.   Number of Cities with Population of 10,000 or Over, Number of Replies Received, Number of Usable Replies, and Percentage of Such Replies of Total Received from 17 States

Abolition states	Number of cities	Number of returns	Usable returns Number	Usable returns Percentage
Maine	13	6	6	46.2
Michigan	57	33	31	54.4
Minnesota	22	14	14	63.6
North Dakota	5	4	3	60.0
Rhode Island	17	6	6	35.3
Wisconsin	34	22	22	64.7
Total	148	85	82	55.4
Capital punishment states				
Connecticut	44	19	19	43.2
Illinois	72	22	21	29.2
Indiana	39	18	15	38.6
Iowa	23	10	10	43.5
Massachusetts	88	38	38	43.2
Montana	7	2	1	14.3
New Hampshire	10	6	6	60.0
New York	73	37	36	49.3
Ohio	78	34	34	43.6
South Dakota	6	2	2	33.3
Vermont	5	1	1	20.0
Total	445	189	183	41.0
Grand Total	593	274	265	44.8

1. Of the 593 cities, 397 fell into the smallest population group, with populations of between 10,000 and 30,000. One hundred and fourteen had between 30,000 and 60,000 inhabitants; 38 had between 60,000 and 100,000 inhabitants; 33 had from 100,000 to half a million, but all but two—one city in Indiana, and one in Ohio—had fewer than 350,000. Finally, six cities had over half a million, including New York, Buffalo, Cincinnati, Cleveland, Boston, and Chicago in capital punishment states and Milwaukee, Detroit, and Minneapolis in abolition states.

2. 44.8 percent of the cities returned usable schedules, but the percentage was higher for the abolition states—55.4 percent—than for the capital punishment states—41 percent.

3. The smaller the city, the better the response. In abolition

states, 60.4 percent of the cities under 30,000 inhabitants returned usable schedules; so did half of the cities between 30,000 and 100,000 population. In the capital punishment states, 42.4 percent of the smallest class of cities replied and 41.7 and 30 percent respectively of the next two classes in size.

4. No replies were received from Detroit and Minneapolis, nor from New York, Cleveland, or Boston. The largest cities represented in the returns were Chicago, Milwaukee, Cincinnati, and Buffalo.

5. The percentage of cities replying in the various abolition states ranged from 64.7 percent and 63.6 percent in Wisconsin and Minnesota to 35.3 percent in Rhode Island; in the capital punishment states the range was from 60 percent in New Hampshire to 20 percent in Vermont. Of the largest capital punishment states—New York, Illinois, Ohio, and Massachusetts, New York had the best percentage (49.3) and Illinois the lowest (29.2). On the other hand, Chicago submitted the best report and the only one from a truly metropolitan center.

In the analysis which follows, Chicago will be dealt with in a separate section, for during the period 1919–1954 that city had 177 casualties, or 39 more than all the other 264 cities put together. We shall take these 264 cities first.

It will be recalled that the schedule asked for information both on woundings and on killings of police, in the belief that this would yield more probative results. However, an inspection of the schedules returned made it clear that the data on woundings were so incomplete that there was no possibility of using them. All the largest cities reporting (except Chicago) reported only the policemen killed; many others stated that figures on woundings were available only for the most recent years, etc. Hence, only the information on the killing of policemen can be utilized. Since, however, this is the kind of information which always seems to be brought forward in discussions of police safety in capital punishment states, it should suffice for our purposes.

We shall analyze, then, 128 instances or attacks or encounters in which policemen were killed during 1919–1954 in 264 cities in 17 states, six of which are abolition states. In these 128 encounters 138 police were actually killed; in one instance, three policemen were casualties and in each of nine of them, two were killed. It is assumed a priori that it is something of an accident that more than one is shot in an encounter and that the important fact is that the criminal shot at the policeman or policemen, whether one or more happened to confront him. Four of these instances occurred in Michigan and one in Minnesota, one in Ohio, one in Connecticut, and two in Massachusetts.

We have not included in the 128 cases the following:

(1) Seven cases in which the killer was insane: Minnesota, 1; Wisconsin, 1; Connecticut, 1; Iowa, 1; New York, 2; Ohio, 1. Two, then, occurred in abolition states and five in capital punishment states.

(2) One case in Wisconsin (abolition state), where the offender struck the officer with a flashlight; one in New York, where the offender struck the officer with the gun without firing it, and one in Ohio where the offender backed a motor vehicle into the officer in such a manner that he was crushed against another vehicle. It is assumed that these attacks were chiefly meant to disable the officer in each case. These offenders either did not carry guns or did not use them as firearms.

On the other hand, we have included three occurrences, one each in Connecticut, New York, and Ohio, when a suspect during or after arrest, although he was himself unarmed, succeeding in seizing the policeman's own gun and shooting him with it..

Table 2 gives, state by state and by size of city, the number of cities whose schedules have been used, the number of cases reported during the entire period 1919–1954 and the rate per 100,000 population for each state and group of cities, based on the 1950 census. Abolition states and capital punishment states have been separately treated. It might be argued that it is improper to use the 1950 population as the base for the computation of rates that involve cases scattered over a thirty-six year period preceding. It would undoubtedly be possible to arrive at some population figure which would on the surface appear more defensible, but which would on close analysis be found to have equally great defects, for it must be remembered that all the cities involved have undergone the effect of con-

TABLE 2. Cases of Police Homicide, by Cities Grouped According to Size; and Rates per 100,000 Population in Each Group of Cities, by State

Abolition states	10,000–30,000				30,000–60,000				60,000–100,000			
	No. cit.	No. cases	Population	Rate	No. cit.	No. cases	Population	Rate	No. cit.	No. cases	Population	Rate
Maine	4		54,280	0.0	1		31,558	0.0	1		77,634	0.0
Michigan	24	8	419,904	1.9	4	1	189,609	0.5	2	3	187,912	1.6
Minnesota	14	4	259,461	1.5								
North Dakota	3	1	51,369	1.9								
Rhode Island	3		46,084	0.0	3	1	116,463	0.9			96,056	3.1
Wisconsin	13	2	207,940	0.9	7	4	252,580	1.6	1	3		
Total	61	15	1,039,038	1.3	15	6	590,210	1.0	4	6	361,602	1.6

Abolition states	100,000–350,000				500,000–650,000				All cities			
	No. cit.	No. cases	Population	Rate	No. cit.	No. cases	Population	Rate	No. cit.	No. cases	Population	Rate
Maine									6		163,472	0.0
Michigan	1	1	176,515	0.6					31	13	973,940	1.3
Minnesota									14	4	259,461	1.5
North Dakota									3	1	51,369	1.9
Rhode Island									6	1	162,547	0.6
Wisconsin					1	5	637,392	0.8	22	14	1,193,968	1.2
Total	1	1	176,515	0.6	1	5	637,392	0.8	82	33	2,804,757	1.2

Capital punishment states	10,000–30,000				30,000–60,000				60,000–100,000			
	No. cit.	No. cases	Population	Rate	No. cit.	No. cases	Population	Rate	No. cit.	No. cases	Population	Rate
Connecticut	11	1	190,746	0.0	5	1	212,213	0.5	1		74,293	0.0

	100,000-350,000				500,000-650,000				All cities			
	No. cit.	No. cases	Popu-lation	Rate	No. cit.	No. cases	Popu-lation	Rate	No. cit.	No. cases	Popu-lation	Rate
Illinois	14	4	206,214	1.9	6	1	225,701	0.4	1	1	92,927	1.1
Indiana	10	3	170,785	1.7	4	7	171,048	4.1	1		72,296	0.0
Iowa	6		85,429	0.0	2	2	64,244	3.1	1		66,112	1.5
Massachusetts	31	6	499,841	1.2	5	1	221,877	0.4				
Montana	1	1	17,581	5.7								
New Hampshire	4		59,809	0.0	1	1	34,469	2.9	1		82,732	0.0
New York	24	3	426,631	0.7	7		290,304	0.0	2	4	171,546	2.3
Ohio	21	7	371,623	1.9	7	3	223,303	1.3	2	1	146,379	0.7
South Dakota	2		24,920	0.0								
Vermont	1		12,411	0.0								
Total	125	24	2,065,990	1.2	37	16	1,443,159	1.1	9	7	706,285	1.0

Capital punishment states	100,000-350,000				500,000-650,000				All cities			
	No. cit.	No. cases	Popu-lation	Rate	No. cit.	No. cases	Popu-lation	Rate	No. cit.	No. cases	Popu-lation	Rate
Connecticut	2	3	263,186	1.1					19	4	740,438	0.5
Illinois									21	6	524,842	1.1
Indiana	1	1	133,607	0.7					15	11	475,440	2.3
Iowa	1	6	177,965	3.3					10	8	399,934	2.0
Massachusetts	1		203,486	0.0					38	8	991,316	0.8
Montana									1	1	17,581	5.7
New Hampshire									6	1	177,010	0.5
New York	2	3	434,019	0.7	1	8	580,132	1.4	36	18	1,902,632	0.9
Ohio	3	14	635,389	2.2	1	13	503,998	2.6	34	38	1,880,692	2.2
South Dakota									2		24,920	0.0
Vermont									1		12,411	0.0
Total	10	27	1,847,652	1.5	2	21	1,084,130	1.9	183	95	7,147,216	1.3

siderable migratory changes due to a depression and a world war and that no one can determine with any real accuracy what population basis is preferable. It is believed that the rates reflect with reasonable faithfulness the *comparative* size of the problem in the different states and in the two types of states. Whatever categories are compared, these comparisons are, of course, more useful the larger the number of cities and populations involved. If one city alone is found in a particular class and if it has a small population, a single case of police homicide would give it a rate which could be very high and yet meaningless.

Let us first compare the *rate* of fatal attacks on police in 6 abolition state cities (82), with a total population of 2,804,757, with the corresponding rate for 11 capital punishment state cities (182), except Chicago, with a total population of 7,147,-216 in 1950. The rate per 100,000 population in the former is 1.2 and in the latter 1.3. They prove to be the same, for the difference is hardly significant.

If we take the cities of the smallest class—those between 10,000 and 30,000 inhabitants—and use only rates from states with at least ten such cities reporting, we find the following comparative rates:

Abolition states		Capital punishment states	
Michigan	1.9	Ohio	1.9
Minnesota	1.5	Illinois	1.9
Wisconsin	0.9	Indiana	1.7
		New York	0.7
		Connecticut	0.0
		Massachusetts	1.2

In the group of cities with populations between 30,000 and 60,000, the abolition cities have a total rate of 1.0 and the capital punishment cities 1.1, but there are considerable variations among the states, ranging from a high of 4.1 in Indiana to a low of .4 for Massachusetts. In the third to fifth groups of cities the number reporting is, of course, small but it may be observed that compared with Milwaukee's (Wisconsin) rate of .8, the rates for Cincinnati, Ohio—2.6 and Buffalo, New York—1.4—are somewhat higher.

It is obvious from an inspection of the data that it is impossible to conclude that the states which have abolished the death penalty have thereby made the policeman's lot more hazardous. It is also obvious that the same differences observable in the general homicide rates of the various states are reflected in the rate of police killings. This can be readily observed by comparing the Middle West states with and without the death penalty with corresponding states in the Eastern part of the country, as is done in the following tables, where the appropriate rates of police homicides are presented.

Middle West states			
Abolition states		Capital punishment states	
North Dakota	1.9	Iowa	2.0
Minnesota	1.5	Illinois	1.1
Michigan	1.3	Indiana	2.3
Wisconsin	1.2	Ohio	2.2

Eastern states			
Abolition states		Capital punishment states	
Maine	0.0	New Hampshire	0.5
Rhode Island	0.6	Massachusetts	0.8
		Connecticut	0.5
		New York	0.9

Another interesting comparison is afforded by the material, namely, the trend of the killings. Table 3, in which the cases for the thirty-six-year period have been grouped into six-year periods, shows clearly that the 1925–1936 periods were the most hazardous and that the hazards have greatly declined.

In only two of the killings was a knife the weapon used; the others were committed by firearms, usually described merely as a gun, a pistol, or a revolver. In one case, a rifle was used and in three cases a shotgun. A machine gun was used in a single instance—in connection with a bank robbery in Needham, Massachusetts, in 1934, when two police officers were

TABLE 3. Trends in Cases of Police Killings, 1919–1954,
as Reported by 266 Cities in 17 States

Years	Cases Abol. states	Cases C.P. states	Police killed Abol. states	Police killed C.P. states	Both combined Cases	Both combined Police killed
1919–1924	8	25[e]	12	25	33	37
1925–1930	8[a]	31[e]	9	31	39	40
1931–1936	5[a]	24[a]	5	26	29	31
1937–1942	4	9	4	11	13	15
1943–1948	5[b]	5[a,d]	5	5	10	10
1949–1954	3	1	4	1	4	5
Total	33	95	39	99	128	138

[a] Excluding a case in which the killer was insane.
[b] Excluding a case in which officer was struck by flashlight.
[c] Excluding three cases in which the killer was insane; excluding a case in which the killer used gun as club.
[d] Excluding a case in which officer was crushed by car operated by the killer.
[e] Including three cases in which the killer seized the officer's gun and killed him.

killed, one during the robbery and the other during his pursuit of the criminals.

The letter which asked for data also requested that the reporter indicate whether or not he believed that the existence of the threat of possible execution gave the police a certain amount of protection which was lacking in the abolition states. Only 69 replies to this request were received from cities in capital punishment states and 27 replies from abolition states, i.e., 36.5 percent of the responding cities in the capital punishment states and 31.7 percent of the cities in the abolition states gave an opinion. In the death penalty states, the police officer reporting believed in the added protective force of the death penalty in 62 out of 69 cities, or 89.8 percent. In the abolition states, 20 out of 27, i.e., 74.1 percent, did *not* believe that there was any connection between the possible threat of the death penalty and the likelihood of a criminal using a lethal weapon in encounters with the police. In view of the results from this study, this opinion seems to be the correct one.

The Chicago Data

The largest cities, which presumably would have the best records and the most accessible ones, generally failed to return the schedules, as has already been mentioned. One prominent exception is Chicago, a city which in 1950 had a population of 3,620,962. Due to the courtesy of Edward C. Erickson, Director of Records and Communications of the Chicago Police Department, rather complete data were returned for the period 1919–1954, both on the number of police killed each year and on those wounded in encounters with criminals. These data made it possible to discover in what connection the killings occurred—the crime or situation involved—and for a brief span of years, 1923–1931, this information could also be secured in relation to the woundings. Injuries were not recorded before 1923, nor were they classified by type of crime after 1931. Table 4 contains, in summarized form, the information given about each death. Unlike the preceding presentation, each police officer killed is counted rather than cases.

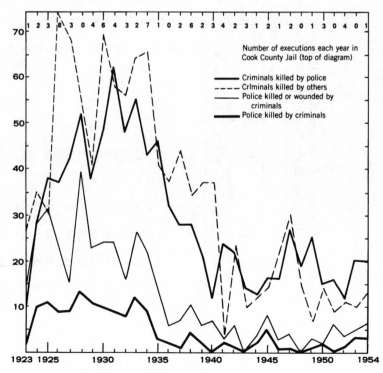

Number of police killed or wounded by criminals; criminals killed by police or private persons; number of persons executed in the Cook County Jail; Chicago, 1923–1954.

TABLE 4. Members of Chicago Police Department Killed or Wounded by Lethal Weapons in the Hands of Criminals or Suspects, 1920–1954

Year	Total killed or wounded			Crime or situation involved — Robbery			Murder			Attempted arrest or escape			Investigation or search			Other crimes			Number of executions in Cook County
	K.	W.	Tot.	K.	W.	Tot.	K.	W.	Tot.	K.	W.	Tot.	K.	W.	Tot.	K.	W.	Tot.	
1920	10			5						3						2			8
1921	5			2						1			1			1			10
1922	6			2						1						3			1
1923	2	13	15		3	3					9	9	2		2		1	1	1
1924	10	18	28	6	5	11		1	1	2	9	11	1		1	1	4	5	2
1925	11	20	31	4	9	13				6	5	11	1	1	2		5	5	3
1926	9	14	23	2	7	9				3	4	7	3		3	1	3	4	8
1927	9	7	16	4	3	7				4	3	7				1	1	2	3
1928	13	26	39	7	9	16	2	1	3	3	16	19				1	1	2	
1929	11	12	23	3	4	7				2	7	9	2		2	4	1	5	4[a]
1930	10	14	24	3	7	10				2	6	8	3		3	2	1	3	6
1931	9	15	24	6	13	19				2	2	4	1		1				4
1932	8	8	16	4						3						1			3
1933	12	14	26	7			1		1	2						2			2
1934	9	13	22	5												4			7
1935	3	10	13	3															1

Year									
1936	2	4	6							2
1937	1	6	7	1				1		6
1938	4	6	10	2		1				2
1939	2	4	6	2						3
1940		7	7							4
1941	2	1	3	2		1				2
1942	1	5	6	1		1				3
1943	4									1
1944	2	2	4		2					2
1945	5	3	8	1	1	3				1
1946	1	2	3			1				
1947	1	3	4			1				2[b]
1948		2	2			1				
1949	1	2	3	1					1	1
1950	2		2	1		1	1			3
1951	1	6	6							4
1952	3	4	4	1						1
1953	3	2	5	1		2				
1954	3	3	6	1		3				
Total	168	243	411	75	6	46	16		25	100

[a] First executions by electricity in Cook County.

[b] National execution statistics published by U.S. Bureau of Prisons reports only one execution in Illinois in 1947. Warden of Cook County Jail, where electric chair for county is found, reports two.

A study of Table 4 and the diagram[1] based on it shows that in a general way the experience in Chicago follows the trend shown in Table 3. The 1920's and the first half of the 1930's were especially hazardous to the police in Chicago, peaks in the number of killed and wounded being reached in 1925 and 1928, gradually declining to a fairly stable and comparatively low level after 1938. The table also gives the annual number of executions in Cook County, which has its own electric chair. These executions were not necessarily for the murder of police officers, such cases not having been segregated. However, the curve of executions follows generally the trend of the homicide curve. There is nothing to suggest that there is any other relation between the two than that when there are more homicides there are more executions and when there are fewer homicides there are fewer executions.

The table, furthermore, indicates that most of the killings of policemen occurred in encounters with robbers. All but 26 of the 168 cases occurred either when police officers interfered with hold-ups, were trying to arrest a person or search him, or were investigating some complaint, which brought them into contact with a suspect. . . .

Conclusion. The claim that if data could be secured they would show that more police are killed in abolition states than in capital punishment states is unfounded. On the whole, the abolition states, as is apparent from the findings of this particular investigation, seem to have fewer killings, but the differences are small. If this, then, is the argument upon which the police are willing to rest their opposition to the abolition of capital punishment, it must be concluded that it lacks any factual basis.

EDITORIAL POSTSCRIPT

During 1961–1963 there were 140 policemen criminally killed in the United States by offenders or suspects, an average of 47 per year. Nine of them were killed in the then abolition states—two in Michigan, four in Wisconsin, two in Minnesota, and one in North Dakota. No policeman was killed in Maine or Rhode Island.

In nine death-penalty states bordering on the above states, 21 policemen were killed—four in Massachusetts, four in Indiana, four in Illinois, five in Ohio, three in Iowa, and one in Connecticut. No policeman was killed in New Hampshire, South Dakota, or Montana.

If we compute the risk of a policeman being killed, using as base the number of police in these 15 states according to the 1960 census, we find that the annual average risk for the three years was 1.312 per 10,000 police in the abolition states and 1.328 in the bordering states. There was, then, no significant difference. We need not stress that 131 of the homicides occurred in death-penalty states.

Police organizations demand the retention of the death penalty as a protective device because of the great occupational hazards to which they are exposed. Police work undoubtedly is hazardous, but those who engage in such work accept occupational risks just as people do who enter other occupations, many of which are more dangerous, such as high-rise steel construction, lumbering, etc. In 1960 there were 225,000 police in the United States. In addition to the 140 police killed criminally in 1961–1963, 97 died in accidents—a total of 237. This means an average annual rate of 3.1 per 10,000 police. The corresponding risks of being killed on the job by accident were 11 in the mining industries, 7.7 in contract construction, 6.5 in agriculture, and 4.2 in transportation and public utilities. During 1963, five of every 10,000 male workers between 20 and 64 years of age in the United States died because of homicide or accidents at work. Had the same rate applied to policemen, 127, instead of the actual 69, would have died from homicide or work injuries.

In a recent report from the national Bureau of Labor Statistics on occupational work injuries in 1961, we find that the total injury frequency rate, i.e., the average number of disabling work injuries per million employee-hours worked, was 36.3 for policemen and 36.7 for firemen; the average number of days of disability per case was 64 for policemen and 82 for firemen. That year, at least, accidents hit firemen harder than the police.

Hazardous as police work is, there are occupations more hazardous; yet people enter them for the same reason people become policemen—for their livelihood.

Prison Homicides

THORSTEN SELLIN

Frequently one hears the death penalty defended as an indispensable measure to safeguard the lives of inmates and staff in penal institutions. Those who advance this argument believe that murderers who are sentenced to life imprisonment or receive a commutation of their death sentences will be deterred by the threat of execution from committing a homicide in prison, even though that threat did not prevent them from killing someone in the first place.

The validity of this argument could be ascertained by a study of homicides in state and federal prisons. Therefore, the author sent a schedule to prison administrators in the United States early in 1966 requesting certain information on fatal and non-fatal assaults in their institutions during 1965. In order to eliminate the common variety of petty fights that result in no real injuries, data were requested only on assaults in 37 jurisdictions (10 reported that none had occurred such as death, hospitalization, or some other incapacitation.

The response to the inquiry was most gratifying. Schedules were returned from 45 states, the District of Columbia, and the Federal Bureau of Prisons. Most of these 47 jurisdictions reported on the situation in all their institutions housing felons, but in some jurisdictions one or more institutions were not heard from. Also, no informatilon on non-fatal assaults could be given—in any case, it was omitted—on the schedules returned by Louisiana, Tennessee, South Carolina,

Virginia, and the Federal Bureau of Prisons. County and municipal correctional institutions were not covered by the inquiry. Only five states failed to provide any data at all: Alabama, Arizona, Arkansas, Idaho, and Maine.

A total of 603 persons were reported as victims of assaults in 37 jurisdictions (10 reported that none had occurred in their institutions: Alaska, Delaware, Nevada, New Hampshire, New Mexico, North Dakota, Oregon, South Dakota, Vermont, and West Virginia; of these states, Alaska, North Dakota, Oregon, and West Virginia were abolitionist states).

Of the 603 victims of assaults, 61—8 staff members and 53 inmates—died. Nine of the inmates were slain by unidentified persons (all in jurisdictions having the death penalty). These "anonymous" homicides occurred in California (one at San Quentin, one at Soledad, and two at Los Padres), the Indiana State Prison, the Georgia State Prison, the South Walpole State Prison in Massachusetts, and the Federal prison at Leavenworth (two cases). Except for the two cases in which some blunt instrument was used, the weapon was a knife; in six cases the motive was unknown, in two cases racial conflict was indicated, and in one an unpaid debt. Three of the California victims were Youth Authority wards; the fourth was said to be a former Nazi leader. The Indiana victim was a mental case, struck by a chair in the presence of several witnesses, whose silence was dictated by the inmate code.

There remain 52 victims whose killers are known. These victims were slain in 46 incidents, in which a total of 59 assailants were identified. The incidents occurred in 23 states and the Federal system, and we shall now describe them, the victims, the known perpetrators, and the circumstances.

In two cases a prisoner killed more than one person. In Tennessee, at the Fort Pillow State Farm, an inmate serving a 3-year term for burglary, third degree, and petit larceny, killed a security guard and a fellow inmate, and a prisoner serving a double life term in the Virginia State Penitentiary for robbery and murder killed the assistant superintendent of industries and a prison physician.

Seven events, on the other hand, involved two or more assailants and one or more victims, 20 offenders and 11 victims in all. The most serious occurred in Hawaii, an abolition state, and in Illinois. The Hawaii incident happened in the state prison yard on December 29. Five prisoners suspected of belonging to a faction trying to smuggle barbiturates into the institution engaged in a gang fight armed with two smuggled pistols and two knives. One of the participants, serving a sentence of 10 years for assault with a deadly weapon, was fatally stabbed by a car thief serving a five-year sentence; he, in turn, was shot by a tower guard. Another participant, a burglar on a 20-year sentence, was killed and two other participants—an inmate serving 20 years for attempted murder and one serving 40 years for robbery—were charged with the crime.

The Illinois affray occurred at the state prison at Menard on November 23, when a riot started in the dining hall. Before the riot ended two lieutenants and a guard had been stabbed to death and five guards and a steward wounded, three seriously. Charged with these homicides were a murderer serving a sentence of 25 years, a thief serving 3 to 7 years, a forger serving 3 to 10 years, and an armed robber serving 3 to 5 years.

In the Georgia State prison two inmates—one serving 20 years for voluntary murder and the other 4 to 10 years for assault to murder—killed an inmate in revenge arising from a struggle between rival cliques. Two inmates of the Kansas State Penitentiary—one serving sentences of 20 to 42 years and life for robbery and murder and one 1 to 5 for grand larceny—killed a prisoner as a result of a sex affair. In the Minnesota State Reformatory, two inmates serving a 5-year term for burglary and a 40-year term for robbery, respectively, armed with a butcher knife and a cleaver, attacked three inmates, killing two of them. In the Missouri State Penitentiary, two robbers serving 10 and 15 years killed a fellow prisoner in revenge, and at San Quentin, three prisoners —two robbers serving terms of 5 years to life and a prisoner serving 1 year to life for a previous assault in prison—killed an inmate during a fight arising from pressure being brought on the victim to sell his drug business.

Six of the eight staff members killed appear in the events

just reviewed. In addition, a San Quentin inmate serving a sentence of 5 years to life for selling narcotics stabbed a shop foreman during a disciplinary action, and in an unidentified institution in Pennsylvania, an inmate, described as a mental case, who was in prison on a 30- to 60-year sentence for aggravated robbery, killed a sergeant for no known reason.

In 35 events one prisoner killed one fellow inmate.

THE OFFENDERS

We have already noted the crimes for which some of the offenders were serving sentences when they committed the homicides in prison. The 59 assailants, altogether, were serving sentences for:

Murder	16
Manslaughter	1
Assault to murder	2
Rape	1
Assault	3
Kidnapping	1
Robbery	19
Burglary	4
Theft	7
Selling narcotics	1
Dyer Act violation	2
Possessing sawed-off shotgun	1
Delinquency	1
Total	59

The striking feature in this enumeration is that 43 of the offenders were in prison for crimes of violence against the person. Only 11 had been sentenced for burglary or theft and five for miscellaneous crimes. The largest single group of offenders was the robbers, followed closely by those guilty of some form of homicide.

Five of the 16 murders had not been punishable by death: two of them had occurred in the abolitionist states of Iowa and Michigan; the other three were second-degree murders reported from California, Nebraska, and North Carolina.

In addition to the 11 sentences for capital murder—four in Louisiana, and one each in Georgia, Illinois, Indiana, Kansas, South Carolina, Texas, and Virginia—nine prisoners were serving time for other capital crimes: one for assault to murder in Georgia, one for rape in Louisiana, two for armed robbery in Missouri, four for robbery in Virginia, and one for the Federal crime of kidnapping. Altogether, 20 of the 59 assailants were serving time for some capital offense, and an additional five had been convicted of noncapital murder.

In eight of the 46 events in which the known assailants participated, the reason was unknown. In 22 instances, the homicide occurred during an altercation. Four events involved homosexuality and revenge. Two events arose from racial conflict. One involved a disciplinary action, one a gang fight, and one a riot. Two events were reported as due to mental disturbance; before one of them the offender had said that he was looking for a "ticket" to court so that he could receive a death sentence—he was serving 99 years in Leavenworth for kidnapping.

The weapon used in 35 events was a homemade knife. In the other 11 events the following weapons were employed: sharpened screwdriver (two), glass dagger, guns and knives, knives and firebomb, butcher knife and cleaver, baseball bat, club, axe, razor blade, fists.

All of the 56 surviving offenders were referred to public prosecutors for action, except two who as strong suspects were still under investigation, both in Federal institutions. Three of the offenders at the Hawaii State Prison had been killed. The results of the prosecutions were not reported, except for the three events at the Virginia State Farm, where one offender committed suicide before his trial, the case of one was dismissed, and the third received five years added to his earlier nine-year sentence for robbery.

The geographical distribution of the offenders and their victims is shown in the table. There were no fatal assaults in the abolitionist states of Alaska, North Dakota, Oregon, Rhode Island, West Virginia and Wisconsin. Maine supplied no data. On the other hand, four such states reported a total of eight killings, of which two were committed by prisoners serving time for felony murder (Iowa) or second-degree murder (Michigan).

Of jurisdictions having the death penalty, 17 were reported free from prison homicides in 1965: Connecticut, Delaware, the District of Columbia, Florida, Kentucky, Maryland, Montana, Nevada, New Hampshire, New Jersey, New Mexico, New York, Ohio, South Dakota, Utah, Vermont, and Wyoming. Nineteen retentionist states and the Federal system reported 53 homicides.

Among the perpetrators of these crimes there were 11 murderers, six robbers, one assaulter, one rapist, and one kidnapper, who were all serving sentences for crimes for which they could have been sentenced to death. If, instead, they *had* been so sentenced and executed, many lives would have been saved, no doubt. But what courts or juries could have had the wisdom to know that these particular persons, among all those convicted of similar crimes, would kill in prison, if they were spared a death sentence? The answer is, none. Courts or clemency authorities had decided for some reason that they should not be executed, and as for the other 39 offenders, the law had not provided a death penalty for the crimes for which they were in prison.

The hazards of life in prison have just been illustrated. To imagine that they can be completely removed is visionary, but it is equally visionary to believe that the threat of the death penalty could play any role in reducing them. They can be lessened only by institutional management. This is a task which challenges the imagination and intelligence of administrators, because prisons are unnatural institutions, especially the maximum-security ones where the most serious offenders are most likely to be found. They bring into enforced daily contact, within a relatively confined area, hundreds and sometimes many thousands of persons of the same sex, usually males in early adulthood or early middle age, most of whom come from social groups in which a resort to physical violence is familiar. Their associations and relationships in prison at times lead to frictions ending in arguments settled by a physical encounter. This is, after all, not unknown in the world outside, which provides a more normal milieu for a man.

In the society within walls, real or fancied wrongs, jealousy, fear, revenge are potent forces that may create situations where violence may end in the killing of an adversary, in spite of the great odds against escaping the consequences of such an act.

Geographical Distribution of Prison Homicides, 1965[a]

		Victims			
			Inmates		
Jurisdiction	Known offenders	Staff	Known offenders	Unknown offenders	Total
California	8	1	5	4	10
Colorado	2		2		2
Georgia	2		1	1	2
Hawaii	5		2		2
Illinois	4	3			3
Indiana	1		1	1	2
Iowa	2		2		2
Kansas	2		1		1
Louisiana	5		5		5
Massachusetts				1	1
Michigan	2		2		2
Minnesota	2		2		2
Mississippi	1		1		1
Missouri	2		1		1
Nebraska	1		1		1
North Carolina	1		1		1
Oklahoma	1		1		1
Pennsylvania	2	1	1		2
South Carolina	2		2		2
Tennessee	1	1	1		2
Texas	2		2		2
Virginia	5	2	4		6
Washington	1		1		1
Federal	5		5	2	7
Total	59	8	44	9	61

[a] Abolition states italicized.

Homicides and Assaults in Canadian Prisons

DOGAN D. AKMAN

In March, 1966, the Canadian House of Commons debated a motion to abolish the death penalty. After an exhaustive debate the motion was defeated by a vote of 143 to 112, the narrowest margin ever recorded in Canada. During the debate, an amendment proposing the maintenance of the penalty for murder of prison staff and inmates, as well as of police officers on duty, was defeated by the combined vote of the retentionists, who argued among other things that the death penalty is a unique deterrent for protecting the life and limb of prison staff and inmates, and the abolitionists, who were not willing to make any concessions.

Since 1961, capital punishment has been mandatory in Canada for capital murder. Before then, the Criminal Code did not distinguish between capital and non-capital murder, and all culpable murders were punished by death. Since late 1957, however, successive governments (Progressive Conservatives and Liberals), using the prerogative of mercy sanctioned by the Governor General, have commuted the death penalty to life imprisonment in 69 out of 85 cases. These commutations have been forcefully opposed by those advocating the death penalty.

This exploratory study will examine the contention that the policy of commuting death sentences to life imprisonment creates additional safety hazards for prison staff and inmates.[1] The data presented in the following pages cover the years 1964 and 1965 and are based on reports from all Canadian penal institutions to which those sentenced to two years and more for felonies are committed.[2]

During 1964 and 1965 a total of 102 assaultive events occurred involving 106 offenders and 107 victims (37 officers and 70 inmates). The offenders included 6 women. The identity of 19 offenders remained unknown. Most of the assaults occurred in maximum-security institutions, where there were 91 victims (32 officers and 59 inmates).

To answer the question about commuting death sentences to life imprisonment, let us first examine some characteristics of the assaults.

Offenders

Most of the offenders were between 20 and 29 years of age; they accounted for over 60 percent of the assaults. In terms of their offenses of conviction, most of the offenders were serving time for robbery or theft. The robbers accounted for one third of the assaults on officers and inmates and the thieves for one third of the assaults on officers and nearly half of the assaults on inmates. In total they accounted for over 70 percent of the assaults.[3] One offender (convicted for theft) committed two assaults on two different occasions during the two years covered.

Victims

The officer-victims were 35 correctional officers and two superior officers. The inmate-victims, considering their offenses of conviction, showed that robbers and thieves were not only the most aggressive inmates but also the most aggressed against, as they, particularly the thieves of whom 35 were assaulted, represent over 70 percent of the casualties.[4] Of interest are the facts that in 15 assaults out of 23, thieves assaulted thieves, in 8, robbers assaulted robbers, in 6, robbers assaulted thieves, and in 3, thieves assaulted robbers.

Causes and Circumstances of Assaults

Because of space limitations in the schedule used for the collection of the data, the complexity of psychological events, and the difficulties of obtaining from victims, offenders and witnesses unbiased information on the incidents, the information on these topics is meager. The causes of assaults on officers cluster around psychiatric problems (8 events), personal complaints (8 events), and disciplinary problems (8 events), while the causes of assaults on inmates cluster around personal complaints (48 events). In 17 cases no causes were reported. In 13 events involving inmate victims, the offender was provoked by the victim.[5]

Weapons Used

The most common means of assault was bodily assault, which occurred in half of the events. In the remaining cases, stabbing and cutting weapons were used in one third of the events, slightly more often against officers (12 out of 37 assaults) than inmate victims (20 out of 72). Blunt weapons and miscellaneous types of objects at hand used as weapons accounted for 10 percent and 15 percent, respectively, of all the assaults. In general, the cutting and stabbing instruments were more often used by robbers and young offenders between the ages of 20 and 29. Interestingly enough, with the exception of one case, where the victim resorted to a blunt instrument, the victims did not use weapons to defend themselves.

Physical Consequences of Assaults

Death. During 1964 and 1965 two homicides occurred. The first involved a guard fatally assaulted by an 18-year-old inmate serving a 12-year sentence for violent robbery. The second occurred in 1965 and involved an inmate victim who was assaulted by a 27-year-old fellow prisoner serving time for armed robbery.

Aggravated Assaults.[6] During the same period 11 officers (3 in 1964 and 8 in 1965) and 31 inmates (17 in 1964 and 14 in 1965) were the victims of aggravated assaults.

Simple Assaults.[7] Fourteen officers (9 in 1964 and 5 in 1965) and 4 inmates (1 in 1964 and 3 in 1965) suffered no physical injuries and 11 officers (9 in 1964 and 2 in 1965) and 34 inmates (17 in 1964 and 1965 respectively) suffered only minor injuries.

An examination of the assaults in terms of age and the offenses of conviction of the offenders indicates harmfulness to be predominant among inmates between the ages of 20 and 29 and those convicted of robbery or theft. Those committed for manslaughter (3), attempted murder (1) and non-capital murder (1) inflicted only three minor injuries on three officers and one minor injury (requiring medical aid only) and three more serious injuries (resulting in hospitalization and temporary disability following hospitalization) to three inmates. This finding is remarkable when contrasted with the record of the robbers and thieves.

The examination of the consequences of the assaults according to the victims' offenses of conviction indicates that robbers and thieves not only caused the most harm but also sustained most of the serious injuries. Out of 16 robbers victimized, seven required hospitalization, one suffered temporary disability following hospitalization, one required a change of work because of the nature of the disability, and one was killed. Out of the 35 thieves victimized, as many as 12 required hospitalization, and five sustained temporary disability following hospitalization. Among the victims, one convicted of non-capital murder and another convicted of manslaughter sustained temporary disability following hospitalization.

Disciplinary Measures

The punishments given to the offenders comprise a number of different combinations of penalties which are routinely meted out by the warden's court of each institution. This makes it rather difficult to present systematically the patterns of punishment, as we do not have a scale for assigning a weighted score to different types of punishment. As one might expect, it generally seems that assaults on officers were more severely punished than assaults on inmates and that the severity of the punishment was related to the gravity of the physical consequences of the assault.

Four offenders (including two woman inmates) originally convicted of theft (2) or armed robbery (2) who assaulted four officers were tried in a criminal court and two were sentenced to an additional two years to be served concurrently, while in the other two cases the outcome of the trial is pending. The latter include the homicide case where the offender has been charged with capital murder. Two other offenders (including one woman), both convicted of robbery, who assaulted three officers, were transferred to a mental hospital.

Five offenders convicted of armed robbery (2), manslaughter (1), theft (1), and assault and wounding (1) who assaulted inmates were also charged in a criminal court and received sentences of death, two, five, seven, and 10 years, respectively. In the cases tried in criminal court, two victims suffered no injuries, one sustained temporary disability without hospitalization, one was hospitalized, two suffered from temporary disabilities following hospitalization, and two were fatally injured.

LIFE AND OCCUPATIONAL HAZARDS IN PRISONS

In the light of the evidence that has been presented, it is timely now to examine the question posed at the beginning of this study: Does the policy of commuting death sentences to life imprisonment create additional safety hazards for the prison staff and inmates?

From 1960 until May, 1965, in Canada, of the 39 persons who had been tried and convicted of capital murder and sentenced to death, only five were executed. This rate of executions (12.8 percent) is unprecedented in Canadian penal practices. Previously, the rates of execution ranged from a low of 28.9 percent (1870–1879) to a high of 74.9 percent between 1930 and 1939.[8] The present dramatic decrease noted earlier is due both to the desire of the government to prevent an execution whenever possible and to changes made in the Criminal Code in 1961.

If we accept for a moment the thesis of the retentionists we should expect to find an increase in the number of murderous and serious (aggravated) assaults in Canadian prisons by those whose sentences have been commuted. This is certainly *not* the case. During 1964 and 1965, among the 87 offenders who were known, *none* was serving a commuted sentence for capital murder; and we cannot assume that the unknown offenders group comprised such offenders;[9] the homicides, as noted above, were committed by robbers.

Information on inmate killings before 1964 is unfortunately not available. However, with respect to officer killings, the records going as far back as 1945 indicate that until 1964, only three guards had been killed, none by a lifer, convicted of homicide. One was killed in 1948 by a robber, one in 1961 by an unknown offender and, finally, one in 1963 by fellow officers when in a panic they blindly fired into a cell where the victim was held hostage by two inmates convicted of robbery.[10]

Of course, it may be argued that "the reason why convicted murderers whose sentences are commuted show such a good record is that the worst types have been executed."[11]

A comparison of the mental characteristics of those executed and those whose sentences were commuted between 1957 and 1965 contradicts this contention. Indeed, among the 16 persons who were executed, six were considered "normal" (or without any symptoms), five had no independent psychiatric reports, and in five cases where the offenders were reported to display mental deficiencies, only two exhibited mental illness (psychopathy and the possibility of delirium tremens and hallucination). On the other hand, among the 69 whose sentences were commuted, we find only 16 cases where the offender was diagnosed as "normal," as free of symptoms, or as not being mentally ill; 12 had no independent psychiatric reports, and one was a borderline mental case. The remaining offenders (40 out of 69) included not only those mentally deficient but a large number of offenders diagnosed as schizophrenic, psychotic, perverts, sociopaths, psychopaths, schizoid, etc.[12] Also, in the face of this evidence, one can no longer argue that "the conduct of murderers whose sentences have been commuted for extenuating reasons is no reliable guide to what will be the conduct of other murderers."[13]

It may be pointed out that if the commutation of the death sentence does not appear to result in increased risks to prison staff and inmates, it is because of the fact that these offenders had, so to speak, the rope dangled in front of them until the executive clemency was exercised, and this might have been responsible for deterring them from further violence. This hypothesis may be examined in relation to those who are serving sentences for offenses other than capital murder, but who might exhibit increased physical aggressiveness, since in the case of a prison homicide their chances of not being executed are currently slightly better than 87 percent. The calculation of the life and occupational hazards for prison staff and inmates indicates that the hazards caused by most offenders are infinitesimal. The rates of hazards for the prison staff are .68 percent (1964) and .45 percent (1965) and for the inmates .47 percent (1964) and .48 percent (1965). The differences between the two groups are due to the small size of the prison staff as compared to the inmate population, since the number of victims among the former was much smaller than among the latter group.[14] Assuming that the prison staff employed in strictly custodial duties are likely to face greater hazards, we still find a rate that barely reaches 1 percent.

Actually, what is surprising is that given the abnormal living conditions in prisons and the extraordinarily high concentration of persons committed to a criminal career, the rate is not significantly higher than it is. Of course it may again be argued that the risks are not equally distributed in each institution and that in some the risks would be much higher than in others. This is true. However, an examination of these risks (for all the prison staff) in selected institutions where the greatest number of assaultive events occurred does not affect the observations to any meaningful extent. For the officers the hazard rates ranged from 4.9 percent (1964) in the women's prison to nil in the majority of other institutions.[15] In only five institutions did the rates rise above 1 percent and these rates (1.7, 1.2, 1.1, and 1 percent) were, with one exception, maintained for two consecutive years in these institutions. For the inmates the hazard rates ranged from 1.9 percent (1965) to nil. The preceding rate of 1.9 and a rate of 1.4 percent were reached only during one year at two different institutions. Actually, these rates exaggerate the facts, as 18 victims (10 officers and 8 inmates) did not sustain any injury whatsoever and 45 victims (11 officers and 34 inmates) sustained minor injuries, requiring only medical aid. This is particularly true in the women's prison, where two victims sustained no injuries, two required only medical aid, and two were temporarily disabled without requiring hospitalization.

Such minor altercations occur in everyday life without being brought to the attention of the police. What causes them to be recorded in prison is the extreme susceptibility of the prison staff to any disruption of their psychological security and the discipline and order of the institution.

Given these extremely low rates, it is highly unlikely that the commutation of the death sentence has caused any increase in the life and occupational hazards for prison staff and inmates, and it is very difficult to believe that the hazard rates were lower before the policy of commutation was adopted by the government.

We may conclude the discussion by stating that, within the limitations of this study, the argument that the commutation of death sentences increases the life and occupational hazards in prison finds no empirical support. Not only has commutation not led to further violence by those whose sentences have been commuted, but the attenuation of the threat of the death penalty resulting from an unprecedented high rate of commutations has not resulted in a general increase of homicidal and assaultive behavior in Canadian prisons.

The Paroling of Capital Offenders

G . I . G I A R D I N I A N D R . G . F A R R O W

This survey was conducted by correspondence. A questionnaire was sent to each state, asking for information about commutation of the death penalty and the procedure for subsequent parole of commuted capital offenders, and requesting statistics on this group. Forty-six states responded to the questionnaire. When the information was summarized, the resulting statements were submitted to the respective states for approval or correction.

Following is the current practice in the paroling of capital offenders in forty-six states, as revealed by this survey.

Alabama. Before 1951, prisoners whose death sentence had been commuted by the Governor to life imprisonment were eligible for parole at the discretion of the Board of Pardons and Paroles. Since 1951, the law has required that the commuted "lifer" must serve fifteen years before he is eligible for parole consideration by the Parole Board. Parole continues for life unless a pardon is granted by the Board of Pardons and Paroles. Parole may be revoked by action of a quorum of the board.

Arizona. Parole of prisoners with death sentences commuted to life imprisonment is granted by the Governor on recommendation of the Board of Pardons and Paroles. The board itself has power to terminate or revoke parole.

Arkansas. After death sentence has been commuted to life, further commutation to a specific term is required for parole purposes. A prisoner is eligible for parole consideration when he has served one-third of the specific term imposed. Expiration of the minimum sentence of the specific term ends parole.

Reprinted, by permission, from *The Annals of the American Academy of Political and Social Science*, 284:85–94, November, 1952.

Parole is granted and may be revoked by the Board of Pardons, Paroles and Probation.

California. Parole may be granted after the prisoner has served seven years of the life sentence commuted from the death penalty, unless the Governor's commutation order stipulates that parole shall not be granted. The Governor may remove this stipulation through further clemency. Parole on life sentences continues for life unless terminated by the Governor, or unless revoked by the Adult Authority for violation.

Colorado. Capital sentences may be commuted to life by the Governor. The Parole Board has authority to parole a life prisoner only after the Governor establishes a minimum sentence and this sentence is served. Further clemency by the Governor is needed to terminate parole, but the Parole Board may revoke for violation.

Connecticut. The Board of Pardons, before July 1, 1951, had power to commute death sentences to life and later to commute the life sentence or grant conditional pardon to lifers, subject to further action and conditions of the Board of Parole. Lifers were eligible for parole in twenty years if they had earned the time given for good behavior. Since 1951, juries have been permitted to recommend mercy in cases of conviction for a capital offense. The judge *must* sentence the offender to life imprisonment. This sentence cannot be reduced, and the offender does not have the privilege of applying for commutation or parole. However, capital sentences will still be subject to commutation by the Board of Pardons, but the possibility of subsequent clemency from a life sentence has not been determined.

Delaware. Capital offenders serving life sentences can be paroled by the Board of Parole after serving fifteen years in prison. Paroles can be terminated by commutation action of the Board of Pardons, or by revocation order of the Board of Parole after violation.

Florida. Parole consideration may be given to lifers, including commuted capital offenders, after six months have been served on the sentence. The Parole Commission can release the parolee from supervision or return him for violation; but only the Pardon Board, on recommendation of the

Parole Commission, can restore civil rights lost through conviction for felony.

Georgia. Since 1943, commutation from death penalty to life imprisonment has been a power of the Board of Pardons and Paroles, rather than of the Governor. Prisoners serving life sentences are eligible for parole consideration after serving seven years. Parole on life sentences can be terminated after five years, through application for commutation and restoration of civil and political rights. The board may order return to prison of a parolee who violates.

Idaho. The Board of Pardons may commute the death penalty to life in prison. In order to be eligible for parole, a life prisoner must serve ten years. Parole may then be ordered by the State Board of Correction, which, incidentally, has the same membership as the Board of Pardons. Parole may be terminated after one year by the Board of Correction, which may also order return for violation.

Illinois. Commutation of death sentences to life imprisonment is effected by the Governor, acting upon recommendation of the Parole and Pardon Board. Parole of commuted capital offenders may be ordered by the Parole and Pardon Board. This same body may order the return of parolee to the institution for violation, and may discharge a parolee from supervision after he has served honorably on parole for five years.

Indiana. The Governor has authority to commute a sentence from death to life. He may then grant parole by executive order or may commute the life sentence to a minimum term of time-served. In the latter instance, the Parole Board may grant parole.

Iowa. Parole of capital offenders serving life sentences through commutation of the Governor appears to be a legal possibility, provided commutation of sentence to a definite term is later effected by the Governor. However, the reply from this state reports no known paroles in such cases in the past twenty years. Termination of parole would have to be through action of the Governor.

Kansas. The Governor may commute death sentences to life imprisonment. Legally, the Governor could parole such cases or could commute the sentence to an indeterminate sentence, after which the Parole Board could take jurisdiction; but no paroles have been granted to date. Paroles on all sentences can be terminated only by the Board of Administration which grants them, except in cases of Governor's parole, which may be revoked by the Governor.

Kentucky. Commutation of the death penalty is a power of the Governor. Capital offenders may be paroled by the Division of Probation and Parole after serving eight years. Parole may be terminated only by pardon or by executive clemency restoring citizenship. A life parolee may be returned to prison as a parole violator, but if he is again released, the act is a reinstatement, not a reparole.

Louisiana. No reply received.

Maine. The death penalty is not imposed in this state.

Maryland. The Governor may commute death to life sentences. Commuted capital offenders serving life sentences are eligible for parole consideration after serving fifteen years. The Parole Director automatically reviews each case at that time. He must make a favorable recommendation to the Governor before the Governor may grant or refuse parole. An unfavorable decision by the Director is final. Paroles on life sentences are not terminated short of life except by revocation by the Parole Director for violation of parole. The Governor may grant a conditional pardon, which also may be revoked for violation.

Massachusetts. The Governor, with consent of the Council, may commute the death penalty to life imprisonment. Parole may be effected through a Governor's conditional pardon or a subsequent commutation by the Governor with release power exercised by the Parole Board. Parole may be terminated by a complete pardon or by revocation order of the Governor and Council for conditional pardon cases, and by the Parole Board for commutation cases.

Michigan. The death penalty may be imposed for treason only. There is no known case of its use.

Minnesota. There is no death penalty in Minnesota.

Mississippi. No reply received.

Missouri. Capital sentences may be commuted to life imprisonment by the Governor. After commutation, parole may be effected at any time by the State Board of Probation and Parole. Termination of parole requires further commutation by the Governor. Return to prison for violation may be ordered by the board.

Montana. The State Board of Pardons may commute death sentences to life imprisonment, upon recommendation of the Governor. A prisoner serving life may be paroled when he has served twenty-five years less possible "good time" of eleven years and three months. Parole must be approved by unanimous action, in writing, of the Board of Pardons. There is no provision for termination of parole, but the Board may order return for violation.

Nebraska. The Board of Pardons may commute death to life imprisonment. Parole may be granted by further commutation to a definite number of years. Parole may be terminated by the Board of Pardons after satisfactory completion of the required period—usually nine months. Revocation may also be effected by the board if the parolee violates.

Nevada. Commutation of death to life sentences is effected by the Board of Pardons and Paroles, consisting of the Governor, three Supreme Court judges, and the Attorney General. A prisoner serving life is eligible to apply for parole after seven calendar years. Parole may be terminated or revoked at the discretion of the Board of Pardons and Paroles.

New Hampshire. The Governor and Council can commute the death sentence to life imprisonment. Parole may be effected by the Governor and Council's granting conditional pardon which may later be changed to complete pardon to terminate sentence. Return of the parolee to prison for violation may be ordered by the Governor and Council.

New Jersey. Capital sentences may be commuted to life imprisonment by the Governor, who may extend further clemency in order to permit release on parole. Parole is ordered by the State Parole Board and supervised by the Parole Division of the Department of Institutions and Agencies. No capital case has been released under the present system, which was adopted in 1947. Parole for capital offenders can be terminated only by further clemency by the

Governor, but the State Parole Board may order return for violation.

New Mexico. The Governor has power to commute death to life sentences. A life prisoner who is not a fourth offender, has not escaped or attempted to escape, and has not violated parole may be granted parole by the penitentiary warden. Such parole is terminated only by violation, with return ordered by the warden. However, capital parolees report for only one year and are then placed on probation for life without any requirement to report or to be supervised.

New York. The Governor has commutation power in capital cases except for the offense of treason, which is subject to the State Legislature. In commuting the death sentence, the Governor may establish a life term or he may set a minimum and maximum term to the sentence. If the term is life, subsequent commutation to a shorter time is needed before parole may be considered by the Parole Board. Parole extends for life or for the duration of the sentence as set by the Governor. The Parole Board may order return for violation.

North Carolina. The Governor may commute death sentences to life sentences. No further commutation is required before parole. However, it is customary to reduce life sentences to a definite term of years before parole is granted by the Governor. Paroles are terminated through further commutation order or through revocation by the Governor.

North Dakota. There is no commutation of death sentences to life imprisonment and therefore no parole of capital offenders. The only capital offense is murder while serving a life sentence for murder.

Ohio. Prisoners serving life sentences after receiving commutation of the death sentence are not eligible for parole without extension of further clemency by the Governor to reduce the offense from first-degree murder to a lesser offense, such as second-degree murder. A prisoner serving life for second-degree murder is eligible for parole consideration after serving ten years. Paroles of first-degree murder cases reduced to second degree by executive clemency can be terminated only by action of the Governor. Return for violation may be ordered by the Parole Commission.

Oklahoma. Capital offenders serving life sentences are in

the same category as other prisoners with life terms and are eligible for parole consideration by the Pardon and Parole Board after serving fifteen years. The Criminal Court of Appeals has the power to modify sentences in cases on appeal. The Pardon and Parole Board has authority to recommend clemency to the Governor. Paroles may be revoked on application from the Pardon and Parole Officer to the Governor. The Governor has authority to grant pardons after they have been recommended by the Pardon and Parole Board.

Oregon. Capital sentences may be commuted to life imprisonment by the Governor. All persons serving life sentences are eligible for parole consideration by the Board of Parole and Probation after serving seven years. By law, any parolee is eligible for discharge after one year, but by rule of the Board of Parole and Probation this period is extended to ten years for life sentences. In the past twenty years, only two commutations from death to life have been granted. There have been no paroles granted to capital offenders.

Pennsylvania. The Governor, on recommendation of the Board of Pardons, may commute death to life. Further commutation is required before the prisoner may be paroled by the Board of Parole. The life maximum stands unless reduced by commutation. The Board of Parole may revoke for violation.

Rhode Island. This state has the death penalty for only one offense, murder committed by a person under sentence of imprisonment for life.

South Carolina. The Governor has power to commute death sentences to life terms, and to grant reprieves. The Probation, Parole and Pardon Board may parole capital offenders serving life sentences after ten years of imprisonment. The board may terminate parole for a capital offender by granting a complete pardon.

South Dakota. Death sentences may be commuted by the Governor to life imprisonment, but capital prisoners in this status are not subsequently paroled. The Governor has authority to parole and could terminate parole by revocation or by extending further clemency.

Tennessee. The Governor can commute the death penalty to life imprisonment. The commuted capital prisoner is eligible for parole by the Board of Pardons, Paroles and Probations after serving thirteen years and seven months. Parole cannot be terminated except by revocation by the board for violation.

Texas. The Board of Pardons and Paroles recommends various form of executive clemency which the Governor may grant or refuse. Commutation from death to life is granted by the Governor on recommendation of the Board of Pardons and Paroles. All other executive clemency may be granted and terminated through the same procedure. Executive clemency may take the form of reprieve and stay of execution, conditional pardon, reprieve, emergency reprieve, commutation of sentence, or full pardon.

Utah. The Board of Pardons may commute the death penalty to life imprisonment, and later commute the life sentence to a definite period of time at expiration of which parole may be granted by the board. Parole may be terminated by the Board of Pardons. No paroles were granted to commuted capital offenders from January, 1920, to January, 1952.

Vermont. The Governor may commute a death penalty to life imprisonment. He may extend further clemency in the form of pardon or conditional pardon to release the prisoner. However, in the past twenty years the only prisoner whose capital sentence was commuted to life has not been paroled. During this period there was one other capital conviction, which resulted in execution. If a conditional release is granted, the Governor has power to revoke or terminate it.

Virginia. Death sentences can be commuted by the Governor to life imprisonment. The Governor may also grant a pardon or conditional pardon to prisoners serving life sentences. The conditions of the pardon may be set by the Governor and may be the conditions of parole, including supervision by a parole officer. Such conditional release can be terminated by a specification in the pardon designating a definite period at the end of which the conditions of the pardon will be satisfied, or by absolute pardon or revocation by the Governor. Parole supervision may be ended at the discretion of the Parole Board, usually after five years.

Washington. The Governor holds the power to commute death sentences to life imprisonment. Before 1951 a life prisoner could be released only by full pardon or conditional pardon. Since 1951 the Board of Prison Terms and Paroles has had jurisdiction over life prisoners and may consider them for parole after they have served twenty years less earned good-time allowance. This cannot be less than thirteen years and four months. Parole on life sentences can be terminated only by full pardon or by final discharge and restoration of civil rights, both actions being solely in the Governor's power. The board, however, may, at its discretion, issue a conditional discharge from supervision, eliminating the reporting requirement of parole. Other conditions of parole remain in effect.

Washington, D.C. No reply received.

West Virginia. Prisoners whose death sentences are commuted by the Governor are eligible for parole after serving ten years, unless they have had two prior felony convictions, in which case they must serve fifteen years. Release from parole can be effected only by clemency action of the Governor.

Wisconsin. There is no death penalty in this state.

Wyoming. There is no commutation of the death penalty to life imprisonment. Death sentence is mandatory for certain offenses unless the jury specifies "without capital punishment," in which event a life term is imposed. These life sentences may later be commuted to an indeterminate term by the Governor on recommendation of the Board of Pardons, making parole possible on expiration of the minimum sentence. Parole may be terminated by expiration of maximum sentence less good-time allowances, and by further commutation action of the Board of Pardons.

STATISTICS ON PAROLING OF CAPITAL OFFENDERS

In Table 1 are presented the data received from twenty-two states on the paroling of capital cases. The table does not include five Pennsylvania cases whose life sentences, after commutation from the death penalty, were terminated by full pardon. Nor does it include several cases whose life terms were commuted to permit deportation to foreign countries. Statistics from five other states had to be excluded for various reasons.

The table shows that 197 capital cases were paroled in 22 states over periods ranging from 1 to 38 years. Eleven cases violated parole by the commission of new offenses, 7 violated by breach of rules, 11 died while on parole, 5 absconded from supervision, 129 are still on parole, and 34 discharged from parole. Combining the three forms of violation of parole, we have 23 cases or 11.7 per cent of the total. This figure compares favorably with violation rates usually reported by parole agencies for all categories of offenders, but its reliability is to be seriously questioned. The small number of cases reported by each state and the wide differences among the states in the laws and policies governing the processing of these cases make any conclusion extremely hazardous.

Of the states that submitted statistics, Pennsylvania and Texas furnished data sufficiently comprehensive to warrant separate treatment. The period covered by the Pennsylvania statistics extended from June, 1914, to March 31, 1952. In 1913 a law was passed providing for the abolition of hanging capital cases in the separate county seats and for the substitution of electrocution of all such cases in a newly built prison in the center of the state. Since that time an electrocution docket has been kept by the warden of the prison. This docket was the principal source of our data.

The Texas statistics cover the period from February 8, 1924, to March 31, 1952. It should be recalled that in Texas capital punishment applies to the crimes of murder, rape, and robbery with arms, whereas in Pennsylvania it applies only to murder in the first degree.

Table 2 shows the number of cases executed and the number commuted to life imprisonment for each of the three crimes for which capital punishment may be imposed. Of 269 cases sentenced to die for murder, 21 percent were commuted to life. Only 7 percent of those charged with rape, and

TABLE 1. Capital Cases Paroled and Their Present Status

State	Years covered	Capital cases paroled	Number of Violators				Still on parole	Completed parole
			New offense	Breach of rules	Absconded	Died		
Arizona	20	2	0	0	0	0	1	1
Colorado	22	1	0	0	0	0	1	0
Connecticut	25	3	0	0	0	0	3	0
Delaware	20	27	0	4	1	0	22	0
Florida	10	12	2	0	0	1	8	1
Idaho	20	1	0	0	0	0	0	1
Illinois	20	1	0	0	0	0	1	0
Indiana	20	3	0	0	0	0	3	0
Kentucky	21	10	0	1	0	0	9	0
Maryland	32	5	0	0	0	0	5	0
Missouri	20	1	0	0	0	0	1	0
Nebraska	20	1	0	0	0	0	0	1
Nevada	20	3	0	0	0	0	3	0
New Hampshire	20	2	0	0	0	0	2	0
New Mexico	20	10	0	0	0	0	0	10
New York	20	18	0	0	2	1	14	1
North Carolina	20	32	5	0	1	0	20	7
Pennsylvania	38	36	3	1	1	7	17	7
Texas	28	21	1	0	1	2	14	3
Virginia	20	3	0	1	0	0	2	0
Washington	1	2	0	0	0	0	2	0
Wyoming	20	3	0	0	0	0	1	2
Total		197	11	7	5	11	129	34

Table 2. Executions and Commutations to Life Imprisonment in Texas, February 8, 1924–March 31, 1952

Offense	Executed Number	Executed Percent	Commuted Number	Commuted Percent	Total numbers
Murder	213	79	56	21	269
Rape	68	93	5	7	73
Robbery	3	37	5	63	8
Total	284	81	66	19	350

Table 3. Capital Cases by Offense and Race, Texas

Offense	White Number	White Percent	Negro Number	Negro Percent	Mexican Number	Mexican Percent	Indian Number	Indian Percent	Total
Murder	88	32.7	147	54.6	33	12.3	1	0.4	269
Rape	12	16.4	56	76.7	5	6.9	0	0.0	73
Robbery	5	62.5	3	36.5	0	0.0	0	0.0	8
Total	105	30.0	206	58.9	38	10.8	1	0.3	350

five of eight cases of robbery, were commuted to life. Of the total of 350 cases sentenced to die, 19 percent were commuted to life imprisonment.

In Table 3 we have presented the same cases segregated according to offense and race or nationality. For the sake of brevity we will use the term "race" loosely.

In Table 4 we have the number of executions and commutations to life imprisonment for Pennsylvania and for Texas. During the period covered by the statistics, Pennsylvania executed an average of 8.6 capital cases a year as compared with Texas' average of 10.1 cases. If we consider only the murder cases for Texas, the average drops to 7.6 cases

TABLE 4. Executions and Commutations to Life Imprisonment, Pennsylvania and Texas

| State | Executed | | Commuted | | Total |
	Number	Percent	Number	Percent	number
Pennsylvania	327	82	72	18	399
Texas	284	81	66	19	350
Total	611	82	138	18	749

per year. If we consider only murder we find that Texas commutes 20 percent of the cases as compared with Pennsylvania's 18 percent. The difference is not significant.

In Table 5 we note that of the 399 Pennsylvania capital cases, 64.2 percent were white, 35.6 percent were Negro. One was Mongolian. When all the Texas cases are considered, regardless of offense, we find that 30 percent were white, 59 percent Negro, and 11 percent included 38 Mexicans and 1 Indian. If we consider only the Texas cases convicted of murder, we have 33 percent white, 55 percent Negro, and 12 percent including 33 Mexicans and 1 Indian.

Table 6 shows the disposition of the cases whose death sentence was commuted to life imprisonment, as far as it is known. Texas does not use the pardon in the fashion used in Pennsylvania. Of the two cases discharged in Texas, one was by order of court and the other by order of the Governor.

The 41 cases conditionally released in Pennsylvania include

TABLE 5. Pennsylvania and Texas Capital Cases by State, Crime, and Race

| State | White | | Negro | | Others | | Total |
	Number	Percent	Number	Percent	Number	Percent	number
1. Pennsylvania	256	64.2	142	35.6	1	0.2	399
2. Texas: all crimes	105	30.0	206	59.0	39	11.0	350
3. Texas: murder	88	33.0	147	55.0	34	12.0	269
Total (1 and 2)	361	48.0	348	47.0	40	5.0	749

TABLE 6. Disposition of Cases after Commutation

| Disposition | Number | |
	Penna.	Texas
Pardoned	5	0
Conditionally released	41	22
Transferred to mental hospital	7	1
Died in prison	7	8
Transferred to county prison	0	1
Escaped from prison	0	4
Discharged	0	2
Still in prison on March 31, 1952	12	28
Total	72	66

TABLE 7. Time Lapses Between Disposition Stages in Capital Cases

Time and stages	Pennsylvania		Texas		Kentucky	
	Number of cases	Average time	Number of cases	Average time	Number of cases	Average time
Time served before death sentence was commuted to life	72	9.6 mos.		No data	12	15.2 mos.
Time served before release from prison	46	14.3 yrs.	22	11.4 yrs.	10	10.0 yrs.
Time served on parole before discharged	7	10.5 yrs.	3	8.2 yrs.		No data
Time served on parole before death	7	4.0 yrs.	2	2.3 yrs.		No data
Time served on parole as of March 31, 1952	17	8.1 yrs.	14	8.5 yrs.	9	6.8 yrs.
Time served by those in prison as of March 31, 1952	12	13.9 yrs.	28	7.3 yrs.		No data

five that were released for deportation. Only one case was released for deportation in Texas.

Of the 41 Pennsylvania cases that were conditionally released, 31 were white and 10 Negro. Of the 22 Texas cases, 8 were white, 11 Negro, and 3 Mexican.

The question of what became of the capital cases conditionally released was answered in Table 1. Of the four cases that were returned for violation in Pennsylvania, two were reparoled. One of these was discharged from parole by commutation of maximum sentence; the other is still on parole. Thus 18 of those originally sentenced to die are still on parole.

One of the questions frequently asked about persons sentenced to serve life terms is how long they actually remain in prison before they are released. With the data at hand it was possible to give a tentative answer to this and other questions. For example, how much time usually elapses between the sentence of death and commutation to life? How long does the capital offender serve on parole before discharge? How long does he remain before he dies? These questions are tentatively answered in Table 7. We have included some data from Kentucky.

It is significant that there are 17 cases in Pennsylvania, 14 in Texas, and 9 in Kentucky that have been on parole on an average of more than seven years with violation in a degree to warrant return to prison. On the basis of the statistics usually published by parole boards the likelihood of violation by these persons in the future is very remote, for it has been shown time and again that more than 95 percent of violations occur within the first three years of parole.

The statistics we have presented point up the need for more thoroughgoing research in this relatively neglected area of criminology.

EDITORIAL POSTSCRIPT

1. During 1945–1954 a total of 342 male prisoners were paroled in California from first-degree murder convictions.

By the end of June, 1956, 37 of them had been declared parole violators, or 10.8 percent; six of them had absconded, 11 had been returned to prison for technical violations, 11 had been returned after convictions of misdemeanors, and nine on new sentences for felonies (two for robbery, two for lewd acts with children; one for a narcotics offense; one for abortion; one for sex perversion; one for assault to murder; and one for second-degree murder).[1]

2. *From July, 1930, through 1961, 63 prisoners convicted of first-degree murder were paroled in New York. Of these, 61 had originally been sentenced to death. Their average age at release was 51 years; 56 had no prior felony convictions. Three of them became delinquent: one was convicted of burglary after 18 months on parole, but the other two were returned to prison for technical violations after 16 months and two years on parole, respectively. None of the paroled first-degree murderers committed a homicide. Five died within a year, two within four years, two within 20 years, and 12 were deported.*

From January, 1945, through 1961, 514 prisoners convicted of second-degree murder were paroled. Their mean age at release was 46 years; of these 417 (81.1 percent) had no previous felony convictions, 77 (15 percent) had one, and 20 (3.9 percent) had two or more. During the period mentioned, 115 became delinquent and were returned to prison: 65 for technical violations, 33 on convictions of misdemeanors, and 17 on felony convictions. Of those 17, two were convicted of first-degree murder. One of them had spent 12 and the other 13 years in prison before being paroled. After a year on parole one was involved in an armed robbery but did no actual killing; after a month on parole, the other killed two drinking companions.[2]

3. "*From 1945 through 1965, a total of 273 former first-degree murderers have been paroled in Ohio. Of this number, 154 have been granted final releases, most of them (143) occurring in 1965. [They had served at least five years on parole.] The other 11 had been reduced still further in sentence to manslaughter or time served and discharged in previous years. Four others were allowed to*

leave the country and not return. A total of 15 first-degree murderers on parole (5.5 percent) became parole violators. Of this number, only two have been returned for the commission of new crimes—0.7 percent of the total paroled. Four of the remaining number of violators were placed again on parole, leaving currently a total of 11 first-degree murderers who are parole violators—seven in institutions and four at large."[3] (Of the two who were returned for new crimes, one had committed armed robbery and the other assault with intent to rob.)

Moral: *Courts had decided that the 514 prisoners paroled in New York should not be executed, having sentenced them for second-degree murder. The Parole Board had decided that they were good risks. No one could have predicted which two of them would again become involved in killing. The only way to have prevented the three homicides by these two parolees would have been either to sentence all 514 to death for first-degree murder—which in most cases would probably have been contrary to law—and execute them all or keep then in prison until they died, which policy would not have been a sure guarantee against their committing a homicide in prison.*

PART IV

The Death Penalty,
and
Judicial Administration

The Death Penalty and the Administration of Justice

HERBERT B. EHRMANN

Armchair criminology is among the least reliable of the social sciences. It is, however, one of the most popular. To qualify as an expert on crime one needs only to be a legislator, a lawyer, a prosecutor, or a judge. Such persons may actually be authorities in the field. Generally, however, they have had no scholastic preparation and no special experience beyond a few sporadic episodes. All too often the opinions of individuals in such positions are accorded a factitious authority merely because of the office which they hold. Unfortunately, the public does not understand the meagerness of experience and inadequacy of data on which such views are so frequently based.

IRRATIONAL VIEWS

Discussions concerning the death penalty have been especially confused by the voices of unqualified "authorities." For nearly a century and a half change has been delayed and the acquisition of real knowledge hampered by sonorous pro-

Reprinted, by permission, from *The Annals of the American Academy of Political and Social Science*, 284:73–84, November, 1952.

nouncements of the eminent but uninformed. When in 1810 Sir Samuel Romilly introduced a bill in Parliament to abolish capital punishment for stealing five shillings or more from a shop, it was unsupported by a single judge or magistrate.[1] Speaking for the unanimous opposition to the bill by his judicial colleagues in the House of Lords, Lord Ellenborough, Chief Justice of the King's Bench, predicted that the repeal of this law would lead to abolition of the death penalty for stealing five shillings from a dwelling house, in which case no man could "trust himself for an hour without the most alarming apprehensions that, on his return, every vestige of his property will be swept away by the hardened robber."[2]

These and similar laws were eventually repealed without any increase in the number of offenders in the particular class of crime. In fact, the absolute number of such offenders diminished.[3] As lawyer and judge, Lord Ellenborough was no fool. Although inclined to be harsh in criminal cases, he did much to bring the civil law into harmony with mercantile practice. He was a profound legal scholar. He knew the value of evidence. Yet, when it came to the death penalty, he felt qualified to pronounce an authoritative judgment without the aid of any evidence whatsoever other than his own emotional reflexes. His contemporaries accorded his words the respect due his high position; but history has proved that the great Lord Ellenborough, in discussing capital punishment, was talking nonsense.

The efforts to remove or modify the death penalty for the crime of murder have run a similar course. Fortunately, there has now been enough experience with abolition and curtailment to establish as a fact that the repeal of capital punishment is not followed by an increase in the number of murders; nor does its restoration result in a diminution. Whatever other purpose the death penalty may serve, it is now obvious that, in a settled community, it is not needed to protect society from murderers.

Nevertheless, even in this narrow area where data are abundant and easy to obtain, pronouncements of the Ellenborough variety continue to confuse the public. As late as 1950, the legislative halls of Massachusetts still rang with dire predictions that the passage of a bill to give juries a chance to designate life imprisonment as a penalty for murder in the first degree would result in loosing upon the people of the Commonwealth a horde of savage murderers. This was at a time when 38 other states and the Federal government already had some form of the alternate penalty and six states had abolished capital punishment!

ALTERNATE AND MANDATORY AREAS COMPARED

A similar disregard of experience frequently marks discussion of the effect of the death penalty on the administration of justice. For instance, it was claimed that the giving of the power to impose the alternate penalty of life imprisonment would result in the complete disuse of capital punishment. Those making the claim seemed to think that this would be very bad indeed. In 1948 the then governor of Massachusetts vetoed the proposed bill granting juries the right to choose life imprisonment instead of death on conviction in murder cases, stating in his veto message that such a law would abolish capital punishment by "indirection"; that it pays "lip service to capital punishment" and then "effectively proceeds to destroy it."

Coming from the governor, the veto message was treated with respect;[4] but it was only another example of armchair criminology. For the ten years ending with 1946, Massachusetts, under a law making death a mandatory punishment for first-degree murder, had 12 executions. For the same period, alternate-penalty states had the following record: New Jersey, with a slightly smaller population, 16 executions; Pennsylvania, with something more than twice the population, 50 executions; and New York, with about three times the population, 118 executions. For the same period, North Carolina, a mandatory state, had 118 executions, and its neighbor, Georgia, somewhat smaller in population, under the alternate penalty, had 102.

There are too many variables—such as homicide rates,

population characteristics, police efficiency, prosecution standards, jury attitudes, executive clemency—for any quantitative comparison of states within these groups, but the figures indicate clearly that capital punishment continues to flourish in states which provide the alternate penalty.

On the other hand, the residents in certain areas have, in practice, virtually abolished capital punishment in both mandatory and alternative penalty jurisdictions. Vermont, a mandatory state, has had only 2 executions in 28 years; New Hampshire, an alternate state, has had only 1 execution in 28 years; South Dakota, an alternate state, has had only 1 in the 10 years since it restored the death penalty; Nebraska, an alternate state, has had only 2 in 28 years.[5] In Massachusetts during a period of 50 years under the mandatory penalty, Worcester County, with a half-million population, had only 2 executions; Bristol, a sizable county, only 1; Berkshire County, of moderate size, none; and some of the smaller counties, none. The failure to use the death penalty in certain counties of Massachusetts is dramatically shown in Table 1.

TABLE 1.   Convictions on Murder Indictments, Certain
Massachusetts Counties, 1925–1941

County	Indictments for murder	Convictions			Executions for murder
		1st degree	2nd degree	Man-slaughter	
Berkshire	11	0	5	1	0
Bristol	36	0	16	3	0
Essex	26	1	12	2	1
Hampden	27	1	12	9	1
Hampshire	8	1 (commuted)	1	4	0
Plymouth	21	0	10	4	0
Total	129	3	56	23	2

Data compiled from records in State Prison and reports of the Attorney General by Sara R. Ehrmann, executive secretary, Massachusetts Council for the Abolition of the Death Penalty.

The counties named in the table have about one and a half million population, well over a third of the people in Massachusetts. A conviction rate of about 64 percent of murder indictments indicates an effective administration of justice, but only three of those accused were convicted of first-degree murder (requiring the death penalty), and only two were executed. Here, under a mandatory law, there was a pretty effective abolition of capital punishment.

DEATH PENALTY AND ACQUITTALS

A closely related problem is presented by the claim that the mandatory sentence of death upon a finding of guilty of murder in the first degree results in more acquittals. Some of those who express this opinion are extremely well-informed penologists.[6] The reason given is that the infliction of death is so repugnant to most people that juries tend to avoid a conviction if possible. Curiously enough, proponents of the death penalty seem to confirm this tendency in a backhanded sort of way. In arguing that the danger of a miscarriage of justice is slight in a capital case, they frequently urge that the evidence must be overwhelming before a jury would vote to consign a fellow being to his death.

Convincing data on this subject are not available. We may, however, accept the reasoning and observations that the reluctance of jurymen to convict, where death is the penalty, leads, in some cases, to acquittal. Nevertheless, one may well question the conclusion that the net over-all result is a larger percentage of acquittals. There are complicating factors working in the opposite direction. For instance, numbers of prospective jurors are frequently excused from serving in capital cases because of opposition to the death penalty. Sometimes the numbers are so great that the judges assail the veniremen for "jury dodging," and these denunciations reach the newspaper headlines.[7]

This process of weeding out jurors who will not serve because of the death penalty tends to produce an unbalanced jury. Those most likely to lean emotionally toward the defendant are eliminated. No doubt the great majority of those who remain view the death penalty with considerable distaste, but their emotional attitude is likely to be negative. Inevitably, however, on some juries there will be those who favor the use of the death penalty. These people are occasionally forcefully articulate and capable of swaying jurors with less positive attitudes. They are not counterbalanced by those most reluctant to inflict death. Thus hostility toward the death penalty may actually, in some cases, produce juries which are most likely to convict the accused.

EMOTION AND PREJUDICE

There are other factors which work for conviction rather than acquittal in a capital case. Of all crimes, murder is most likely to produce a violent emotional public reaction, a demand for vengeance, a feeling that the perpetrator "deserves" to be put to death. Jurymen cannot help sharing this feeling. The idea that a jury "weighs" the evidence in a criminal case to decide whether the accused is guilty beyond a reasonable doubt conveys a wrong picture of the process. In many cases it is merely a question of what evidence the jury chooses to believe. If the government's case rests largely on identification testimony and the defense is an alibi, the jury does not "weigh" one against the other. If it believes the identification testimony, the alibi is thrown out of the scales of justice entirely, and vice versa. Where there is conflict of testimony, people tend to believe that which they would like to believe. The emotional drive to punish someone for an atrocious murder frequently plays an important part in conditioning a jury to believing the evidence which proves the guilt of the accused.

In a recent Massachusetts case the only issue was the criminal responsibility of the defendant, who had killed his wife. According to the opinion of the Supreme Judicial Court, the evidence portrayed "the sudden destruction, while in apparent good health, of one member of a harmonious and cultured household by the only other member, in a series of acts paradoxically done, it is confessed, solely in kindness to benefit the victim, yet revoltingly achieved in the grossest barbarity with the crudest of weapons."[8] Two eminent psychiatrists testified that the defendant was not criminally responsible at the time of the killing. There was no medical testimony that he was responsible. Nevertheless, the jury returned a verdict of guilty. The conclusion that the accused was sane beyond a reasonable doubt can be explained only on the ground of emotion aroused by the sheer horror of the deed itself. Although there was no error of law, the Supreme Judicial Court ordered a new trial under a statute passed in 1939 for the review of capital cases.[9] The defendant was tried a second time, found insane, and committed to a mental institution.

When prejudice is added to the emotional reactions induced by a slaying, the jury finds even greater difficulty in believing evidence offered for the accused.[10] If the jury is composed of the dominant or "in-group" and the defendant and his witnesses belong to an "out-group"—as they frequently do—the defendant's evidence is often discounted to zero. The jury tends to believe that foreigners, Negroes, or members of any minority group will lie for one another and "stick together" under all circumstances.

The United States Supreme Court has recognized this human failing, in holding that the exclusion of Negroes from a jury trying a Negro is a denial of equal protection of the laws.[11] Massachusetts had a case where a Chinese, arrested and tried with others for a tong killing, was convicted of murder although no witness identified him or implicated him in the affair.[12] In Kentucky it used to be said that if a Negro killed a white man it was murder, if a white man killed a Negro it was unfortunate, but if a white man killed a white man it was self-defense, unless the affray was over a woman, in which case the cause of death was apoplexy.

PUBLIC HOSTILITY

If to a brutal killing and prejudice there is added the element of public hostility against the accused, the jury listens to the defendant's evidence with ears that are stone-deaf. This is the combination which produces most of our *causes célèbres* subsequently believed by many to be miscarriages of justice, such as the cases of Leo Frank, Tom Mooney, and Sacco and Vanzetti. In the last-named case, the jury, after thirty-five days of trial, received the case in the afternoon and returned a verdict of guilty in the evening. According to one of the jurymen, his colleagues were ready to vote a guilty verdict immediately at the close of the case, but he forced an hour's discussion because he thought such precipitate action was improper.

Regardless of the eventual verdict, the jury could not possibly have considered the mass of testimony in favor of the defendants or weighed the improbabilities in the government's case in so brief a time. Even without the benefit of the subsequent revelations which threw new doubt on the defendants' guilt, a relaxed and unprejudiced jury would have debated at great length the validity of the fleeting and even silly identifications and would not have lightly assumed that a large number of reputable Italian alibi witnesses were perjurers.

Strip the case of the then current antiradical hysteria, change the defendants into Massachusetts veterans of World War I, the identifying witnesses into Italians, and the alibi witnesses into native New Englanders, and it becomes inconceivable that the weaknesses of the prosecution and the massive evidence for the defense would have received such brief consideration by the jury.

DEATH PENALTY AND SECOND-DEGREE CONVICTIONS

Whether or not the mandatory death penalty results in more acquittals, there seem to be some general data indicating that it produces a smaller proportion of convictions for first-degree murder and a larger proportion for second-degree murder.[13] Opponents of capital punishment claim that this is due to the fact that juries shy away from the infliction of death; proponents allege that the possibility of the extreme penalty produces more pleas of guilty to murder in the second degree, for which the sentence is imprisonment. Without further and more precise research, it is impossible to draw any general conclusions. People and conditions differ. Doubtless both theories are valid, but it is not known to what extent.

How difficult it is to generalize about these questions may be seen in the contrasting experience with the death penalty of the two most populous counties in Massachusetts—Suffolk and Middlesex. These two counties are contiguous, being separated, for the most part, only by the Charles River. During the test period they were approximately the same size in population[14] (Middlesex was actually about 5 percent more populous). The criminal courts handling murder cases are presided over by judges who rotate their sittings in the various counties, so they are not indigenous to either Suffolk or Middlesex. Nevertheless, respective records of the two counties for disposing of murder cases are strangely different.

State Prison records for the years 1900 to 1949, inclusive, show that 23 individuals were executed for murder in Middlesex and only 10 for the crime in Suffolk. More detailed reports of the Attorney General for the years 1925 to 1941, inclusive, indicate that of 113 indictments for murder in Middlesex, 19 were convicted of first degree (of whom 17 were executed), 23 of second degree, and 30 of manslaughter; of those not guilty, 18 were insane, 10 received a verdict of not guilty, and 13 were nol-prossed meaning that the district attorney refused to prosecute. For the same period in Suffolk, 3 were convicted of first degree (of whom 2 were executed), 16 of second degree, and 24 of manslaughter; of those not guilty, 10 were insane, 22 received a verdict of not guilty, and 4 were nol-prossed. The approximate percentages are shown in Table 2.

The period covered by Table 2—seventeen years—and the number of cases involved are sufficient to smooth out any substantial distortions due to unusual cases. From these figures it appears that one indicted for a capital offense in Middlesex stood nearly a 17 percent chance of being convicted of first-degree murder and a 15 percent chance of being executed; whereas if the murder were committed in Suffolk, he would stand only a 4 percent chance of being so convicted, and only a 2.5 percent chance of being executed. Those guilty of second-degree murder, whether by plea or after trial, were

TABLE 2. Disposition of Capital Cases, Middlesex and Suffolk Counties, Massachusetts, 1925–1941[a]

Middlesex County	
Convicted	
First degree	16.8
Executed	15.0
Second degree	20.4
Manslaughter	26.4
Total	64.0
Not convicted	
Not guilty	9.0
Nol-prossed	11.4
Not guilty and nol-prossed	20.4
Insane (not tried)	16.0
Total	36.0
Suffolk County	
Convicted	
First degree	3.9
Executed	2.55
Second degree	20.2
Manslaughter	30.4
Total	54.0
Not convicted	
Not guilty	27.8
Nol-prossed	5.0
Not guilty and nol-prossed	32.8
Insane (not tried)	12.65
Total	46.0

Compiled from data collected by Sara R. Ehrmann.
[a] By percentage of all cases.

approximately the same in percentage in both counties, as were those guilty of manslaughter. The accused had three times the chance of being acquitted after trial in Suffolk that he would have had in Middlesex, but in the latter county the district attorneys may have nol-prossed weak cases more freely than their opposite numbers in Suffolk.

Explanations may be offered for these startling differences. Suffolk contains a larger percentage of more recent immigration; its racial, religious, and ethnic proportions of population vary substantially from those in Middlesex; its residents, on the whole, are on a lower economic level; they are less suburbanite; there is a tradition of "hanging" prosecutors in Middlesex. The very nature of these explanations, however, indicates the complexity of the problem. If citizens of the same state, living in adjoining counties, operating under the same administration of justice, differ so drastically in their attitude toward the death penalty, how is it possible to generalize for an entire state or nation?

DEATH PENALTY AND NUMBER OF TRIALS

Again, it is claimed that fewer trials are required in abolition states because obviously guilty defendants are more likely to plead guilty where they do not have to battle for their lives. There are, indeed, some instances where this appears to be the fact. On the other hand, there are those who claim that it is harder to secure pleas of guilty in abolition states because the prosecutor has less inducement to offer the guilty defendant. The answer necessarily depends upon the attitude of prosecutors in a death penalty state. If, for instance, the prosecutor insists on first degree with death as the penalty, the accused has nothing to lose by trial; if the prosecutor is willing to trade for a plea of guilty in the second degree, the defendant has much to gain by not risking a trial. How do we know, however, what prosecutors will do?

The application of armchair psychology to forecast the conduct of prosecutors—or any other public authority—is no easier than the Ellenborough method of predicting the reaction of criminals. For instance, as early as 1900, Hosea M. Knowlton, then attorney general of Massachusetts, recommended the commutation of the death sentence of a seventeen-year-old murderer whose crime was particularly vicious, on the ground that Massachusetts public sentiment would not tolerate the execution of so young a boy.

In 1942, after forty years' development in the field of handling juvenile delinquency, another Massachusetts prosecutor insisted on the death penalty for a seventeen-year-old offender despite the suggestion of the judge that the case was a proper one for a plea of guilty to murder in the second degree. The boy's previous record had been good, and there was a conflict of medical testimony as to whether the cause of the victim's death was the wound or a heart ailment, since the victim lived for seven weeks and his injuries had apparently healed. Nevertheless, the lad was allowed by the governor to be electrocuted, with the assent of the parole board acting in an advisory capacity.

A few years later, in another case involving a seventeen-year-old boy, another Massachusetts judge took the initiative and accepted a plea of guilty to second-degree murder on the ground that no Massachusetts governor would ever allow so youthful an offender to be electrocuted.

A very conscientious district attorney will sometimes secure a conviction which the facts require, in the belief that the governor will take care of mitigation. Such a case was *Commonwealth v. Desatnick*,[15] where the father of an illegitimate child, plagued by accusing parents and a religious sense of guilt, murdered the infant. Instead of commuting, however, the governor sent for clerics of the defendant's faith and asked them whether illegitimacy was a more serious offense than murder. On the basis of the obvious answer, the young man was electrocuted. Within a short time, however, another Massachusetts district attorney, regarded by many as more hard-boiled than the one who prosecuted Desatnick, nol-prossed the case of a mother who had abandoned her illegitimate child to die, on the ground that, although the crime would ordinarily be murder, "society needs no penalty for this, unfortunate as it is."

These instances are sufficient to indicate the futility of generalizing on insufficient data. Research alone, in a wide area and covering a period of years, could establish what prosecutors tend to do in the death penalty states by way of accepting pleas of guilty to second-degree murder.

DEGREES OF MURDER

Degrees of murder present such a confusing problem that they create a further obstacle to predictability in the administration of criminal justice. In states where capital punishment has been abolished, the situation is not too serious. An intelligent parole board may ultimately adjust any gross errors in the jury's verdict or in the pleas. But where the penalty is death, a confused jury may eternalize its mistakes.

The principal variety of "first-degree" murder is generally defined as including "malice aforethought," and involves "premeditation" and "deliberation." However, judicially defined "malice" does not necessarily involve malice against the victim in the ordinary dictionary sense. Moreover, the courts have explained "deliberation" and "premeditation" in such a way that these words also have lost their usual meaning. Under judicial definition, "premeditation" and "deliberation" can both occur within a few seconds of the killing itself. In the now rather celebrated case of *Fisher v. United States*,[16] a Negro of low-grade intelligence, suddenly feeling that he was insulted by his victim, struck her, and then killed her "to stop her from hollering." The jury by its verdict found deliberation and premeditation, essential to first-degree murder.

Mr. Justice Frankfurter, in his dissenting opinion in the United States Supreme Court, referred to the judge's charge on the subject as the "dark emptiness of legal jargon." According to Mr. Justice Frankfurter, the insult "pulled the trigger of Fisher's emotions." We shall never know how many defendants have been hanged or electrocuted for a "deliberate" and "premeditated" killing where some unexpected incident "pulled the trigger" of the accused's emotions.

"Is it possible," asked Sir Ernest Gowers of Mr. Justice Frankfurter at hearings held by the Royal Commission on Capital Punishment in 1950, "to express premeditation clearly and logically without mumbo-jumbo entering into it?" Mr. Justice Frankfurter thought that it was possible, but conceded that "the charges given by trial judges in the United States are often not very helpful." The Royal Commission appeared to think this observation to be an understatement.[17]

Another type of first-degree murder is usually defined as a homicide occurring in the act of commiting a serious felony. Here again the situation may be far from clear. If the jury believes that the accused, at the time of the killing, had given up all intention of committing the felony and killed the victim because of fear for his own safety, the crime is not first-degree murder. In a close case, how is the jury to read the defendant's mind in order to apply the instructions of the judge?

It would be unfair, however, to blame the judges for their inability to explain clearly the different degrees of murder. The fact that so many do not succeed suggests that the real blame rests with the rather fanciful distinctions between first-degree and second-degree murder. Mr. Justice Cardozo himself found it difficult, if not impossible, to draw a satisfactory line:

> I think the distinction is much too vague to be continued in our law. . . . The statute is framed along the lines of a defective and unreal psychology. . . . The present distinction is so obscure that no jury hearing it for the first time can fairly be expected to assimilate and understand it. I am not at all sure that I understand it myself after trying to apply it for many years and after diligent study of what has been written in the books. Upon the basis of this fine distinction with its mystifying psychology, scores of men have gone to their deaths.[18]

Degrees of murder were introduced into the law originally in order to give juries an opportunity to mitigate the harshness of the death penalty. No doubt in many cases they have accomplished their purpose. Some juries find second degree despite the facts and the judge's instructions; other juries, more conscientious than merciful, find first degree where warranted; still others muddle through the "mystifying psychology" to a bewildered finish. In conjunction with the death penalty, these degrees of murder have created a combination which tends to produce a most haphazard application of the criminal law in capital cases. Once the death penalty has been abolished, however, the criminal law may safely drop such metaphysical distinctions and relate the period of imprisonment to modern penology for the protection of society and the rehabilitation of the convicted.

MENTAL RESPONSIBILITY

Another cause for the haphazard application of the death penalty is the submission of the issue of mental responsibility to juries under legal definitions of insanity which are completely at variance with medical science. Most jurisdictions still apply the century-old rule in M'Naghten's case, namely: Did the defendant know that his act was morally and legally wrong? The rule has been somewhat qualified by such exceptions as the "irresistible impulse" test, but on the whole, M'Naghten still dominates judicial charges and decisions.

Under this definition of insanity, the lowest-grade morons and the most disturbed psychopaths are repeatedly convicted because they "knew the difference between right and wrong." It has also provided astute defense counsel with a handy means of getting guilty clients off without any penalty whatever, through a verdict of "not guilty by reason of insanity," and a subsequent speedy cure of nonexistent mental disease.

In Massachusetts, under the Briggs law, the issue of insanity in capital cases is now usually decided before trial by the report of two impartial psychiatrists. In most states, however, the juries must continue to choose between contending alienists who are paid for their opinions by the side which calls them to the stand. Since there can be no reconciliation between the legal test for insanity and a conscientious psychiatrist's ideas about mental disease, the expert testimony from the witness stand is given under conditions which often confuse rather than assist a jury in reaching a verdict.

If imprisonment or confinement were the result in any event, then a finding of either sanity or insanity would provide opportunity for further study and possible treatment. Under the present system, a mistaken finding of guilty or not guilty where insanity is pleaded may result in irrevocable error. It is the presence of the death penalty that hinders a new approach to the entire question of mental responsibility.

DEATH PENALTY AND COST OF TRIAL

Whether there is actually a larger proportion of pleas of guilty without trial where capital punishment has been abolished is also largely unexplored territory. The trial of murder cases is an expensive process. The ordinary murder trial may cost the county thousands of dollars, and some of the more bitterly contested cases may run high up in five figures. In Massachusetts, the trial of the Millen brothers and Abraham Faber in 1934 for murder in the commission of robberies ran for nearly eight weeks at very great cost to the county. These criminals and their lawyers knew that the government's case was overwhelmingly strong and that public feeling ran high against them. Slim as their chances were, however, they went to trial because no prosecutor in a mandatory death penalty state, on the facts of their outrageous crimes, would have accepted a plea of second degree. Under the same conditions in an abolition state, would the accused have pleaded guilty?[19]

California was put to a great expense in the trial of the sensational Hickman case involving the fiendish sex killing of a child. Would the defendant have pleaded guilty in an abolition state? Shortly after the Hickman trial, Michigan had a murder case almost exactly the same in its gruesome details, apparently induced by the lurid press treatment of the California crime. The accused, one Hoteling, promptly pleaded guilty, thereby sparing the state much expense and the public a recital of the macabre details.

The money spent on the trial of capital cases would pay the salaries of a substantial number of additional parole officers, badly needed in a constructive effort to reduce crime. It might repay any state to investigate the probability of saving the cost of these expensive murder trials through repeal of the death penalty.[20]

Whether or nor capital punishment increases the expense of administering justice by forcing to trial a greater number of murder cases, there can be no doubt that the cost of cases actually tried is greatly increased because of the reluctance of jurors to serve where they may feel compelled to decree death to the accused. This is a universally observed phenomenon. Where the cases are notorious, the delay in securing a jury may be fantastic. In the trial for the murder of "King" Solomon in Boston, only one of 90 veniremen failed to disqualify himself on the ground that he was opposed to capital punishment. After 160 had been interrogated, there still were not enough to make up a jury.[21] In the case of Sacco and Van-zetti, four days were consumed in impaneling a jury.[22] These instances may be extreme, but they underscore a fact which should properly be considered in any evaluation of the death penalty in the administration of justice.

DEATH PENALTY AND SENSATIONALISM

Expert observers also agree that the trial of murder cases where death may be the penalty tends to be more sensational than where imprisonment is the only punishment. The spectacle of a human being fighting for his life is stirring drama inside and outside of the courtroom. Frequently, in order to sway a jury toward the fatal verdict—and possibly to reassure his own conscience—a prosecutor will inflame the jurors against the accused by playing upon every prejudice and ghastly detail. It is generally recognized that some prosecutors, because of political ambition or simple vanity are not above deliberately seeking the headlines.

Of course, noncapital cases may also tend toward sensationalism; but where this occurs, it is because of reasons other than the penalty involved. Generally speaking, the trial of cases where the penalty may be death is surcharged with an emotional tension not present in other prosecutions. Defense counsel, witnesses, judges, and even prosecutors have been visibly affected by the strain. This atmosphere, created by invoking the specter of death to destroy the life in the dock, is hardly a help to calm consideration of the evidence.

DEATH PENALTY DISTORTS ADMINISTRATION OF JUSTICE

Indeed, the one conclusion on which practically all criminologists agree is that the death penalty tends to distort the course of the criminal law. In the phrase of Professor Sheldon Glueck, it "bedevils the administration of justice."[23] Data may indicate that in some instances it may result in acquittals or findings not merited by the accused; in others, in convictions and executions not justified by an unemotional consideration of the evidence. In either case, the normal is deflected. The penalty is erratically inflicted at different times in different places. It retards progress in the criminal law by maintaining concepts which should have little to do with the process of ascertaining guilt, innocence, or responsibility.

Just as the death penalty is a paradoxical block in a modern system of penology, so does the fear of its finality hinder reform in the administration of criminal justice. Professor Sam Bass Warner, then on the faculty of the Harvard Law School, declared to the Joint Judiciary Committee of the Massachusetts Legislature in 1935 that "the existence of the death penalty for first-degree murder is one of the principal reasons, if not the main reason, why it is extremely difficult to get judges and legislators to remove procedural barnacles from our law."

It may be said that all human processes are imperfect, and that those of justice are no different; but the fact of human fallibility is not a good reason for increasing it. If to err is human, then it becomes all the more important to reduce the probability of errors—especially fatal ones. On the massive evidence now available dealing with the use and disuse of the death penalty, there would seem to be no sufficient compensating advantage in retaining it. Its disappearance could only improve the administration of justice.

The Errors of Justice

OTTO POLLAK

> I shall ask for the abolition of
> the penalty of death until I have
> the infallibility of human judgment
> demonstrated to me.
>
> LAFAYETTE

To recognize the fallibility of human judgment and still to act, but act wisely in the light of such fallibility, is one of the great challenges of mankind. For this reason the fact of irrevocability has always been among the arguments for the abolition of the death penalty. It was brought up in the French National Assembly of 1791.[1] In 1948 it was brought up in the debate on the Criminal Justice Bill in the British House of Commons.[2] It was brought up on all conceivable occasions in the time span between these two cornerstones of legislative consideration of the abolition of capital punishment. In all probability it will continue to be brought up until capital punishment has disappeared from the practice of civilized society.

The strength of this argument is revealed by the counter-arguments which it has evoked. Apparently very few opponents of the abolition of capital punishment have had the courage to say: Yes, errors of judgment have led to the execution of innocent persons and may do so in the future, but this is a necessary item of social cost. Significantly enough, many efforts to meet the argument have followed other lines. They have resorted to avoidance or to the denial of the obvious. Thus they have shown reactions typically associated with fear, and it is this fear which suggests that the argument is considered to be serious even by those who try to deny its validity.

Reprinted, by permission, from *The Annals of the American Academy of Political and Social Science*, 284:115–123, November, 1952.

RISK OF ERRONEOUS EXECUTION
MINIMIZED

The records show that French, English, Belgian, German, and American lawyers have repeatedly made statements to the effect that because of the safeguards of the jury system, because of the protection furnished by the pardoning power, or because of the possibility to resort to the alternative punishment of lifetime imprisonment, the risk of executing an innocent person did not exist or almost did not exist.[3] A district attorney in Worcester County, Massachusetts, is reported to have said in the 1920's: "Innocent men are never convicted. Don't worry about it, it never happens in the world. It is a physical impossibility."[4] Sir John Anderson, for ten years permanent Head of the Home Office, said in the British House of Commons on April 14, 1948:

It is fair to say, and there was a wealth of testimony to that effect in the evidence before the Select Committee, that the risk, under the conditions as they exist in this country, of the capital penalty being executed on any one who was not in fact guilty of the crime of which he had been convicted is so small, indeed so infinitesimal, that that consideration can be dismissed.[5]

Statements of similar nature have been made not only by practicing lawyers in the heat of public pronouncement, but also by professors of criminal law. Even a man of the international reputation of Wilhelm Kahl asked, on the occasion of a lawyers' convention, where those cases of executing innocent persons had occurred which justified stressing the argument of human fallibility in discussing the pros and cons of capital punishment.[6] Interestingly enough, in 1910 the *American Journal of Sociology* contained an article by Arthur McDonald in which the following statement can be found:

It is said that the death penalty is irrevocable and thus an innocent man might suffer it. It is well known to prison officials and the police that such instances are mostly mythical and seldom, if at all, can be proved beyond a doubt.[7]

If such denials can be made by practitioners and scholars alike, the argument apparently cannot be countered with Bentham's question: "Is there, or could there be devised, any system of penal procedure which could insure the judge from being misled by false evidence or the fallibility of his own judgment?"[8] The obvious must be corroborated by facts, and such attempts have been undertaken repeatedly and in various countries.

REPORTS OF MISCARRIAGES OF JUSTICE

Actually, by the time Kahl and McDonald made the statements quoted above, they could have found books devoted to reports of miscarriages of justice. The number of these books is large enough to make disregard or lack of knowledge of them by these scholars an interesting psychological phenomenon. Certainly McDonald might have been expected to be acquainted with the writings of Charles Phillips and Alfred H. Dymond.[9] Equally, Kahl might have been expected to be acquainted with the works of Mühlfeld, Katscher, Lailler and Vonoven, and Péan.[10]

Since McDonald's and Kahl's statements were made, there have appeared Sello's careful analysis of 153 cases[11] and Borchard's classic *Convicting the Innocent* which carries the identification of erroneous verdicts in the United States into the first three decades of the twentieth century.[12] To be sure, these works show some overlapping in their reports and show various degrees of reliability. However, they contain a sufficient number of solidly documented reports on actual executions of innocent persons to make the questioning of the real risk in this respect a hardly tenable position. They contain, further, a large number of cases which show to what degree life imprisonment, because of the time element involved and because of the continued interest in the victim which such life terms safeguard, permits the discovery of errors in convicting a person of a capital crime. They show, finally, that the sources of errors in judgment are frequently the same whether the error has led to an actual execution or to a life sentence. Thus they dispel the notion that errors may have occurred in the past but do not occur in the present, and also the notion that though errors might occur in the cases of sentencing a person to a life term they do not occur in the cases of actual execution.

Meaningful examples which might illustrate all this can, of course, be taken only from a time span in which the principles of procedure and the rules of evidence were sufficiently close to the present to make the risk which these cases demonstrate a still plausible one. Because of this consideration, the illustrations given below do not go back of the period of the French Revolution. In order to show the persistence of the same sources of error over the time span, the procedure followed in this paper will be to give for each source of major error an example from the late eighteenth or early nineteenth century on the one hand, and one from or close to the twentieth century on the other.

Circumstantial Evidence

As might be expected, circumstantial evidence is a frequent source of error in judgment. This category might be illustrated by the two following cases.

Case 1

On January 31, 1811, the barns of the mayor of a French village, Noyelles, were destroyed by a fire which had all the appearances of arson. Public opinion directed suspicion immediately at Maximilien Flament, who was a relative of the mayor. He was known to have lived in enmity with the latter, and some witnesses reported that three days before the fire Flament had voiced threats against him. Others reported that at the time of the fire the wind had blown in a direction such as to drive away the flames from Flament's house, which was situated close to the barns which were consumed. Flament increased suspicion against himself by repeatedly declaring himself innocent before a direct accusation had been made. Finally, the detectives discovered in the hedge which separated Flament's property from that of the mayor's a hole big enough to permit the arsonist to get through; and close by were footprints which fitted Flament.

On the basis of this circumstantial evidence Flament was arrested. He attempted to establish an alibi by only one witness, who first supported him but later showed uncertainty in his depositions. During the trial thirty-one witnesses testified against Flament; only the one produced by him in his defense supported him, and that one only weakly. On that basis he was found guilty and sentenced to die. Clemency was denied to him by the Emperor, and he was executed. Six years later his innocence became manifest in the following manner.

On October 20, 1817, a certain Felix Moreau was executed for murder in the same place. Immediately before the dropping of the knife Moreau, who was attended by the same priest who had stood by Flament at his last hour, confessed having committed the arson for which Flament had been executed, and asked for forgiveness. In recognition of the error in judgment which had sent his father to the guillotine, the National Assembly of 1850 granted Flament's son a pension.[13]

Case 2

On the morning of October 17, 1901, a railroad engineer, H. E. Wesson, was found dead in the shop yard of the Florida Southern Railway at Tilgham's Mill in Palatka, Florida. He had been shot at close range in the back of his head, and his pockets had been turned inside out. Close by a .38 caliber pistol was found from which one shell had been fired. Under the pressure of public indignation the authorities right away rounded up a number of suspects and put them into jail. Among them was a yard night watchman, Lucius Crawford. Apparently on the afternoon after the arrest, the jailer observed a colored man approach a crack in the fence of the jail yard and call for Lucius Crawford who happened to be in the yard at that time. The jailer reported that the colored man was J. B. Brown and that he had heard him say to Crawford, "Keep your mouth shut and say nothing."

Brown was arrested and a chain of circumstantial evidence began to form against him. First of all it was reported that two months earlier Brown had had a fight with the murdered man and had threatened to kill him. On October 16, the day before the murder, Brown was reported by one witness as having been without money and having tried to borrow a quarter from him. In answer to the witness' refusal of his request, Brown was reported to have said "Never mind, I'll catch 209 away from here tonight, that is the train going south to meet 208." Two hundred and eight was the train on which the murdered man had worked as an engineer. On the morning after the murder, Brown had been observed to have money when he joined in a card game with a number of men, among whom there was one by the name of Johnson. Brown was reported to have been excited when he arrived for the game and to have taken Johnson aside for a whispered conversation.

After these items of apparent evidence had been collected against Brown, the other suspects were released. The clouds over Brown thickened further when two cell mates of his reported to the authorities that Brown had confessed to them that he had, together with Johnson, committed the murder for purposes of robbing Wesson of his money.

On the basis of all that, Brown and Johnson were indicted for murder in the first degree and Brown was brought up for a separate trial in which he was convicted and sentenced to be hanged. His appeal for clemency having been denied, he was finally led to the gallows. However, at the last minute, the rope having been put around his neck, the executioner was interrupted because of an almost unbelievable event. When the death warrant was read in the course of the execution procedure it was found that by mistake it ordered the execution, not of Brown, but of—the foreman of the jury which had found Brown guilty. Brown was returned to jail, and under the impact of this occurrence his capital sentence was commuted to life imprisonment. The prosecution seemed to have lost the taste for continuing against Johnson, for the case against the latter was nol-prossed.

More than ten years later, Johnson confessed on his deathbed that he alone had committed the murder and that Brown had not been connected with the crime at all. On October 1, 1913, Brown, on the basis of Johnson's confession, was granted a full pardon, and in 1929 the Florida legislature granted him "for faithful service . . . during the period of his wrongful imprisonment the sum of $2,492 to be paid in monthly installments of $25."[14]

False Identification

Another possible source of errors in judgment of criminal cases is false identification of the accused by witnesses. This phenomenon of faulty perception is well known to lawyers, and on occasional instances also reaches the awareness of the public because of the weight of tragedy with which its consequences may strike an innocent person. One of the earliest cases of this kind which falls within the time span here considered is the execution of Joseph Lesurques.

Case 3

In the year 1796, a mail coach was attacked by robbers on the road between Paris and Melun. The coachman and his assistant were killed. Only five persons could be considered as the criminals, the only passenger of the coach and the four members of the group of horsemen who had attacked it. The four horsemen had left Paris on the day of the crime in the early morning. During the day they had stopped at two inns where they had spent enough time and behaved conspicuously enough to be observed by many persons. Seven of these recognized Lesurques as one of the four riders who had committed the crime.

The identification convinced the jury of Lesurques's guilt in spite of the fact that he presented fourteen witnesses in support of his statement that he had spent the whole critical day in Paris. Unfortunately, one of these witnesses, Legrand, referred to a business entry in his ledger as the reason for his remembering the day. When the ledger was produced in court it was found, however, that this transaction had first been booked for the day following the day of the crime and that the date had been corrected later on. When, because of this, another witness who was supposed to have met with Lesurques and Legrand on the day of the crime became uncertain of the date, the jurors disbelieved also the twelve other witnesses for Lesurques's alibi.

After the jury had retired, a woman asked to be seen by the presiding judge and told him that Lesurques was the victim of a resemblance to her lover who had been one of the real criminals. The judge, however, told her that it was too late because the jury had already retired. After the verdict, Couriol, one of Lesurques's codefendants, stated repeatedly that Lesurques was innocent and asserted this even on his way to the place of execution. After Lesurques had been executed, two other persons, Laborde and Roussy, were found guilty of the crime in separate trials and both asserted the innocence of Lesurques. If some question could still be raised as to whether Couriol had not lied in order to save Lesurques, no such question can be raised with regard to the other two, who made the statements regarding his innocence years after he had been executed.[15]

Roughly a hundred years later a case of mistaken identification caused the sentence to death by hanging of a youth who escaped his fate and lived to see his rehabilitation only because the knot around his neck untied after the trap was sprung.

Case 4

In 1893 the Whitecaps, an organization formed to suppress criminality among the Negroes by private action, took punitive measures against the servant of one of its own members, in Marion County, Mississippi. His employer, a certain Will Buckley, decided to denounce the organization before the Grand Jury of the County, which led to an indictment of three members of the organization. On his way back, Will Buckley, who was accompanied by his brother Jim and the Negro servant who had been flogged by the Whitecaps, was killed from ambush. After he saw Will Buckley fall from his horse, the murderer jumped out into the lane and fired one more shot at the companions of his victim, but they managed to escape.

Close to the place of the murder was the home of the Purvis family. Two days after the murder, bloodhounds picked up a scent which led them in the direction of the Purvis place; and a neighbor, who was an enemy of the family, directed suspicion at young Will Purvis. He was arrested and while in jail admitted that he had been a member of the Whitecaps, but insisted that he was innocent of the murder. However, Jim Buckley, the brother of the murdered man, positively identified Will Purvis as the killer. This, together with the admission of the accused that he had belonged to the organization which Will Buckley had exposed, made the defense, which was based on an alibi, unconvincing, although it was supported by creditable witnesses. Will Purvis was found guilty and sentenced to capital punishment.

As already indicated, the execution was attempted, but the rope did not tighten around his neck when the trap was sprung. This was a public execution, and the onlookers made it unmistakably clear that they would not let the executioner make another attempt to hang Purvis. Purvis was taken back to jail, and a new execution was ordered to be carried out on July 31, 1895. Public indignation about this court order ran high. On the eve of the execution Purvis was liberated by a group of friends and hidden from the authorities. This case played a role in the following elections for state governor of Mississippi, and the candidate in favor of commuting the sentence won. When he assumed office Purvis surrendered himself, and the governor commuted the sentence to life imprisonment.

Two years after this commutation, Jim Buckley, who had been the principal witness against Purvis, admitted that he might have made a mistake in his identification of the accused, and Purvis received a full pardon on December 19, 1898. Roughly nineteen years later, that is twenty-three years after the execution which Purvis escaped by so gruesome an incident, an old man, Joe Beard, experienced a religious conversion at a revival meeting and confessed himself a terrible sinner, without, however, revealing the details. Shortly afterwards, when grievously ill, Beard confessed that he and another man, Louis Thornhill, had been chosen by the Whitecaps to punish Will Buckley, that they had been in the ambush, and that Thornhill had fired the deadly shot. In 1920 the legislature of Mississippi granted Will Purvis a compensation of $5,000 "for service done and performed . . . in the State Penitentiary under the provisions of an erroneous judgment."[16]

False Confession

It is probably true that nothing alleviates doubt in jurors and judges as much as a confession on the part of the defendant. It is probably even more true that nothing is harder to believe than the possibility that a person accused of a capital crime would wrongly confess to having committed it. Yet this seems to have happened a number of times. Spurious confessions led to death sentences in the frequently mentioned case of Jesse and Steve Boorn.

Case 5

In the year 1812 these two Vermont farmers once worked together with their brother-in-law, Russel Colvin, in the fields. They were observed to quarrel with him. That was the last that was seen of Russel Colvin. Since he was known to have the habit of disappearing for periods sometimes as long as eight or nine months, no suspicion was aroused at first. In the ensuing years, however, a fantastic chain of events seemed to point to the two brothers as the probable killers of their sister's husband.

An enumeration of the individual items of occurrence which led to the formation of this suspicion would take up too much space and it would not be pertinent to the point which this case illustrates. At any rate, seven years after the disappearance of Colvin, the suspicion which had accumulated against the brothers led to their arrest. In the course of the proceedings, first one and then the other brother—probably despondent under the weight of the apparent evidence speaking against them and hoping for mercy—confessed their guilt. Although the confessions were made piecemeal and were in part contradictory, the brothers were sentenced to hang.

Jesse's sentence was commuted to a life term, but Steven's plea was denied. Under the threat of the apparently certain execution he marshaled his powers of defense and asked his attorney to advertise for the whereabouts of his brother-in-law. This was done, and Colvin was located in Dover, New Jersey. Due to the fortunate coincidence that a person knowing him happened to learn about the advertisement and managed to persuade Colvin by ruses to return home, the innocence of the brothers was established.[17]

For the twentieth century, mention might be made of the case of Louise Butler and George Yelder, which occurred in Alabama in 1928.

Case 6

Louise Butler was a Negro woman who lived with her daughter Julia, aged twelve, and a small son, as well as two nieces, Topsy Warren, aged fourteen, and Anne Mary, aged nine. Louise Butler had won the affections of George Yelder, and she was very jealous of his attentions. One day upon returning home she learned that George had visited in her absence and had found in the house only Topsy, who was now in possession of a new one-half-dollar piece. Louise Butler's jealousy was aroused and she beat the young girl severely, even threatening to kill her. After this incident Topsy was seen no more.

Rumors that Louise Butler had killed her niece brought the police into action. Incredible as it sounds, the two children, Anne Mary and Julia, accused Louise Butler and George Yelder of having killed Topsy, and gave many gory details. First Louise denied having killed Topsy, but later she confessed and even showed the authorities the spot where she said that she and George had thrown Topsy's body into the river. Afterwards she withdrew her confession but found no credence from the jury, in true accordance with the frequent experience that a prisoner is believed when he incriminates himself but mistrusted when he asserts that he is innocent.

Both Louise Butler and George Yelder were found guilty and sentenced to life imprisonment. Shortly after their having been sent to the penitentiary, Topsy was found well and alive, staying with relatives in another county. The sheriff later learned that the children had been coached by an enemy of George Yelder's to make the false accusations. The sheriff suggested that Louise

Butler might have felt in her ignorance that she would curry favor by doing what the "white folks" wanted her to do, and had confessed for that reason. One cannot help wondering how the authorities would have felt about the reappearance of Topsy if a death sentence had been pronounced and executed in this case.[18]

Examples could easily be furnished also for the occurrence of cases in which a wrongly accused person was forced into spurious confessions by mistreatment or promises at the hands of the police. As already pointed out, such confessions, once made, tend to be believed even if the defendant later withdraws his statement.[19]

EXTENT OF RISK OF ERROR

Examples could further be furnished which show that both the hostility of a prosecutor against the psychiatric expert and the mistake of the psychiatric expert himself have led to the conviction and execution of persons who were suffering from severe mental disorders.[20] Space, however, does not permit any further illustration. In any case, the necessarily limited number of examples which can be given in a single paper cannot convey any impression of the real extent of the risk of errors in convictions for capital crimes. These are crimes which, by their very nature, arouse strong emotions in the general public as well as in the officers of the law. Where such emotions are aroused, failures in perception are likely to occur.

For an evaluation of the quantity of risk of executing an innocent person, we must turn to the following considerations. As far as the nineteenth century is concerned, a survey of the literature shows that the collections which have been made of such instances fill books. This, of course, was a period of time in which the number of capital crimes and the number of executions were more frequent than they are today.

For the twentieth century, no such collection has come to the attention of this writer except Borchard's book, which has for its emphasis the problem of indemnification of persons who have been erroneously convicted. This work, therefore, is concerned also with offenses other than capital crime. As the examples presented above show, even this work, with its different focus, contains material showing that the danger of executing innocent persons has not yet completely passed from the American scene. On the other hand, if reports published in the literature are taken as an index of the extent of this problem, executions of innocent persons for capital crimes in this country must have become very rare indeed during the last few decades.

It is the opinion of this writer, however, that no collection of cases known to have been miscarriages of justice can reveal the true extent of such occurrences.

FACTORS IN CONCEALMENT

The effort of the truly guilty person to escape punishment is in itself a force which may lead to error in judgment by keeping correct information away from the courts. Furthermore, if crime goes together with strenuous efforts at concealment, so does erroneous judgment in a capital case. If it has led to the execution of an innocent person, the feelings of guilt and regret on the part of those involved in such a judgment cannot but work against the acceptance of the fact of error. Borchard reports that pardons are granted on occasion "without indication or admission of an erroneous conviction probably in order to save the prestige of the prosecuting officials."[21] If such face-saving comes into play where a measure of reparation to the innocent person is still possible, how much stronger must the same factor be in cases when reparation can no longer be made! We are justified, therefore, in assuming that the efforts of the police and of a district attorney's office cannot be relied upon to reveal executions of innocent persons to any extent which might approximate reality.

Even in cases where innocent persons have been sentenced to a life term, it is usually the deathbed confession of the murderer or some effort of an outside person which brings about the elucidation of the facts. However, if an innocent person has been executed, the interest of outsiders will probably be much less active than it will be in cases where there is still the motivation of saving a person from the continuation of his wrongful punishment.

CRITERIA OF RELIABLE REPORTING

It is now accepted theory in criminal statistics that a crime in order to be reliably reported must have three characteristics: (1) it must be considered serious enough to ensure intensive effort on the part of law enforcement officers to elucidate it; (2) it must ensure the co-operation of the victim, or those interested in the victim, with the police; and (3) it must leave public traces.[22]

If one were to apply these criteria to the question whether executions based on errors in judgment are likely to be reliably reported, it is clear that the answer would be negative on all three counts. Such cases will not arouse law enforcement officers to great effort, because that would mean enthusiasm for professional self-indictment. Obviously, they cannot ensure the co-operation of the victim. Furthermore, the impossibility of reparation to the victim of the error will probably weaken the effort also of those who were interested in him as long as there was hope. Finally, the efforts of the actual killer to remain undetected, together with the fact that the case has been decided and led to the punishment demanded by the law, tend to conceal a miscarriage of justice rather than leave public traces of its occurrence.

Thus it is highly probable that erroneous convictions for capital crimes are greatly underreported. This does not mean, however, that we have to assume any considerable number of occurrences every year. The actual figures, absolutely taken, are probably very small—as are the figures of actual executions at present.

THE ETHICAL ASPECT

However, this does not meet the core of the problem, which is ethical and not utilitarian. Ethics cannot be argued in figures. It shows the strange humor of history that the essence of the ethical position involved has never been better expressed than by Robespierre in the National Assembly of 1791. Participating in the debate on the abolition of capital punishment, he said:

> Listen to the voice of justice and of reason! It tells us and tells us that human judgments are never so certain as to permit society to kill a human being judged by other human beings. . . . Why deprive yourselves of any chance to redeem such errors? Why condemn yourselves to helplessness when faced with persecuted innocence?[23]

The Death Penalty and Fair Trial

WALTER E. OBERER

The right of the accused in a criminal case to be tried by a jury of his peers is a cornerstone of American justice. One might therefore expect this principle to be most honored in the most serious of criminal cases—those in which the defendant's life is in jeopardy. Ironically, certain mechanics of these "capital" trials, as presently conducted, operate to defeat this principle. The situation has been strangely neglected to date by lawyers, judges and libertarians.

It becomes increasingly difficult to obtain a jury in capital cases, the reason being that such juries must be "death-qualified." This means that, to sit on such a jury, a person must first declare under oath that he is willing to return a verdict of death if the evidence seems to him to warrant it. If he has "conscientious scruples" against death as a punishment for a crime—that is, if he himself would be unwilling to vote for such a verdict—he is subject to "challenge for cause" by the

Reprinted, by permission, from *The Nation*, 198:342–344, April 6, 1964.

prosecution and is excused from service by the trial judge. Indeed, as frequently administered, mere *hesitance* to vote for a death verdict is sufficient to disqualify a prospective juror.

What this means in practice is that a multitude of prospective jurors must be examined by the prosecutor and defense counsel before a jury of twelve can be obtained. Recently, I observed part of the examination of jurors in a rape case in Texas, where rape is a capital offense. Of the nine persons examined while I was present, six were challenged and excused for cause by reason of death scruples. In another Texas case of which I have personal knowledge, a murder case tried in 1961, eighty-eight prospective jurors were examined before a jury of twelve was selected. Forty-two of these were challenged for cause by the prosecution and excused from service by the trial judge because of scruples against capital punishment. Moreover, the prosecution exercised eleven *peremptory* challenges (differing from challenges for *cause* in that no reason need be given for their exercise) for the apparent purpose of eliminating other jurors who, while affording inadequate basis for a challenge for cause, none the less evinced a "weakness" on the death penalty.

The foregoing are not isolated examples, or peculiar to Texas. The condition is general. Nor are the Texas figures I have cited by any means high-water marks. In a New Jersey case in 1959, for example, more than 300 prospective jurors were reported to have been examined before a jury could be obtained. Public-opinion surveys conducted in recent years cast some light upon this problem. A Gallup poll in 1960 showed 51 percent of the nation in favor of capital punishment. A Roper poll in 1958 showed 42 percent in favor, 50 percent opposed and 8 percent undecided. What these polls do not reveal, however, is that a substantial percentage of those who express themselves as favoring capital punishment are speaking in the abstract; they want no part of such awesome responsibility themselves, and so would fall before the prosecution's challenge for cause.

A particularly pertinent and revealing commentary is made by Lindley R. McCelland, a member of the Pennsylvania bar, in the March, 1959, issue of the *Pennsylvania Bar Association Quarterly*. He reports the case of one Miner Davis, tried for murder in Erie in 1958. The prosecuting attorney and defense counsel, one of whom was Mr. McClelland,

examined 142 prospective jurors . . . before we were able to accept 12 jurors and 2 alternate jurors. We exhausted the original panel of 100 jurors, and on three occasions sent the sheriff out into the highways and byways of Erie for 20 more citizens. Why?

The answer, in large part, is that the prospective jurors had conscientious scruples against bringing in a penalty of death.

The presiding judge . . . was most liberal in permitting the defense to attempt a rehabilitation of the jurors. [Defense counsel] continually asked them—"granted the death penalty is revolting in most cases, couldn't you bring in such a verdict against a professional killer, a hired assassin or the brutal murderer of a little child?" Many of the jurors said no. Others replied, in such extreme cases, they could return a death verdict. All of them fell before the Commonwealth's challenge for cause.

The result has been that a jury in a capital case is no longer representative of the community from which it is drawn. While community attitudes toward the death penalty have changed, the attitude required by law of the capital jury remains frozen. Such a jury represents, today, a fragment of the community—those who not only *condone* capital punishment but *believe* in it to the extent of being willing personally to vote for the death sentence. Viewed in this light, it becomes almost irrelevant to argue, as some do, that many prospective jurors merely utilize the death-scruples device to avoid serving on a capital jury. To the extent that this is true, it may tend to aggravate rather than mitigate the minority character of the capital jury. It can be argued that those who survive the examination, and thus man the jury box, become almost *volunteers*—that they are not merely impartial on the death penalty, but affirmatively support it.

What is the bearing of the minority complexion of the capital jury on fair trial and due process of law? This question leads to three more specific questions: (1) Does such a jury constitute a "jury of one's peers"? (2) Can such a jury be expected to answer guilt-innocence questions (such as the question of whether the defendant was sane or insane at the time of his alleged offense) as favorably to the defendant as a jury not death-qualified? (3) Can such a jury, in the event it convicts, be expected to decide impartially on the nature of the punishment?

Inherent in this line of inquiry are questions of psychology: To what extent does a death-qualified jury take with it into the jury box a pattern of *other* attitudes not characteristic of the community at large? To what extent are such other attitudes, if they exist, prejudicial to the defendant? Searching the reports of court decisions in capital cases, one discovers that these questions have not only not been answered, they have never really been asked. I have turned, therefore, to the psychologists and others in the behavioral sciences, to whom I have access on a university campus, for their ideas. Through them I have been led to the vast literature on the "authoritarian personality," the suggestion being that a death-qualified jury would tend to be a jury of "authoritarians." The fount of the concept of "authoritarianism" is *The Authoritarian Personality* by Adorno, Frenkel-Brunswik, Levinson and Sanford, published in 1950.

While the book is essentially an inquiry into prejudice, it develops two pertinent propositions. The first is that a person's ideas and values may tend to run to a coherent, discernible pattern, however oblivious he may be of the pattern. The second is the "authoritarian-nonauthoritarian" antithesis. The *authoritarian* personality is seen as one involving, in the language of psychology, the following characteristics: moralistic condemnation; extrapunitiveness; distrust-suspicion (people threatening, victimization, survival of the fittest, world as a jungle); hierarchical conception of human relations; non-love-seeking; exploitive-manipulative opportunism.

In contrast, the characteristics of the *nonauthoritarian* personality are: permissiveness; impunitiveness or intrapunitiveness; trustingness (people essentially good until proved otherwise); equalitarianism-mutuality; love-seeking.

If the "hunch" of my psychologist friends is accurate—that a death-qualified jury would be culled from nonauthoritarians in favor of authoritarians—the due process and fair-trial implications are not only obvious, but gravely disturbing. I say "hunch" because at present there is nothing more definite to go on. Perhaps "nothing" is too strong a statement. There is some supporting evidence of an empirical nature in the practice of some prosecuting attorneys in the state of Texas. (I do not mean to single out Texas from the other death-penalty jurisdictions for any reason other than that I live there and, as a result, have better information as to its practices.)

The prosecution practice of which I speak is the death-qualification of juries in capital cases where there is no bona fide intention on the part of the prosecutor to seek the death penalty. The explanation of this practice, where it exists, is that through death-qualification the prosecution expects to get a "better" jury for its jurpose—one that will be more responsive to the prosecution's case on the guilt-innocence issue and also on the punishment issue. Since, in Texas, the punishment on a conviction of murder may range from a two-year suspended sentence to death in the electric chair, the scope of discretion entrusted to the jury is unusually broad. I have heard defense counsel remark that a death-qualified jury "thinks it's doing you a favor with a life sentence."

How did we fall into the curious practice of death-qualifying jurors in capital cases and, having fallen into it, why have lawyers and judges not been more astute to examine the fair trial and due process implications? The reasons lie in the historical evolution of capital crimes and proceedings.

The earliest statutes assessing the death penalty left only one question to the jury—that of guilt or innocence. Upon conviction of the offense made capital, the penalty of death was mandatory. Since the sole function of the jury was to determine guilt or innocence, it was deemed necessary that the jurors be qualified on the death penalty. If they were not so qualified, it was feared they would not convict, thus subverting the administration of criminal justice. As a result, the capital jurisdictions either enacted statutes which disqualified jurors who could not for reasons of conscience impose the death penalty or adopted the same rule through judicial decision. In this context, the logic of death-qualification was difficult to assail.

But the situation has changed drastically. A humanitarian trend away from capital punishment as a mandatory penalty for certain offenses began long ago. The statutes establishing capital crimes have been amended in almost every jurisdiction in the United States so as to give juries the discretion to assess or withhold the death sanction. Under the current statutes *two* issues are presented to the jury for decision: (1) guilt or innocence, (2) degree of punishment. In this altered context, the logic of death-qualification leaves much to be desired.

No longer can it be said that without death-qualification a guilty man may go free. The most that can be said is that a guilty man may not receive the death penalty. But despite this fundamental change, jurors with scruples against capital punishment continue to be challenged for cause and excused from service on capital juries. To some extent, this continuance of the old practice in the changed environment has been the result of inertia. The old practice went unchallenged, out of habit, until it had deepened its roots in the new environment. When challenge was finally made, it was prejudiced by the delay. As stated by the Supreme Court of Oregon in *State* v. *Leland,* a 1951 decision (which is, incidentally, the most pertinent of any I have discovered to the questions raised herein):

During the thirty years that have elapsed since capital punishment was reinstated in Oregon [in non-mandatory form] it has been the uniform practice to apply the provision now challenged [death-qualification of the jury] in first-degree murder cases. This practice is not conclusive against the defendant's contention; it does, however, fortify the conclusion that it is without merit.

Where the challenge of the practice of death-qualification has been made, however belatedly, under the new, non-mandatory, two-issue capital statutes, a new theory for justifying the old practice has been developed. The theory is that the prosecution (the "People," the "State," the "United States") is entitled to an impartial jury on the issue of punishment. This new theory raises more questions than it answers. For example: Why, in the qualification of the jury, should the prosecution's interest as to the *punishment* issue be given precedence over the defendant's interest as to the more fundamental *guilt* issue? On what basis is it presumed that a death-qualified jury is as impartial on the *guilt* issue as one not so qualified? In a state such as Texas, where the jury has a broad discretion on the punishment issue itself (term of years, life sentence or death), on what basis is it presumed that a death-qualified jury is impartial from the defendant's standpoint *even on the punishment issue?* Why should the defendant in a capital case be denied the same kind of jury on the *guilt* issue as that accorded in non-capital cases? In summary, what are the constitutional implications of trial before a jury which, by reason of changing community values not yet reflected in the law, is drawn from a shrinking and therefore increasingly extremist fraction of the community?

None of these questions is adequately considered, much less answered, in any court report I have been able to find. It is, however, interesting to note that in England, where they have loved liberty and justice and also tried and executed criminals for ages longer than we, the practice of death-qualifying jurors is unknown.

The Dynamics of Executive Clemency

SOLIE M. RINGOLD

On November 3, 1964, the people of Oregon voted to abolish the death penalty. The next day Governor Mark Hatfield commuted the sentences of three persons awaiting the gas chamber. Clearly, Governor Hatfield was carrying

Reprinted, by permission, from the *American Bar Association Journal*, 52:240–243, March, 1966.

out the voters' mandate as expressed by the repeal of capital punishment, and his actions evoked little criticism. His predecessor, Robert D. Holmes, had conscientious scruples against capital punishment and expressed his personal opposition to the death sentence by commuting every one that arose during his term. Governor Holmes's actions were not unchallenged: they resulted in an appeal to the Oregon courts to enjoin him from commuting a death sentence.

Billy Junior Nunn was convicted of the murder of Alvin Eacret and was sentenced to death. Eacret's parents filed a lawsuit against Governor Holmes, contending that because of his publicly expressed views against capital punishment he would commute Nunn's sentence unless restrained by the court. The Eacrets requested a declaration by the Supreme Court of Oregon which, in substance, would inform the Governor that he must not exercise his power to commute a sentence of death because of his personal convictions.

So was posed an intriguing question. What standards shall a governor use in exercising his power of commutation?[1] Why shouldn't a governor who opposes capital punishment commute the sentence, when he has been given the power by the electorate? Does clemency require any reason other than compassion or mercy?

In approximately half the states the awesome power of commutation is vested solely in the governor. Commutation procedures and power vary from state to state, but they can be classified generally as being lodged in: (1) a board alone; (2) a board alone, with the governor sitting as a member; (3) a board alone, the governor sitting as a member with grant, conditional on his being in the majority; (4) the governor, empowered to act only if a board makes a favorable recommendation (governor can overrule, denying commutation); (5) the governor with the advice and consent of an executive council, an elected body.[2] Under the Federal Constitution the President alone has the power to abrogate a death sentence, derived from the power to grant reprieves and pardons.

In the United States the concept of commutation is derived basically from the principles of executive clemency inherited from our colonial history. Throughout the early history of England, the kings were engaged in struggles for power with the earls, the feudal courts, the Church and Parliament. A recurring matter of contention was possession of the pardoning power. During a temporary lull in the contest between Parliament and Henry VIII in 1536, the King was given the sole responsibility for the exercise of clemency.[3]

Colonial charters provided for the exercise of the pardoning power. In the royal colonies the governor was permitted to pardon in all cases except treason and willful murder. In other colonies the chief executive, with occasional assistance from other colonial officers, dictated the exercise of clemency. The Revolutionary struggle created distrust of royal governors and executive departments in state governments, and in only five of the original thirteen states was the pardoning power unconditionally vested in the governor. With increasing confidence in the executive, after the establishment of the nation, the constitutions of the states later admitted to the Union almost uniformly conferred the power of clemency in the absolute discretion of the governor.[4] Today, Connecticut is the only state that does not provide for the clemency power in its constitution, but by statute it is lodged in a board partially appointed by the governor. (The board consists of one judge appointed by the Supreme Court of Errors; four persons appointed by the governor, two of whom must be attorneys, one a social scientist and one a physician; and no more than three to be of the same political party.)

Some state constitutions have qualified executive clemency. In California the governor may not commute the sentence of any felon previously convicted of a felony, unless he first secures the recommendation of a majority of the justices of the state supreme court. (A majority of the court refused to make the recommendation in the case of Caryl Chessman.) Other limitations or requirements, either constitutional or statutory, such as open hearings, reasoned decisions, reports to the legislature, and notice to the public, prosecutor and judge may be found. But no criteria or standards to be considered by the clemency authority have been enacted. This seems to leave a governor free to grant clemency, if he personally opposes the death penalty.

In an early case Chief Justice John Marshall pronounced that

A pardon in an act of grace, proceeding from the power intrusted with the execution of the laws, which exempts the individual on whom it is bestowed from the punishment the law inflicts for a crime he has committed. It is the private, though official, act of the executive magistrate. . . .[5]

NEED A PARDON BE ACCEPTED?

As far as the courts were concerned (with a couple of exceptions later noted), mercy or grace was the sole reason for a pardon or commutation. In 1915 the United States Supreme Court emphasized this when confronted with the issue whether acceptance of the pardon by the person to be pardoned is part of the pardoning process.

George Burdick, city editor of the *New York Tribune,* had been called to testify before a federal grand jury as to sources of his information regarding frauds under investigation. He declined to answer, claiming that his answers might tend to incriminate him. He was directed to appear at a later date, and when he returned he was handed a Presidential pardon. The United States attorney demanded that he answer the inquiries of the grand jury, as he was now absolved from the consequences of every criminal act. Burdick refused to accept the pardon and again declined to testify, claiming the protection of the Fifth Amendment.

A conviction for criminal contempt followed, but it was reversed by the Supreme Court. The Court followed the lead of Marshall and ruled that a pardon is a private act of grace and must be accepted before it is valid. Burdick was within his rights in his refusal to accept it, and therefore could not be compelled to testify.[6]

It is sometimes said that hard facts make bad law, and that is what happened in the case of Vuco Perovich, who was convicted in Alaska of murder. On September 15, 1905, he was sentenced to be hanged. Respites were granted from time to time, and on June 5, 1909, President Taft executed a document purporting to be a commutation of sentence to life imprisonment. From the Alaska jail he was transferred to several penitentiaries. Two requests for a pardon were denied. On February 20, 1925, he applied for a writ of habeas corpus and his release from Leavenworth on the ground that his removal from jail to a penitentiary and the order of President Taft directing the moves were without his consent and without legal authority. The district judge agreed and ordered his release.

A perplexing dilemma was before the Supreme Court on the appeal. Justice Holmes put it this way:

> When we come to the commutation of death to imprisonment for life it is hard to see how consent has any more to do with it. . . . Supposing that Perovich did not accept the change, he could not have got himself hanged against the Executive order. Supposing that he did accept, he could not affect the judgment to be carried out.
>
> The considerations that led to the modification had nothing to do with his will.[7]

And the court had no desire to set Perovich free. So Justice Holmes held:

> . . . A pardon in our days is not a private act of grace from an individual happening to possess power. It is a part of the Constitutional scheme. When granted it is the determination of the ultimate authority that the public welfare will be better served by inflicting less than what the judgment fixed.[8]

STANDARDS FOR CLEMENCY DIFFER WIDELY

Today pardoning authorities hold differing philosophies and concepts concerning clemency, display varying abilities to withstand influences of all sorts and exercise the pardoning power in different ways. Abramowitz and Paget, in their study cited in footnote 2, state:

As a general proposition, the reasons, or standards, for granting commutation, as observed in the states visited, do not differ greatly. Upon close observation, however, clearly discernible differences appear in the depth of commitment of various states to a given standard: further, some states exclude from consideration matters deemed critical in others. In most cases, the grant of commutation depends upon a combination of factors, rather than upon a single determinant. Because of this cumulative approach, it is difficult to draw anything other than a rough sketch of the hierarchy of standards within given jurisdictions.

They attempt to classify the criteria used by various pardoning authorities for commutation:

1. *The nature of the crime.* The degrees of community shock, horror and offensiveness are considered. "The more heinous the crime, the less chance for clemency."

2. *Doubt as to guilt.* In Arizona this is the only standard considered, and the governor may commute only after the board has made a favorable recommendation. Obviously, it is a rare event for an innocent man to be convicted and sentenced to death; there has been but one commutation by the Arizona authorities in thirty years.

3. *Fairness of trial.* This refers to community hysteria or undue publicity that does not amount to a constitutional denial of due process but is of sufficient magnitude to concern the clemency authority.

4. *Relative guilt and disparity of sentences.* When two or more persons have been convicted of the same offense under the principle that the act of one constitutes the act of all, the personal involvement of each is considered and weighed.

5. *Geographical equalization of sentences.*

6. *Mitigating circumstances: duress, provocation, intoxication, self-defense* and

7. *Mental and physical condition of the defendant.* This latter category emphasizes the general dissatisfaction with the McNaghten rule in determining legal insanity. Factors that shed light on the reasons for the crime and the character of the defendant, most of which were probably inadmissible as evidence during the course of the trial, are considered. Governor Rockefeller "expressed incredulity that the massive

evidence of an unstable home life, mental retardation, and years in a mental institution was revealed for the first time at the clemency hearing" of Salvatore Agron. To permit the jury to consider evidence of mitigation, New York, California, Connecticut and Pennsylvania have adopted a two-trial system. If the jury returns a verdict of "guilty," the trial proceeds then into the "penalty phase," in which these matters are revealed to the jury (including the defendant's prior criminal record) before it determines whether or not to impose the death penalty.

8. *Rehabilitation.*

9. *Dissents and inferences drawn from the courts.*

10. *Recommendations of the prosecution and trial judge.*

11. *Political pressure and publicity.*

12. *Precedent.* Though clemency authorities deny that these factors carry much weight, Abramowitz and Paget are convinced that they are important considerations.

13. *The clemency authorities' views on capital punishment.* Former Governor Peabody of Massachusetts and Governor Brown of California both publicly stated their opposition to capital punishment. Massachusetts provides that the governor may commute with the advice and consent of an executive council, and during his term of office Governor Peabody recommended commutation of every death penalty. Governor Brown, however, has not commuted every case. He has devoted considerable time and energy to the reform of clemency procedure and has held a hearing in every case involving the death sentence.

GOVERNOR UPHELD IN OREGON CASE

In the *Eacret* case, Governor Holmes had the sole power to commute in death cases, and he had exercised it as an act of clemency, mercy and grace in support of his moral opposition to capital punishment. The Supreme Court of Oregon, sitting *en banc,* sustained his right to do so. The court held that the parents had no standing to maintain the action. The alleged wrong of which they complained, the court said, was public in character, and the plaintiffs were in effect seeking an advisory opinion respecting the proper exercise of the governor's pardoning power. "Putting all this to one side," it continued, "it is not within judicial competency to control, interfere with, or even to advise the Governor when exercising his power to grant reprieves, commutations and pardons. The principle of separation of powers written into the constitution . . . forbids it."

After declaring that there was nothing to decide, the court gave its advisory opinion:

> Where the constitution thus confers unlimited power on the Governor to grant reprieves, commutations and pardons, his discretion cannot be controlled by judicial decision. The courts have no authority to inquire into the reasons or motives which actuate the Governor in exercising the power, nor can they decline to give effect to a pardon for an abuse of discretion. Concerning such matters, the courts "are not authorized to express an opinion." . . . We know of no court which has expressed dissent from these views. . . . If perchance, the Governor should abuse the power, the only recourse that the people have is at the polls. . . .[9]

More than fifty years ago, the Criminal Court of Appeals of Oklahoma reluctantly concluded it was powerless to direct or overrule the Governor in the exercise of his pardoning power—but it tried![10] Lee Cruce was Governor of Oklahoma from 1911 to 1915. Because of strong and determined scruples against the death penalty, he commuted every one (twenty-two) imposed during his administration. The Oklahoma court took the opportunity to castigate him in colorful, virulent language, and to make an impassioned plea for capital punishment.

Newton Henry had had trouble with Charley Lucas. Charley owed him sixty cents, and "The crazy son-of-a-bitch is after my woman," a witness testified Newton had stated shortly before Lucas was knifed. Henry was convicted of murder and sentenced to death. On appeal to the Criminal Court of Appeals, the court found no error in law. Judge Furman, speaking for the court, said:

> It is a matter known to all persons of common intelligence in the state of Oklahoma that the Governor takes the position that legal

executions are judicial murder; and that he refuses to permit them to be carried into effect upon the ground that he would thereby become a party thereto; and that he has expressed his fixed determination to strictly adhere to this policy until the expiration of his term of office. As this is a capital conviction, and as the Governor's action presents an absolute bar to the enforcement of the law in Oklahoma, we cannot, without a failure to discharge our duty, omit to take judicial notice of, and pass upon, this position of the Governor, as unpleasant as it is for us to do so.

The court insisted that the Governor's position was "utterly untenable," because he is not required to approve a death verdict and he is not responsible. The court castigated the Governor:

. . . No Governor has the right to say, directly or substantially, either by words or by actions, which speak louder than words: "I think that capital punishment is wrong. I know that it is taught in the Bible, and is provided for in the laws of Oklahoma; but I occupy a higher plane than this. I am not such a barbarian as to believe this is right. I am a better judge of what punishment should be inflicted than is taught in the Bible, or than the ignorant, savage and bloodthirsty people of Oklahoma have provided for in their laws. Therefore, notwithstanding my official oath, I will place my judgment above the law, both human and divine, and make my will supreme in this state, and will not permit capital punishment to be inflicted in Oklahoma, no matter what the law is, or how atrocious the offense committed may have been. . . ."

The opinion continues in the same vein, quoting statistics and Scriptures, vehemently defending capital punishment and condemning the Governor.

GOVERNOR HARRIMAN AGREES
WITH THE COURT

While Governor of New York, Averill Harriman publicly reflected on his power of commutation in an article entitled "Mercy Is a Lonely Business." Siding with the Oklahoma court, he criticized the position of the former Oklahoma Governor: "As an individual, Governor Cruce had every right to

oppose capital punishment, but as the state's highest executive, I think he was perverting his power of clemency. It
is for the people of the state to decide—through their legislators—if capital punishment is to exist in their state. In my
own state, capital punishment is accepted as a deterrent to
crime and as governor of New York I must accept that condition."[11] (The omission of any reference to Governor Holmes
must be attributed to gubernatorial courtesy.)

The excoriation by the court had little effect on Governor
Cruce. On April 4, 1914, he commuted Newton Henry's death
sentence to life imprisonment. Henry subsequently had
several leaves from the penitentiary, and on May 2, 1924,
Governor Trapp commuted his sentence to fifteen years. He
was released from incarceration on May 12, 1924, and passed
into obscurity.[12]

Whatever rationalizations may be given for the grant or
denial of commutation, it is evident that a governor's personal
views on the merits of the death penalty influence the determination. This is manifestly true when the governor is vested
with the sole power. Abramowitz and Paget report: "With
few exceptions, all the clemency officials interviewed favored
the death penalty, with varying degrees of enthusiasm and
different opinions as to when it ought to be applied." This
diversity enforces the position of the governor who grants
commutation because he opposes capital punishment. No
constitution or legislature has ever imposed standards, and
the courts have consistently recognized that the criteria to be
considered and the ultimate decision to be reached are within
the executive's sole discretion. What better reason can there
be than his assertion of a strong-driven conscience?

WHY SHOULDN'T A GOVERNOR
FOLLOW HIS CONSCIENCE?

Executive clemency should be just what its name implies
—mercy, compassion and forgiveness. Aspects of a case involving doubt as to guilt, unfairness of trial, mental incom-
petency—these should be solely within the province of the

courts. When the death penalty comes before the governor, all legal procedures have been exhausted. The defendant is no longer seeking legal technicalities to escape from the imposition of the death sentence. He is asking but one thing—mercy. Why is that not an adequate reason for a governor to grant commutation? And perhaps in the process his actions will lead, as did Governor Holmes's, to the removal of the death penalty from the laws of his state.

PART V

Summation

The Inevitable End of
Capital Punishment

THORSTEN SELLIN

Death is the rarest of all punishments for crime. In 1965, only seven persons were executed in the United States. This is the lowest annual figure since 1935, when 199 met that fate. Since then there has been a steady and steep decline in the use of capital punishment, especially since World War II. This drop is not due to a lack of candidates, for at the end of 1965 there were 331 inmates of our prisons under sentence of death. Of these, 67 had been admitted during the year. If none of them were to benefit from commutations or new trials, it would take nearly 48 years to expedite the executions at the present rate, not counting the annual contingents of new admissions during the period.

The dilemma created by this situation is one important reason for the present widespread agitation for the abolition of capital punishment. It is evident that our growing reluctance to execute murderers necessitates a reform of the law to prevent trial courts from imposing death sentences that merely result in an increasing backlog of candidates for execution and throw upon appellate courts and pardon au-

Slightly revised and up-dated version of an address delivered in Toronto, Canada, February 7, 1965, and printed in its original form in *The Criminal Law Quarterly*, 8:36–51, 1965.

thorities the task of reducing its size. This reduction is done by commutation or reversals of judgments, vacating sentences or granting new trials, but the delays involved are lengthening, so the backlog keeps on growing.

The trial courts have not been immune to the spreading objections to the death penalty. There has been a constant decrease over several years in the number of defendants sentenced to death. We are apparently getting ready to join the civilized countries of the world, which have abolished capital punishment, at least in peace time. Quite a number of our states have already done so. Indeed, the first sovereign state in the world to abolish the death penalty during the nineteenth century was Michigan in 1846. Since then it has been joined by Maine, Rhode Island, Wisconsin, Minnesota, North Dakota, Alaska, Hawaii, Puerto Rico, the Virgin Islands, Oregon, Iowa, New York, West Virginia, and Vermont.

In Europe the strongholds of the death penalty are the Communist countries. Of the rest, Turkey, Greece, Eire, France, and Spain alone cling to it, now that the United Kingdom has abolished it. In Latin America most countries have renounced it, including Argentina and Brazil. Elsewhere in the world, Israel, New Zealand, and New South Wales have abandoned it, either totally or at least for murder. A strong abolition movement in Canada is lending support to a substantial number of members of Parliament who hope that an end to capital punishment in that country will soon occur.

Considering how rarely we now execute the death penalty, compared with the number of persons convicted of murder annually, the strong emotional reaction to any move challenging its propriety is amazing to the objective observer of the social scene. We do not question the sincerity of those who debate the issue, but feelings tend to be substituted for facts, the Holy Writ quoted in support of both positions, and statistics derided unless they favor the argument. In that kind of debate, the social scientist is at a disadvantage, for he is, professionally, not concerned with the retention or the abolition of the death penalty. He knows that social policy is not dictated solely—and at times never—by what is demonstrated by scientific inquiry. But, since capital punishment is a social institution, it can be studied empirically in order to learn if it serves the useful functions attributed to it and operates in a manner to fulfill the expectations of the legislator.

Basically, capital punishment probably survives because many believe strongly that it possesses a certain moral fitness, that it is the only just penalty for murder, especially when the murder is particularly brutal. In such instances, they say, simple justice demands "a life for a life." Such a murderer, it is claimed, has forfeited the right to live. In a sense, these advocates adopt the Mosaic law of retaliation and thus support a publicly regulated substitute for private vengeance, but they disregard the fact that the strict law of talion once found in criminal codes of centuries ago has disappeared, except for murder. Furthermore, they find nothing illogical in entertaining, side by side with their desire for retaliation for murder, a favorable attitude toward a host of radical innovations in correctional treatment based on theories of rehabilitation and reformation.

We have to admit that while the social scientist may be able to study the extent and the intensity of a retributive sentiment in a population, the rebuttal of the argument will have to come from the moral philosopher. I will, however, point out a few facts.

First of all, what of the claim that death is the only just punishment for a deliberate murder? If we look back at history, we find that capital punishment was once thought to be the only just punishment for thieves, adulteresses, heretics, and forgers. The sentiment of justice went so far as to require the robber to have his bones broken and his still living body left to expire tied to the spokes of a wheel fixed on a pole on a scaffold. We now find such punishments revolting; we use the death penalty only to remove life, and we perform the operation in the seclusion of a prison chamber. The point is that justice is a relative concept that changes with the times. A sense of justice must exist among all people to regulate their living together. This is an immutable requirement of social life, but what justice *means* is not immutable. Therefore, the belief that a murderer should forfeit his life differs from the old belief that a thief should also lose his life only in the fact that social sentiments still uphold the former but have renounced the latter,

Furthermore, can people who hold such a concept of justice —a life for a life—maintain that they alone know what justice requires in dealing with the murderer? Are the people of the abolition states of the United States, the people of Argentina, Brazil, New Zealand, the Scandinavian countries, the Netherlands, Belgium, Switzerland, West Germany, Italy, and the rest of the countries that have abolished capital punishment to be branded as deficient in their conception of justice? Obviously not. These countries have simply decided that they do not—whatever the reason—believe that it is just to execute murderers.

In addition, retribution seems to be unworkable. It is neither efficient nor equitably administered. This concept of justice would properly demand that every person who commits a capital murder should receive his just deserts. Of course, all such persons are not detected or brought to justice, but once proved guilty, retribution should operate as stated. What are some facts? The gap between what the theory demands and what happens in reality is enormous. It begins to show in the courtroom, where the skilled defense lawyer may stave off conviction for capital murder or a jury may inequitably determine a verdict or a sentence, depending on its attitudes toward a defendant or the feelings of the community, rather than on the strict character of the crime. It is a well-known fact that the proportion of women murderers sentenced to death is disproportionately low compared with the proportion of male murderers so sentenced. In Ohio, for instance, from 1955 to 1958, 31 percent of the males and 8 percent of the females prosecuted for capital murder were found guilty of that crime; 8 percent of the males were executed, but no female was. As for members of minority groups, such as the Negroes, we are all familiar with newspaper reports from the Southern states. They reflect racial sentiments which even today make a travesty of justice. In Mississippi, for instance, no white man has ever been executed for the murder of a Negro.

But if a sentence of death is imposed, we still have the pardon authorities, who may commute sentences. In the last resort, the execution of a murderer depends on such authorities. At times a governor opposed to capital punishment may commute every death sentence; another holding opposite views may commute few or none; furthermore, studies have shown that if private counsel has handled the case of the defendant, he has a better chance of receiving a commutation than if he was represented by court-appointed counsel. In Pennsylvania, from 1914 to 1958, the chance of a white felony-murderer to receive a commutation was three times the chance of a Negro convicted of such a murder.

Finally, if we conservatively assume that there are now about 2500 capital murders annually in the United States and but seven executions, it is obvious that a life for a life is rarely taken. It is vain to expect any material change. The experience of history and the changing climate of opinion in states that have retained capital punishment do not favor it.

Whatever we may think of the claim that capital punishment is the only *just* penalty for murder, that claim is impervious to attacks by science. Its proponents do not assert that this penalty produces any tangible results; they rest their case purely on moral grounds. Being concerned with abstract justice they are not interested—or should not be—in the mundane effects of the death penalty. They may be open to conversion to another philosophy of punishment, but they are not—or should not be—influenced by empirical facts. Were they logical, they would persist in their views even if one could prove that capital punishment is neither effective nor equitable. Their reply would be that what is needed is to see to it that it becomes more widely and consistently used.

Not often, however, do those who voice a retributive philosophy in connection with murder stick to their guns. Whether from a lack of complete conviction or from a feeling that in a world in which scientific ways of thought have gained ascendancy a retributive philosophy alone is not socially acceptable, they tend to add other reasons why capital punishment should be retained. Then it is said that we need the death penalty, not only because it is morally right, but because it serves certain utilitarian ends. This is where the social scientist comes in, because these ends or aims of capital punishment are of a kind that can be examined in the light of experience and subjected to testing by research.

Some of the utilitarian arguments can be dismissed as being so trivial or uninformed that they should not need consideration. Nowadays one rarely hears the death penalty defended because it helps to improve the human stock by eliminating the unfit. Even if it were assumed that murderers are carriers of highly undesirable inherited traits, seven executions a year in a population of 190 million would have no effect. After all, other members of the murderer's family may also pass on these traits to future generations and, furthermore, sterilization would be as effective and less radical.

A great many feel that to substitute life imprisonment would mean adding to the financial burden of the government. This cynical argument is unfounded. Those who use it are ignorant of the often mountainous cost of capital trials and their aftermath of appeals, nor do they know the realities of prison administration. Some prisoners, it is true, including some lifers, are no doubt incapable of making adequate return, measured in dollars and cents, to the state, but most lifers work in prison. They perform domestic services, work in shops, do clerical work. If they were paid a wage commensurate with their services, they would be able to pay the cost of their maintenance, but since they receive little or nothing, it is easy to forget that they are a source of financial profit to the institution in one way or another. Any prison warden will testify to the fact that it is from the group of lifers that he draws a considerable number of trusted inmate workers.

In the last analysis, the only utilitarian argument that has to be given attention is the one that defends capital punishment as being a uniquely powerful means of protecting the community. Those who hold this belief say that the death penalty is needed as a threat or warning to potential murderers, and that murderers, if they were kept alive, would remain a constant threat to fellow prisoners or to prison officers while in institutions and would endanger the lives of fellow citizens if they were paroled or pardoned and thus allowed to return to a life in freedom. Life imprisonment as a substitute for death would thus be too risky, nor would the threat of that penalty have the same power to inhibit murderous impulses.

I propose to examine this matter of deterrence on the basis of what factual data are available. First of all, does capital punishment have any effect on capital murder rates? If this were so, we would expect to find that such rates are higher in states that do not have this penalty, that abolition results in an increase in murder, and that the institution of the death penalty is followed by a decrease.

Before reporting the results of research designed to inquire into the validity of these assumptions, it is only fair to say that no one knows with any certainty how many capital murders are committed. A body is found. Was the death due to natural causes, accident, or malice? If natural death and accident are both excluded, was the death caused under circumstances that would define it as due to premeditation and malice on the part of the killer, or could it involve a non-capital murder or a manslaughter? Unless the offender is found and his motives clarified, these are matters for some conjecture. Even then, the lack of probative evidence may hamper prosecution and reduce the number of cases that actually result in a finding of guilt and a conviction for capital murder. In other words, our police and judicial statistics are neither complete nor sufficiently refined to permit us to determine the actual number of capital murders in any given area.

We do have one other source of data. All states today have developed rather complete mortality statistics based on death certificates, and one cause of death revealed is willful homicide. These statistics are commonly used today in the study of homicide rates, but they do not give us information on the number of *capital* crimes, a special form of homicide. Therefore, we are compelled to make an assumption: whether we use police or mortality statistics, the proportion of capital murders to all criminal homicides remains constant, so that if such homicides increase, capital murders increase correspondingly, and vice versa.

Abolitionists in the United States used to show with enthusiasm that homicide rates were much higher in capital punishment states than in the states that had discarded this penalty. The facts were correct, but they were improperly used. When the Royal Commission on Capital Punishment requested me in 1949 to make a statistical study of homicide, I decided that the only proper way of comparing homicide death rates would be to compare the rates of abolition states with the rates of their neighbor states, on the assumption that such clusters of states were essentially similar in population and in their social, economic, and political conditions. When the study was completed and the homicide rates were compared, it was found that both the size of the rates and their trends over several decades were the same, whether or not the death penalty was found in the law and whether or not executions actually took place, for in the last analysis it is the execution that demonstrates the existence of capital punishment and presents a unique risk to a potential murderer. More of that later.

In connection with the study mentioned, I also assembled homicide rates for years before and after abolition of the death penalty, including rates for years after the re-introduction of capital punishment in several states. The result was inconclusive. In some states re-introduction was followed by a temporary decline, in others by a rise in rates. In either event homicides were related to changing population and social conditions and not to the presence or absence of executions.

About 30 years ago, an investigation was made of the effect of executions on homicides in Philadelphia, a city which then had close to two million inhabitants. We began the study with the assumption that if executions have a deterrent effect, this effect should be most powerfully shown in a community where the person executed had lived and where his crime and trial had been highly publicized and his execution equally well covered by the local press. We located five cases between 1927 and 1932 that met these conditions and also were sufficiently far removed from earlier or later executions to remove any possible influence from such events. Three of the cases were notorious; in one of them four men were executed on the same night, and one local newspaper devoted its entire front page to the story.

We proceeded to list all homicide deaths in the records of the police and the coroner's office during the 60 days before and the 60 days after each execution. We eliminated accidental, excusable, and justifiable homicides, and deaths due to abortion. The rest we checked for date of occurrence and for the charge made by the prosecutor's office. We retained only cases presumed to be criminal homicides, whether the offender was known or unknown, had committed suicide, or had been dealt with by the courts. We then plotted these crimes on calendars, with the execution date in the middle, and tried to discover if the execution led to any temporary lag in homicidal crimes. Combining the five 60-day periods before the executions and comparing them with the combined periods after the executions, we found 105 days free of homicides before, and 74 free days after, the executions. Of the 204 homicides covered by the investigation, 19 resulted in convictions for capital murder. Nine of them had been committed some time during the pre-execution periods and 10 in the post-execution periods. Two of them had been committed during the 10 days just before the executions and five of them during the 10 days immediately following. A similar study based on convictions was made a few years ago in Philadelphia and arrived at the same negative results.

Now and then some organization passes a resolution demanding the retention of capital punishment. The most persistent of such organized opposition is represented by the police. State associations of chiefs of police in the United States have on more than one occasion successfully put a stop to legislation favoring abolition. "Who would speak with greater authority than those in constant contact with criminals and exposed to danger at their hands?" seems to be the attitude of legislators. No one disputes the fact that police service, like fire-fighting, steeple-jack work, testing planes, and a number of other occupations, involves a risk to life, but the claim of the police that the existence of the death penalty reduces such hazards is a myth and like other myths is accepted as fact in states that still have capital punishment. That the police have failed to test the validity of the myth is clear from the statement made in 1954 to the Joint Committee of the Senate and the House of Commons in Ottawa by the then president of the Chief Constables Association. He began by saying: "Our main objection is that abolition would adversely affect the personal safety of police officers in the daily discharge of their duties." He then interjected this statement: "If time had permitted I would have tried to obtain this vital information as to the number of policemen murdered in the execution of their duty in those parts of the world where capital punishment had been abolished." He had no time to do so, but this did not prevent him from arriving at a conclusion. He continued: "I submit that it will be found that the number is much higher than in those countries where the death penalty is still in effect." Having made up his mind and expressed the view of his Association without taking time to find the facts, he ended with these words: "This point is the main one in our submission that our government should retain capital punishment as a form of security." Oh, blessed logic!

The constables' spokesman was quite correct in assuming that he would have had to conduct some research into the matter, because none had previously been done to test the truth of his assertion. The Joint Committee had asked me to give them some assistance, and I had previously spent two days with them discussing statements I had prepared for them on capital and corporal punishment. Now it occurred to me that the time had come to subject the beliefs of the police to a test. Nowhere could such a test be better made than in the United States, where abolition states and capital punishment states bordered on each other. The test was made in 1955 and submitted to the Joint Committee, which published the results in its proceedings. Briefly, the study was based on a questionnaire sent to all police departments in cities with more than 10,000 inhabitants, according to the 1950 census, in the six states that had no death penalty at that time and the 11 states that bordered on them. Information was requested on the number of policemen killed by lethal weapons in the hands of criminals or suspects each year, beginning with 1919 and ending with 1954. Full reports were returned by 265 cities, representing 55 percent of the cities in the abolition states and 41 percent of those in the capital punishment states. [The procedure has been described in detail in "The Death Penalty and Police Safety."]

Several interesting facts appeared from an analysis of responses. First, when comparing groups of cities in the two types of states, according to the size of the cities, it was found that there was no difference in the rates of policemen killed. Second, it was found that in the Northeastern states, police were killed more rarely than in the Middle West. Third, the decade of 1920–1930 had been most hazardous to the police in both types of states, and the number of police killed had since then declined regularly, whether the state had the death penalty or not. It is impossible, then, to conclude that capital punishment offers a unique protection to the police not offered by life imprisonment. (Recent data on police killings supplied by the F.B.I., covering 1961 through 1963, show no significant differences between the two classes of states used in the previously reported study.)

It may be of interest to note that 9 out of 10 of the police officers from capital punishment states who responded to the questionnaire believed in the protective value of the death penalty, but that 3 out of 4 of the respondents from abolition states did not share that view.

Why should we assume that the fear of the gallows is more potent in regulating our actions than the fear of dying in prison or of spending the best part of our life in the abnormal setting of such an institution, separated from family and friends? The assumption is completely gratuitous. I do not deny that the prospect of legal punishment—any kind of punishment—plays some role in regulating our conduct, but there is ample evidence for believing that it does not, or cannot, operate in the case of murder. No social value is stronger than that attached to the preservation of life. When, in spite of this general social aversion to murder, killings do occur, it means that the perpetrators have either not been taught the proper respect for life or that they find themselves in a situation where hatred, desire, sudden anger, greed, necessity, or the mores of a group to which the offender belongs acquire such dominance that all else is forgotten, including the legal consequences of their acts. The person who carefully plans his crime so as to avoid detection has no fear of consequences because he expects to escape them. Discounting war and revolution, all but a very few people—even most murderers who eventually are convicted—consider the taking of life a great moral wrong. It is this feeling that ultimately is the great deterrent.

If we were to take the ultracynical view that people obey the law only because they want to avoid the consequences of disobedience and not because they live by a moral code which also finds its expression in some laws, we would have to assume that potential offenders fear the consequences of their acts somewhat in proportion to the risk of suffering them. But we have practically nullified the risk of execution. There were 809 felony murders known to the police in the United States in 1963, i.e., murders occurring during the commission of certain felonies. Most of them occurred in capital punishment states and would there be threatened by the death penalty. In addition there were 6740 willful homicides that year. Let us conservatively estimate that at least 1000 of these homicides were capital murders. When added to the felony murders we would get around 1700 in the death penalty states. There were 21 executions in 1963. If the present trend in executions continues, the risk of dying on the gallows, in the electric chair, or in the gas chamber will be still further reduced.

Supporters of the death penalty would probably feel that if anyone merits it, it is the gangster who in cold blood eliminates a business rival or his henchman. Yet, this is the very group that is immune to punishment. From 1919 to 1963 there were 982 gangland murders in Chicago alone. It is fair to assume that both the one ordering the killing and the one executing it were guilty of capital murders and that many of the killings were committed by two or more executioners. This would raise the number of actual murderers from 982 to, let us say, at least 1500. There were 19 convictions, usually resulting in prison sentences. Several were reversed on appeal. No one was executed for these crimes.

If risk is important, it is not the risk of execution that is greatest for the potential murderer but the risk of being killed by the police, the intended victim, or some bystander. In Chicago, during 1934–1954, policemen killed 69 and other people killed 261 criminals or suspects involved in homicide, or a total of 331. During the same period there were 45 persons executed for murder in the Chicago jail, a score of 8 to 1.

During the last four months of 1954, the Police Commissioner of New York City conducted a noteworthy experiment. In a district containing about 165,000 people, he quadrupled the size of the foot and motor patrol, added a special squad of 16 patrolmen for the evening and early morning hours, almost doubled the detective squad, and set up a special unit of the Juvenile Aid Bureau. This saturation of the area by the police had some interesting effects on the frequency of crimes of various kinds during the experimental period when compared with what had occurred during the corresponding months of the previous year. Assaults, robberies, burglaries, auto thefts, and grand larcenies known to the police declined, and certain other offenses rose, but what is important in this connection is that eight persons were killed in the precinct during the saturation period, compared with six the year before. The increased risk of discovery due to the greatly strengthened police surveillance in the district played no deterrent role.

We have little space left to discuss the problem of a substitute for the death penalty. Usually, life imprisonment is the substitute, and defenders of capital punishment fear that once a person has killed someone he is especially prone to kill again and therefore would be potentially more dangerous to fellow prisoners and prison staff than would other classes of prisoners.

In all capital punishment states today most of those convicted of capital murder are *not* sentenced to death but are given life sentences, either directly by courts or later by commutation. In other words, these agencies do not seem to share the fear mentioned, and quite properly so, for the belief that a prisoner serving a sentence for capital murder presents a special danger is another myth. Experience shows the contrary. Homicides do occur in prisons, but most of them are committed by people serving time for robbery, forgery, or what have you. For the last hundred years Rhode Island has retained the death penalty for killings committed in prison by lifers; there have been none. Even supposing that such a murder occasionally occurred, what would be the remedy? Since science has not reached the stage where such a potential murderer could be identified beforehand and selectively disposed of, the only alternative would be to make sure that all convicted murderers were executed. Such a rigid policy would never be countenanced, even by the advocates of capital punishment.

But, say the supporters of the death penalty, what of life imprisonment? There is none, they say. Lifers get paroled and are allowed to roam freely again. This is true, but only in part. A considerable number of lifers do serve their sentences. In 1957, in Ohio, for instance, one prisoner was executed, but 11 who were serving definite life sentences died from natural causes. Nevertheless, a large percentage of lifers do receive paroles after terms of varying length. In Pennsylvania, the average time spent in prison before parole is now somewhat over 20 years. In some states this figure is lower, in others higher. What is important is that paroled murderers everywhere have the best record of all parolees. Very few of them are again convicted and then usually of relatively minor offenses. Of 169 first-degree murderers paroled in Ohio in the 15 years between 1945 and 1960 only two were returned to prison—for a robbery and an assault.

Therefore, paroled murderers are not a special menace to the community.

I have attempted to show that, as now used, capital punishment performs none of the utilitarian functions claimed by its supporters, nor can it ever be made to serve such functions. It is an archaic custom of primitive origin that has disappeared in most civilized countries and is withering away in the rest.

If an intelligent visitor from some other planet were to stray to North America, he would observe, here and there and very rarely, a small group of persons assembled in a secluded room who, as representatives of an all-powerful sovereign state, were solemnly participating in deliberately and artfully taking the life of a human being. Ignorant of our customs, he might conclude that he was witnessing a sacred rite somehow suggesting a human sacrifice. And seeing our great universities and scientific laboratories, our mental hospitals and clinics, our many charitable institutions, and the multitude of churches dedicated to the worship of an executed Saviour, he might well wonder about the strange and paradoxical workings of the human mind.

Notes

Notes

THE PROBLEM OF THE DEATH PENALTY
Marc Ancel

[1] See E. Ferri, *Sociologie criminelle* (Paris, 1893), p. 531; A. Prins, *Science pénale et droit positif* (1899), p. 654.

[2] Royal Commission on Capital Punishment (1949–1953), *Report*, H. M. Stationery Office, London, 1953.

[3] *La Peine de mort dans les pays européens*, Comité européen pour les problèmes criminels, Conseil de l'Europe, Strasbourg, 1962; *Capital Punishment*, United Nations, Department of Economic and Social Affairs, New York, 1962.

[4] Ancient law and "European common law" before the reforms at the end of the 18th century consequently had recourse to torments aggravating the execution; expiatory intimidation and vengeance reached perfection in this repressive system. See L. T. Maes, "La Peine de mort dans le droit criminel de Malines," *Rev. hist. de droit français et étranger*, 1950, pp. 372 ff. Also J. Graven, "Le Problème de la peine de mort et sa réapparition en Suisse," *Rev. int. de crimin. et de police techn.*, January–March, 1952 (spec. no.), pp. 4 ff.

[5] See J. Escarra, *Code pénal de la République de Chine* (Paris, 1930), "Introduction," p. xxv, vol. II, part 1.

[6] On the *Shariah*, see Said Moustapha El Said Bey, *La Notion de responsabilité pénale*, in the *Travaux de la Semaine internationale de droit musulman* (Paris, 1951), pp. 122 ff. Cf. L. Milliot, *Introduction à l'étude du droit musulman* (Paris, 1953), pp. 744 ff.

[7] See P. Savey-Casard, "L'Église catholique et la peine de mort," *Rev. sciences crim.*, 1961, p. 773. Cf. J. Vernet, "Le glaive et la croix: position de l'Église devant la peine de mort," *Rev. int. de crimin. et de police techn.*, 1955, pp. 63 ff.; A. Santoro, "La Chiesa e la pena di morte," *Scuola positiva*, 1962, pp. 620 ff.

[8] We know that the shoemaker George Fox, founder of the Quakers, began preaching in 1647 and showed himself to be a resolute adversary of the death penalty. In this respect, he had precursors in England, notably Thomas More (*Utopia*, 1516) and the dramatist Middleton, Shakespeare's contemporary.

[9] See Ortolan, *Cours de législation pénale comparée* (Paris, 1939), vol. II, part 2, sec. iii, "Mouvement de reforme pénale au XVIIIᵉ siècle"; Faustin Hélie, "Introduction" to the translation of Beccaria's *Traité des délits et des peines* (Paris, 1956). Cf. my comparative introduction to the *Codes pénaux européens* (Paris, 1956), p. 18.

[10] It had a predecessor, 1809, in the Society for the Diffusion of Knowledge upon the Punishment of Death and the Improvement of Prison Discipline, founded by the Quaker William Allen. On this movement see L. Radzinowicz, *A History of English Criminal Law from 1750*, vol. I (1948), pp. 301 ff. (note, p. 348).

[11] See the famous speech by Lamartine, "Sur l'Abolition de la peine de mort," reprinted in *La Vie judiciaire*, no. 779, March 13–18, 1961; on Victor Hugo, see P. Savey-Casard, *Le Crime et la peine dans l'oeuvre de Victor Hugo* (Paris, 1956), and his "Les Enquêtes de Victor Hugo dans les prisons," *Rev. sciences crim.*, 1952, pp. 427 ff.

[12] The President of the Republic was equally affected by the rejection in 1908 of the bill to abolish the death penalty. See Garraud, *Traité théorique et pratique de droit pénal français*, 3rd ed., vol. I, pp. 110–111.

[13] See Garofalo, *La Criminologie* (2nd ed., Paris, 1890), pp. 290 ff.; on this aspect of the positivist movement, see also Graven, *op. cit.*, pp. 33 ff.

[14] See the beautiful address by Jean Rostand at the celebration of the fifteenth anniversary of the Declaration at UNESCO, December 10, 1963.

[15] On the reform introduced on this point by the Homicide Act of 1957, see especially Rupert Cross and Elizabeth Ely, "La Responsabilité pénale," in *Introduction au droit criminel de l'Angleterre,* published by the Institute of Comparative Law of the University of Paris, 1959, pp. 35 ff., 57–58. Cf. Kenny's *Outlines of Criminal Law* (18th ed. by J. W. Cecil Turner, 1962), pp. 83 ff.

[16] See *Annuaire de législation française et étrangère* (1961), p. 98.

[17] On recent legislation in the United States, see a note by Professor Mueller in *Rev. sciences crim.*, January–March, 1964.

[18] P. Cannat, "Abolition de la peine de mort à Monaco," *Rev. sciences crim.*, 1963, p. 580.

[19] R. Thompson, "L'Abolition de la peine de mort en Nouvelle Zélande," *ibid.*, 1962, p. 83.

[20] See Paul W. Tappan, *Crime, Justice and Correction* (New York, 1960), p. 239.

[21] "La Peine de mort en U.R.S.S.," *Rev sciences crim.*, 1961, p. 854.

[22] Note especially the discussions at the colloquium of the Rhenish-Westphalian Academy on *Todesstrafe? Theologische und juristische Argumente* (Stuttgart, 1960).

[23] See my report to the United Nations on *Capital Punishment* (New York, 1962), secs. 203 ff.

[24] According to article 23 of the Soviet code of 1963, the death penalty exists in the Soviet Union only as "an exceptional punishment until its complete abolition." Cf. my *Introduction au système de droit pénal soviétique* (Paris, 1962). An analogous position, tending to present the scope of the death penalty as limited to exceptional cases, is taken by an official publication of the Ministry of Justice, Madrid, in *Delitos, penas y prisiones en España* (1963), p. 28.

[25] See Sir E. Gowers, *A Life for a Life?* (London, 1956).

[26] Examine in this connection the discussion at the international colloquium on the death penalty held at Royaumont, June 28–29, 1961, reported in *Rev. sciences crim.*, 1961, p. 855, and at the colloquium organized in Athens in April, 1960, by the Panthios School of Political Science (*Travaux,* publ. in 1961).

[27] See the fine book by Mme Maria Le Hardouin, *A la Mémoire d'un homme* (Paris, 1962). On the repercussions of the Chessman case in intellectual and criminological circles, see Negley K. Teeters, *The Academic Criminologist and His Responsibility for Social Action*, distributed by The All India Prevention Society, Lucknow, India, October, 1963. [For a detailed account of the Evans-Christie case, written for the general public, see Ludovic Kennedy, *Ten Rillington Place* (New York: Simon & Schuster, 1961)—Ed.]

[28].During the last century, this idea was analyzed by Mittermaier in his work, *La Peine de mort d'après les travaux de la science, les progrès de la législation et les résultats de l'expérience* (Paris, 1865), pp. 65 ff. Furthermore, it cannot be fully comprehended unless one blindly accepts

that celebrated *psychological constraint* which, according to Feuerbach, produced the threat of severe punishment (for the conclusions he arrived at, see his *Lehrbuch,* par. 16). Feuerbach, however, later came to entertain doubts of the truth of this doctrine to such an extent that he finally rallied to the cause of the abolitionists. (See K. d'Olivecrona, *De la Peine de mort,* 2nd ed., 1893, p. 105.)

[29] This finding, already stated by Mittermaier (*op. cit.*), has been demonstrated definitively by Thorsten Sellin in *The Death Penalty* (Philadelphia, 1959), pp. 22 ff.

[30] Sir Lionel Fox, *The English Prison and Borstal Systems* (London 1962), p. 11.

[31] See the statements by Albert Naud at the meeting on February 8, 1963, of the *Association française contre la peine de mort,* reported in the *Rev. sciences crim.,* 1963, p. 426. See also his book *Tu ne tuera pas* (2nd ed., 1963) and the thought-provoking little work by Dean Richard, *La Mission méconnue de la justice pénale* (Paris, 1956).

[32] See "Jean XXIII et la criminologie." *Rev. sciences crim.,* 1962, p. 157; cf. A. Santoro, "Un Insegnamento definitivo: la parola del Sommo Pontifice sull'antropologia criminale e sulla rieducazione dei rei," *Scuola positiva,* 1961, p. 429.

[33] One might refer to the work of the Colloquium of Strasbourg, organized by the International Penal and Penitentiary Foundation in 1959, and especially to the general reports by Lamers and Dupréel (*Travaux-préparatoires,* Bern, 1959, 2nd vol., pp. 441 and 467). Cf. J. Dupréel, "Théorie et pratique dans le traitement des détenus," *Bull. de l'admin. pénit.,* Brussels, 1961, pp. 5 ff. Van Bemmelen also is opposed to the death penalty, not for reasons of humanitarian sentimentality but because of the trend of modern ideas on punishment that now envisage the social readaptation of the offender (*Het Probleem van de doodstraf,* Antverp, 1948).

[34] See Thorsten Sellin, *The Protective Code: A Swedish Proposal* (Stockholm, 1957); cf. my comments on a protective social law in *Rev. sciences crim.,* 1957 (*Chronique de défense sociale,* pp. 938 ff.) On the preparatory work on the project, see *Rev. sciences crim.,* 1956, p. 43 and p. 251.

[35] Albert Camus, "Réflexions sur la guillotine" in *Réflexions sur la peine capitale,* by A. Koestler and A. Camus (Paris, 1957). Concerning the persistence of the idea of "ritual murder," see my comments on "L'exécution de Caryl Chessman et la peine de mort," *Rev. sciences crim.,* 1960, pp. 477 ff.

[36] See my chapter on "L'Abolition de la peine de mort et la peine de remplacement," written for the symposium volume commemorating Sir Lionel Fox and published by the I.P.P.F.

A SURVEY OF CAPITAL OFFENSES
Robert H. Finkel

[1] Whether an execution in fact takes place after conviction for that offense turns on other factors in and other parties to the administration of criminal justice.

[2] The 50 states, the District of Columbia, Puerto Rico, the Virgin Islands, and the Federal criminal jurisdiction.

[3] Minnesota, Iowa, Wisconsin, Michigan.

[4] The 1965 act required that the murder be "premeditated." This qualification was removed in 1966.

[5] Alabama, Arizona, Arkansas, California, Connecticut, Georgia, Illinois, Indiana, Kansas, Louisiana, Mississippi, Montana, Nevada, New Jersey, North Dakota, Texas, Vermont, Virginia, Washington, and the Federal jurisdiction.

[6] The statutes of the two named states carry mandatory penalties; the Federal statute does not.

[7] Arizona, California, Colorado, Georgia, Idaho, Kansas, Missouri, Montana, Nebraska, Nevada, Texas. The mandatory states are Arizona, California, Colorado, Idaho, Montana, Texas.

[8] Arizona, Connecticut, the District of Columbia, Florida, Georgia, Indiana, Kansas, Kentucky, Maryland, Ohio, Pennsylvania, Texas, Virginia, Washington, and the Federal jurisdiction, plus the mandatory states: California, Montana, North Carolina.

[9] Arkansas, Indiana, Maryland, Texas.

[10] Alabama, Arkansas, Connecticut, Georgia, Indiana, Maryland, North Carolina, Texas, Virginia.

[11] Pennsylvania, for example, requires only the entering of a building of another with intent to commit a felony therein.

[12] Alabama, North Carolina, Virginia.

[13] Several statutes add torture to the list.

[14] Pa. Stat. Ann. (Purdon's Statutes), Tit. 18, Sec. 4701.

[15] New York, North Dakota, Rhode Island, and Vermont make only certain special kinds of murder punishable by death.

[16] Florida and Louisiana.

[17] All except the District of Columbia, Massachusetts, Montana, New Hampshire, North Carolina, North Dakota, Pennsylvania, Rhode Island; the mandatory jurisdictions are Arkansas and Louisiana.

[18] Alabama, Arkansas, the District of Columbia, Florida, Georgia, Kentucky, Louisiana (mandatory), Maryland, Mississippi, Missouri, Nevada, North Carolina, Oklahoma, South Carolina, Tennessee, Texas, Virginia, and the Federal jurisdiction.

[19] Arkansas, Florida, Georgia, Indiana, Massachusetts, Mississippi, Nebraska, Nevada, Oklahoma, South Carolina, Texas, Utah, Wyoming.

[20] All except Georgia.

[21] New York, Pennsylvania, Utah; the mandatory jurisdictions are Alabama, Arizona, California, Colorado, North Dakota, Rhode Island.

[22] Alabama, Arizona, Georgia, Kentucky, Missouri, Oklahoma, Virginia, and the Federal jurisdiction.

[23] Alabama, Florida, Georgia, Kentucky, Mississippi, Missouri, Texas, and the Federal jurisdiction.

[24] Despite the assassination of President John F. Kennedy, there seems to be no movement afoot in other jurisdictions to pass similar legislation.

[25] Kentucky, South Carolina, Texas, Virginia.

[26] Maryland, Nevada, South Carolina, Virginia.

[27] It is not clear whether or not this applies to the shotgun-wielding

father of the bride, as well as to the man who abducts a girl to be his bride.

28 This crime is so specific and limited that it was not possible to combine it with the more general Arkansas boat-collision statute to make a crime punishable by more than one jurisdiction.

29 These crimes are found in separate statutes, which are necessary because South Carolina does not follow the Pennsylvania form for the murder statute.

EXECUTIONS IN THE UNITED STATES
Thorsten Sellin

1 William Bradford Huie, *The Execution of Private Slovik*. 152 pp. New York: New American Library, 1954.

ON THE PENALTY OF DEATH
Cesare Beccaria

1 Cantù, *op. cit.*, pp. 372–373.

AN ANCIENT DEBATE ON CAPITAL PUNISHMENT
William McAllen Green

1 Livy, vi, 20, 12; W. E. Heitland, *M. Tulli Ciceronis pro C. Rabirio Perduellionis Reo Oratio ad Quirites*, Cambridge, University Press (1882), 26; George W. Botsford, *Roman Assemblies*, New York, Macmillan Co. (1909), 250.

2 Polybius vi, 14, 7; Livy, x, 9, 4; Sallust, *Cat.* li, 22 and 40; Cic., *Pro Rab. Perd.* iv, 12; Botsford, *op. cit.*, 250.

3 Sir Henry S. Maine, *Ancient Law*, New York, Henry Holt & Co. (fourth American edition, no date), 374.

4 Theodor Mommsen, *Römisches Strafrecht*, Leipzig, Duncker & Humblot (1899), 941.

5 J. L. Strachan-Davidson, *Problems of the Roman Criminal Law*, Oxford, Clarendon Press (1912), 160 ff.

6 *Pro Rab. Perd.* iii, 10.

7 *Att.* xii, 21; *Cat.* i, 2; iii, 14. These passages indicate that Cicero believed he had the right under the *consultum ultimum* to execute the conspirators and that he decided on that course. Strictly speaking, then, the issue was whether the senate's decree gave Cicero a free hand, setting aside the regular law and procedure. Both Caesar and Cato assume that the execution would be irregular, if not positively illegal. Caesar argues for abiding by the laws—*eis utendum censeo quae legibus comparata sunt* (Sall., *Cat.* li, 8). Cato's plea is that it is idle to talk of the laws and proper legal procedure when the existence of the state is at stake (*ibid.*, lii, 4).

[8] Plut., *Cato* XXIII, 3; Sall., *Cat.* LI ff.

[9] Sall., *Cat.* LI, 40.

[10] Reprinted in Beman, *Selected Articles on Capital Punishment,* New York, H. W. Wilson Co. (1925), 247.

[11] Geo. W. Kirchwey *apud* Beman, 233 ff.

[12] Beman, 235, 247, *et saepe.*

[13] *Cat.* 51, 21.

[14] *Capital Punishment,* Clarence Darrow *versus* Judge Alfred J. Talley, New York, The League for Public Discussion (1924), 32 ff.

[15] Sall., *Cat.* LI, 15 and 25.

[16] A. F. Schuster *apud* Beman, 286.

[17] Sall., *Cat.* LI, 20; Cic., *Cat.* IV, 7. For the thought compare *Tusc. Disp.* I, 96–100; *Pro Milone* 101: *mortem naturae finem esse, non poenam.* The notion of death as a refuge from all evils is, of course, a commonplace. That Caesar himself did not fear death is evident both from his daring in battle and his failure at the last to provide himself with adequate guards when he knew his life was menaced (*Suet., Iul.* LXXXVI).

[18] John O. Yeiser *apud* Beman, 316 ff.

[19] Sall., *Cat.* LII, 13.

[20] A. F. Schuster *apud* Beman, 290.

[21] Sall., *Cat.* LI, 19.

[22] Cic., *Cat.* IV, 7 ff.; cf. Sall., *Cat.* LI, 43.

[23] G. Rayleigh Vicars *apud* Beman, 276.

[24] Sall., *Cat.* LII, 18–23; Plut., *Cato* XXIII; etc.

[25] Darrow-Talley, 53.

A CANADIAN DEBATE, 1966

[1] Canada, *House of Commons Debates,* vol. 111, no. 50. First Session, 27th Parliament. Ottawa, 1966, pp. 3263–3266.

[2] *Ibid.,* pp. 3311–3312.

[3] *Ibid.,* pp. 3317–3318.

[4] *Ibid.,* pp. 3848–3849.

[5] *Ibid.,* pp. 3867–3868.

[6] *Ibid.,* pp. 3314–3316.

[7] *Ibid.,* pp. 3894–3895.

[8] *Ibid.,* pp. 3818–3820.

[9] *Ibid.,* pp. 3830–3831.

MOVEMENTS TO ABOLISH THE DEATH PENALTY
IN THE UNITED STATES
Louis Filler

[1] John B. McMaster, "Old Standards of Public Morals," *Annual Report of the American Historical Association for the Year 1905* (Washington, D.C., 1906), pp. 67 ff.

[2] William Bradford, *An Enquiry How Far the Punishment of Death*

Is Necessary in Pennsylvania . . . (Philadelphia, 1793), pp. 14 ff.

³ Bradford, *op. cit.* note 2 *supra*, p. 43.

⁴ Ohio preceded Pennsylvania by accepting this distinction in 1788. See Raymond T. Bye, *Capital Punishment in the United States* (Philadelphia, 1919), p. 5.

⁵ Bradford, *op. cit.* note 2 *supra*, p. 91.

⁶ *Ibid.*, p. 75; Negley K. Teeters, *They Were in Prison: A History of the Pennsylvania Prison Society, 1787–1937* (Philadelphia, 1937), pp. 149 ff.

⁷ Marvin H. Bovee, *Christ and the Gallows; or, Reasons for the Abolition of Capital Punishment* (New York, 1869), pp. 237–238.

⁸ John Edwards, *Serious Thoughts on the Subject of Taking the Lives of Our Fellow Creatures* . . . , Seventh Edition, New York, 1812; Rev. Samuel Whelpley, *Letters Addressed to Caleb Strong, Esq.* . . . , New York, 1818.

⁹ Samuel L. Knapp, *The Life of Thomas Eddy,* New York, 1834; Blake McKelvey, *American Prisons: A Study in American Social History* (Chicago, 1936), p. 7.

¹⁰ *The Complete Works of Edward Livingston on Criminal Jurisprudence* . . . (New York, 1873), Vol. 1, p. 37.

¹¹ William B. Hatcher, *Edward Livingston* (University, La., 1940), pp. 245 ff.

¹² The United States was the leader in this movement; see Bye, *op. cit.* note 4 *supra*, p. 6.

¹³ *The Report of the Honorable S. M. Stillwell, Chairman of a Select Committee* . . . *[Inquiring] into the Expediency of a Total Abolition of Capital Punishment,* Albany, 1832.

¹⁴ *House [Document]* . . . *36* . . . *January 14, 1835,* Boston, 1835; *House* . . . *No. 32, Report Relating to Capital Punishment, January 12, 1836,* Boston, 1836; *House* . . . *No. 43, Report and Bills Relating to the Abolition of Capital Punishment, January 12, 1837,* Boston, 1837; Arthur B. Darling, *Political Changes in Massachusetts, 1824–1848* (New Haven, 1925), p. 215.

¹⁵ See *Senate [Document] No. 58* . . . *Commonwealth of Massachusetts, 1846* (Boston, 1846), for evidence of the pressures put upon the legislature. In 1839 the penalty for armed robbery and for illegal entry into a house at night was reduced from death to life imprisonment. Rantoul also labored for the separation of first- and second-degree murder, by then accepted in eleven states. See also Benjamin Dole, *A Circular Addressed to the Citizens of Massachusetts* (Cambridge, 1846), which gives an antagonistic account of Rantoul's efforts over eleven years to make "proselytes" to what are deemed his evil views on capital punishment.

¹⁶ T. Purrington, *Report on Capital Punishment Made to the Maine Legislature in 1836,* Third Edition, Washington, D.C., 1852. See also *Remarks of John L. Stevens, in the Senate of Maine, February 11 and 12, 1869, on an Order Instructing the Judiciary Committee to Report a Bill Abolishing Capital Punishment,* Augusta, 1869.

¹⁷ Thus, in 1852, Massachusetts adopted the policy of giving the executive discretionary authority (see Purrington, *op. cit.,* pp. 46–47). This did not, however, in fact or in theory, end capital punishment in that state.

[18] Rev. Timothy Alden Taylor, *The Bible View of the Death Penalty; Also a Summary of the Webster Case* . . . (Worcester, 1850), p. 23.

[19] The abolition issue also brought together dissimilar personages; thus, in Ohio, outstanding advocates of abolition included not only Amasa Walker, then of Oberlin College, an antislavery partisan, but the Hon. Clement L. Vallandigham, at that time a brilliant young state representative, partial to the south, later notorious as a defeatist during the Civil War; see Albert Post, "The Anti-gallows Movement in Ohio," *Ohio State Archaeological and Historical Quarterly*, Vol. LIV (1945), pp. 109–110.

[20] Albert Post, "Early Efforts to Abolish Capital Punishment in Pennsylvania," *Pennsylvania Magazine of History and Biography*, Vol. 68 (1944), p. 48; *The Impropriety of Capital Punishment: or the Report of a Committee on Dr. Cuyler's Sermon* . . . , Philadelphia, 1842. For actual debates, see introductory remarks to *Capital Punishment. The Argument of Rev. George B. Cheever in Reply to J. L. O'Sullivan, Esq., in the Broadway Tabernacle* . . . (New York, 1843), and also *An Exercise in Declamation; in the Form of a Debate on Capital Punishment* . . . , Boston, 1849.

[21] Merle Curti, *The American Peace Crusade, 1815–1860* (Durham, N.C., 1929), pp. 83–84.

[22] John L. O'Sullivan, *Report in Favor of* . . . *Abolition* . . . *April 14, 1841*, Second Edition, New York, 1841.

[23] Albert Post, *op. cit.* note 20 *supra*, pp. 48–49. For a progress report, see [James H. Titus] *Fourth Annual Address of the New York State Society for the Abolition of Capital Punishment* (New York, 1848), and *Reports and Addresses of James H. Titus, upon the Subject of Capital Punishment*, New York, 1848.

[24] Purrington, *op. cit.* note 16, *supra*, pp. 33 ff.

[25] Albert Post, "Michigan Abolishes Capital Punishment," *Michigan History*, Vol. 29 (1945), pp. 44–50. The law abolishing capital punishment retained it for treason. Since treason, however, could only apply to an offense against the United States, Michigan's priority as an abolitionist state is unaffected.

[26] *Appleton's Annual Encyclopaedia and Register of Important Events of the Year 1888*, Vol. XIII, Whole Vol. XXVIII, New York, 1889.

[27] *Op. cit.* note 7 *supra*. Reprints of this work, published in all three cases by the author, appeared in 1870 and 1876.

[28] William Tallack, *The Practical Results of the Total or Partial Abolition of Capital Punishment in Various Countries* (London, 1886), pp. 18–19.

[29] Bye, *op. cit.* note 4 *supra*, pp. 8–9.

[30] Frederick H. Wines, *Punishment and Reformation* (New York, 1895), p. 192.

[31] *Ibid.*, pp. 192 ff., 197–198, 292 ff.; Mary Carpenter, *Reformatory Prison Discipline* . . . , London, 1872; Amos W. Butler, "The Operation of the Indeterminate Sentence and Parole Law." *Journal of Prison Discipline and Philanthropy*, New Series, No. 55 (March 1916), pp. 56 ff.; Helen D. Pigeon, *Probation and Parole in Theory and Practice* (New York, 1942), p. 84.

[32] Comment in answer to an inquiry from Torajiro Mogi, quoted

in Mogi's thesis, *Capital Punishment: Historically, Philosophically and Practically Considered* . . . (Ann Arbor, Mich., 1890), p. 40.

33 William Tallack, "Humanity and Humanitarianism," *Transactions of the National Congress on Penitentiary and Reformatory Discipline,* edited by E. C. Wines (Albany, 1871), pp. 204 ff.; E. C. Wines, *The Actual State of Prison Reform Troughout* [sic] *the Civilized World* . . ., Stockholdm, 1878; Bovee, *op. cit.* note 7 *supra,* pp. 241 ff.; Alfred H. Love, "Our Duty to the Prisoner and the Community," *Proceedings of the National Prison Congress* . . . (Chicago, 1887), pp. 92 ff. In 1898 Love embarrassed his organization by writing to the Queen of Spain in a pacifist effort, and resigned his vice presidency of the organization; see Teeters, *op. cit.* note 6 *supra,* pp. 398–400.

34 [Symposium] "The Death Penalty," *North American Review,* Vol. 133 (December 1881), pp. 534 ff.; George F. Shrady, "The Death Penalty," *Arena,* Vol. XI (October 1890), p. 53.

35 Tallack, *Penological and Preventive Principles with Special Reference to Europe and America* . . . (London, 1896), pp. 252–253.

36 N. M. Curtis, *Capital Crimes and the Punishment Prescribed Therefor by Federal and State Laws and Those of Foreign Countries* . . . (Washington, D.C., 1894), [3].

37 "The Death Penalty in the United States," *Harper's Weekly,* Vol. 41 (January 30, 1897), p. 107. This general rule has persisted to the present. McKinley's assassination resulted in a statute making it a capital crime to attempt the life of a high federal official (*Nation,* Vol. 84 [April 25, 1907], p. 377); and the Lindbergh law added kidnapping as a capital crime. The statement in Teeters, *World Penal Systems, A Survey* (Philadelphia, 1944), p. 180 fn., that "the Federal government resorts to capital punishment (hanging) for treason only . . . ," is inaccurate.

38 Brand Whitlock, *Forty Years of It* (New York, 1925), pp. 82 ff.

39 Allan Nevins (Ed.), *The Letters and Journal of Brand Whitlock* (New York, 1936), pp. 49, 69 ff., 155.

40 Bye, *op. cit.* note 4 *supra,* p. 9.

41 These included the International Anti-Capital Punishment League in San Francisco and Los Angeles; the Anti-Capital Punishment League, headed by Charles H. Ingersoll, in New York; the Anti-Capital Punishment Society of America, headed by George W. Hunt, in Chicago; the Massachusetts Prison Reform Association, headed by Mrs. Florence Spooner; and the Anti-Capital Punishment Society, headed by George Foster Peabody, in New York. I am indebted to Mrs. Herbert B. Ehrmann, executive director of the American League to Abolish Capital Punishment, for information and material about modern abolitionist movements.

42 Teeters, *op. cit.* note 6 *supra,* pp. 397–398.

43 "Capital Punishment and Prison Reforms," *Survey,* Vol. 37 (March 10, 1917), pp. 670–671.

44 *Journal of Prison Discipline and Philanthropy,* New Series, No. 57 (March 1918), p. 52.

45 Harry L. Davis, "Death by Law," *Outlook,* Vol. 131 (July 26, 1922), pp. 525 ff.

46 Maureen McKernan, *The Amazing Crime and Trial of Leopold*

and Loeb, Chicago, 1924; "Capital Punishment, 1910–1925 (a Selected Bibliography)," *Journal of the American Institute of Criminal Law and Criminology*, Vol. 17 (May, 1926), pp. 117 ff.

[47] "Abolishing the Death Penalty," *Literary Digest*, Vol. 86 (August 22, 1925), p. 29; "Attacking the Death Penalty," *ibid.*, Vol. 88 (February 13, 1926), pp. 7–8.

[48] *Boston Sunday Herald*, March 9, 1952, p. 38.

[49] Vivian Pierce, *Annual Report of 1931* (New York, n.d.), p. 4.

[50] Mabel A. Elliott, *Coercion in Penal Treatment: Past and Present* (Ithaca: Pacifist Research Bureau, 1947), pp. 34–35.

[51] Raymond T. Bye, "Recent History and Present Status of Capital Punishment in the United States," *Journal of the American Institute of Criminal Law and Criminology*, Vol. XVII (August, 1926) p. 245.

[52] A convenient summary of opinion, pro and con, may be found in *Capital Punishment: The Reference Shelf*, Julia E. Johnson, compiler, Vol. 13, No. 1 (New York, 1939).

[53] *New York Times*, July 18, 1952, p. 21.

EXPERIMENTS WITH ABOLITION
Thorsten Sellin

[1] Thorsten Sellin, *The Death Penalty*, pp. 37–38.

ABOLITION AND RESTORATION
OF THE DEATH PENALTY IN MISSOURI
Ellen Elizabeth Guillot

[1] The writer is indebted to Judge Cave for much of the material for this article. Judge Cave was a member of the Judiciary Committees of both houses of the Legislature during this decade.

[2] *Kansas City Star*, April 4, 1917, p. 2.

[3] *Missouri Historical Review*, Vol. XXXVI, No. 4 (July 1942), p. 310.

[4] William M. Reedy, "Hanging Is a Lost Art," *Kansas City Star*, April 19, 1918.

[5] *Kansas City Star*, April 15, 1917, p. 8A.

[6] *St. Louis Post-Dispatch*, July 5, 1919, p. 14.

[7] *Kansas City Star*, April 15, 1917, p. 8A.

[8] *St. Louis Post-Dispatch*, Jan. 26, 1919, p. 2, Editorial Section.

[9] *Journal of the Missouri Legislature*, 50th General Assembly, Regular and Extra Sessions, Senate, p. 50; *Kansas City Times*, July 3, 1919, p. 13.

[10] *St. Louis Post-Dispatch*, June 18, 1919, p. 17.

[11] *Kansas City Star*, July 3, 1919, p. 13.

[12] *Ibid.*

[13] *St. Louis Post-Dispatch*, June 16, 1919, p. 12.

[14] *St. Louis Post-Dispatch*, June 24, 1919, p. 14.

[15] *Kansas City Times*, July 6, 1919, p. 1.

THE DEATH PENALTY AND POLICE SAFETY
Thorsten Sellin

[1] For the diagram in the original version there is substituted the diagram that appears on page 61 of my monograph, *The Death Penalty*, Philadelphia: American Law Institute, 1959.

HOMICIDES AND ASSAULTS IN CANADIAN PRISONS
Dogan D. Akman

[1] The writer wishes to thank A. J. MacLeod for giving permission to collect the material for this study and R. E. March, Director of Correctional Research of the Penitentiary Service, for his generous and most efficient cooperation in arranging on our behalf the collection of the data.

[2] The study excludes assaults that might have occurred in provincial jails, where those convicted of felonies for terms of two years and more and those awaiting their sentences for such offenses are held temporarily. To the best of this writer's knowledge, during the period studied no homicides were committed by these offenders.

[3] The offenders were convicted for: non-capital murder (1), manslaughter (3), attempted murder (1), rape and attempted rape (2), robbery (armed and violent included) (29), theft (including burglary and possession of stolen goods) (37), assault and wounding (5), fraud (4), possession of drugs (1), forcible confinement (1), escape of custody (1), property damage (1), living on avails of prostitution (1).

[4] The victims were convicted for: non-capital murder (1), manslaughter (2), robbery (16), theft (35), assault and wounding (3), fraud (3), incest (1), procuring miscarriage (1), possession of drugs (1), trafficking in drugs (2), perjury (1), uttering of threatening letter (1), unknown (3).

[5] Among the 13 cases where provocation by the victim was recorded, five were robbers and five were thieves. While the former provoked four robbers and one thief, the latter provoked three thieves and one robber.

[6] For the purposes of this discussion, aggravated assaults are defined as those resulting for the victims in (a) temporary disability without hospitalization, (b) hospitalization, (c) temporary disability following hospitalization, (d) permanent disability—incapacity to work—and (e) disability necessitating change in the type of work.

[7].Simple assaults are defined as those resulting in no injury or minor injury necessitating medical aid only.

[8] *Capital Punishment: Material Relating to Its Purpose*, published by the Minister of Justice, Queen's Printer, Ottawa, 1965, pp. 98 ff.

[9] The victims of the unknown offenders included one convicted of manslaughter, four robbers, nine thieves, two convicted of assault and wounding, one convicted of fraud, and two convicted of trafficking in drugs. Bodily means were used in five assaults, cutting and stabbing

weapons in eight, and a blunt weapon in one case. In five assaults the weapons used were not recorded. In terms of physical consequences, the victims of these offenders sustained minor injuries (6), temporary disability without hospitalization (8), and temporary disability following hospitalization (5).

[10] *Capital Punishment, op. cit.,* p. 108.

[11] From Thorsten Sellin, "The Death Penalty," quoted in *Capital Punishment, op. cit.,* p. 27.

[12] *Capital Punishment, op. cit.,* pp. 102–103.

[13] Report of the Joint Committee of the Senate and the House of Commons on Capital Punishment (Canada), quoted in *Capital Punishment, op. cit.,* p. 24.

[14] Twenty-two officers versus 35 inmates in 1964 and 15 officers versus 35 inmates in 1965.

[15] The rates for officers are calculated on the basis of the number of officers assaulted over the total prison staff population exposed to risk. The latter figure was supplied by the Penitentiary Service for April, 1965, and is unofficial. This figure was used in computing both rates, as the figures for 1964 were not available, and no significant change in the size of the prison staff is reported.

The rates for inmates are calculated on the basis of the number of inmates assaulted over the average yearly population obtained by computing the arithmetic mean of the inmate population present at the first day of the year, the middle of June, and the last day of the year.

THE PAROLING OF CAPITAL OFFENDERS

G. I. Giardini and R. G. Farrow

[1] *Report of the Subcommittee of the Judiciary Committee on Capital Punishment Pertaining to the Problems of the Death Penalty and Its Administration in California* (Assembly Interim Committee Reports 1955–57, vol. 20, no. 3), 55 pp., Sacramento, 1957, p. 12.

[2] State of New York, Executive Department, *34th Annual Report of the Division of Parole for 1963,* Albany, 1964, pp. 53–73.

[3] Ohio Adult Parole Authority, *A Summary of Parole Performance of First-Degree Murderers in Ohio for the Calendar Year 1965 and for the Period 1945–1965,* 2 pp. (mimeo.), Columbus, June, 1966.

THE DEATH PENALTY

AND THE ADMINISTRATION OF JUSTICE

Herbert B. Ehrmann

[1] *Hansard,* May 1, 1810.

[2] *Ibid.,* May 30, 1810.

[3] Second Report on the Criminal Law by His Majesty's Commissioners, 1836, p. 21.

[4] Not, however, by the dean of the Harvard Law School, who commented on the fact that the message ignored available data.

[5] Data from *Memorandum on Capital Punishment,* prepared by Thorsten Sellin for the Royal Commission on Capital Punishment, 1951, pp. 657–660.

[6] For instance, Lewis E. Lawes, former warden of Sing Sing Prison, *Man's Judgment of Death* (New York: G. P. Putnam's Sons, 1925), p. 58; Austin H. MacCormick, formerly Commissioner of Corrections, New York City, then executive director of the Osborne Association, in *Boston Sunday Herald,* December 11, 1949.

[7] See for instance the quoted remarks of Chief Justice Higgins in the *Boston Daily Record,* November 5, 1942; those of Judge Warner in the *Boston Herald,* June 7, 1933; and those of District Attorney Foley in the *Boston Herald,* April 10, 1930.

[8] Mr. Justice Wilkins in Commonwealth v. Cox, 1951 A. S. 857; 100 N. E. 2d 14.

[9] Mass. St. 1939, Sec. 341; G.L. (Ter. Ed.) C. 278, Sec. 33E. This case was an unusual one for Massachusetts, where, under the Briggs law, so-called, insanity is usually determined before trial. G.L. (Ter. Ed.) C. 123, Sec. 100A.

[10] See Arthur Garfield Hays, *Trial by Prejudice* (New York: Covici Friede, 1933).

[11] Smith v. Texas, 311 U.S. 128, 61 S. Ct. 164, 85 L. Ed. 84 (1940); Pierre v. Louisiana, 306 U.S. 354, 59 S. Ct. 536, 83 L. Ed. 760 (1939); Strauder v. W. Virginia, 100 U.S. 303, 25 L. Ed. 664 (1879).

[12] Related by Wendell Murray of the Boston Bar, called in as counsel for Wong Duck after the trial. Three of the defendants were executed, but Wong Duck was among those granted a new trial.

[13] Royal Commission on Capital Punishment, Minutes of Evidence taken before the Royal Commission on Capital Punishment, Thirtieth Day, Thursday, 1st February, 1951. Witness: Professor Thorsten Sellin. [Pp. 647–678] London: H. M. Stationery Office, 1951.

[14] The 1940 Census gave Middlesex, 958,855; Suffolk, 912,706.

[15] 262 Mass. 408 (1928).

[16] 328 U.S. 463, 66 S. Ct. 1318, 90 L. Ed. 1382 (1946).

[17] See Testimony of Mr. Justice Frankfurter before the Royal Commission on Capital Punishment, 1950, pp. 580–582.

[18] Benjamin N. Cardozo, *Law and Literature* (New York: Harcourt, Brace & Co., 1931), pp. 99–101.

[19] Cf. *Boston Globe,* October 14, 1930. "Battle Creek, Michigan [an abolition state]. Only a little more than 12 hours following their capture after the killing of a state policeman and the robbery of a bank, Thomas Martin and James Gallagher were sentenced to life imprisonment in Jackson Prison." The Millen-Faber cases are notable for reasons other than great expense. At the time of the arrest of these criminals, two innocent men, Beret and Molway, were being tried for one of the murders committed by the Millen gang. The trial was nearing a conclusion, and eight reputable witnesses, with good opportunity to observe, had identified Beret and Molway as the robbers, when the real criminals were apprehended, bringing confessions and ballistic evidence to the rescue. No one familiar with the Beret-Molway trial has ever doubted that these men would have been convicted—and executed—but for this timely occurrence.

[20] Commenting on the execution of Irene Schroeder by the State

of Pennsylvania in 1931, Dr. Harvey M. Watkins of Reading, a social worker, is quoted in a bulletin issued by the American League to Abolish Capital Punishment as saying: "It cost the State of Pennsylvania $23,658 to prosecute, convict and electrocute Irene Schroeder at the Western Penitentiary. If one twentieth of this sum had been spent 10 years ago by any social workers on that 22-year-old girl, that electrocution would have been prevented."

[21] *Boston Herald,* June 7, 1933.

[22] Record published by Henry Holt & Co., 1928.

[23] Minutes of Faculty Meeting on Capital Punishment, Twentieth Century Club, January 18, 1936.

THE ERRORS OF JUSTICE
Otto Pollak

[1] Charles Lucas, *Recueil des débats des Assemblées Législatives de la France sur la question de la peine de mort* (Paris, 1831), Part I, p. 38.

[2] *Hansard,* 5th Series, Vol. 449, Col. Nos. 1000–1002.

[3] Erich Sello, *Die Irrtümer der Strafjustiz und Ihre Ursachen* (Berlin: R. V. Decker's Verlag, 1911), pp. 6–7; M. Liepmann, *Die Todesstrafe* (Berlin: J. Guttentag, 1912), p. 127; Gabriel Tarde, *Penal Philosophy* (Boston: Little, Brown & Co., 1912), p. 539; Edwin M. Borchard, *Convicting the Innocent* (New Haven: Yale University Press, 1932), p. vii; *Hansard, loc. cit.*

[4] Borchard, *loc. cit.*

[5] *Hansard, op. cit.,* Col. 1000.

[6] Liepmann, *loc. cit.*

[7] Arthur McDonald, "Death Penalty and Homicide," *American Journal of Sociology,* Vol. 16, pp. 91–92.

[8] Jeremy Bentham, *Works* (Bowring edition, Edinburgh, 1843), Vol. I, p. 447.

[9] Charles Phillips, *Vacation Thoughts on Capital Punishment,* 4th edition, London, 1858; Alfred H. Dymond, *The Law on Its Trial, or Personal Recollections of the Death Penalty and Its Opponents,* London, 1865.

[10] Julius Mühlfeld, *Justizmorde,* Berlin, 1880; Leopold Katscher, *Schuldlos Verurteilt,* Leipzig, 1895; Lailler and Vonoven, *Les erreurs judiciaires et leurs causes,* Paris, 1897; Gaston Péan, *L'erreur judiciaire,* Paris, 1895; Liepmann, *op. cit.* note 3, pp. 129 and 137.

[11] Sello, *op. cit.* note 3.

[12] Borchard, *op. cit.* note 3.

[13] Condensed from Sello, *op. cit.* note 3, pp. 346–348.

[14] Condensed from Borchard, *op. cit.* note 3, pp. 33–39.

[15] Condensed from Sello, *op. cit.* note 3, pp. 327–343.

[16] Condensed from Borchard, *op. cit.* note 3, pp. 210–217.

[17] Condensed from Borchard, *op. cit.* note 3, pp. 15–22; Sello, *op. cit.* note 3, p. 317, and others.

[18] Condensed from Borchard, *op. cit.* note 3, pp. 40–45.

[19] Liepmann, *op. cit.* note 3, pp. 159–160.

[20] Sello, *op. cit.* note 3, pp. 110–128, 291–295; Liepmann, *op. cit.* note 3, pp. 171–172.

[21] Borchard, *op. cit.* note 3, p. viii.

[22] Thorsten Sellin, *Research Memorandum on Crime in the Depression* (New York: Social Science Research Council, 1937), p. 70.

[23] Lucas, *op. cit.* note 1, p. 85.

THE DYNAMICS OF EXECUTIVE CLEMENCY
Solie M. Ringold

[1] *Eacret* v. *Holmes,* 333 P. 2d 741 (Or. 1958).

[2] Abramowitz and Paget, *Executive Clemency in Capital Cases,* 39 N.Y.U.L. Rev. 136 (1964). I am deeply indebted to the authors of this article. It is the only one I found that attempts to analyze the standards and criteria used in granting executive clemency.

[3] 27 Henry 8, c. 24 (1536).

[4] Jensen, *The Pardoning Power in the American States* (1922).

[5] *United States* v. *Wilson,* 7 Peters 150, 160 (1833).

[6] *Burdick* v. *United States,* 236 U.S. 79 (1915).

[7] *Biddle* v. *Perovich,* 274 U.S. 480, 487 (1926).

[8] 274 U.S. at 486.

[9] 333 P. 2d at 744.

[10] *Henry* v. *Oklahoma,* 136 Pac. 982 (Cr. Ct. App. Okla. 1913).

[11] *Saturday Evening Post,* March 22, 1958.

[12] Letter from Hugh M. Collum, Assistant Attorney General of Oklahoma, December 7, 1964.

Selected Bibliography

SELECTED BIBLIOGRAPHY

Articles in this book are not listed.

A good bibliography on capital punishment can be prepared by consulting A. F. Kuhlman, *A Guide to Material on Crime and Criminal Justice* (New York: H. W. Wilson Company, 1929); Dorothy C. Culver, *Bibliography of Crime and Criminal Justice, 1927–1931*, and *Bibliography of Crime and Criminal Justice, 1932–1937* (New York: H. W. Wilson Company, 1934 and 1939); *International Review of Criminal Policy* (New York: United Nations, 1952–   ), containing annually an international bibliography of criminology; *International Bibliography on Crime and Delinquency* (begun in 1963 by the National Research and Information Center of the National Council on Crime and Delinquency, New York, and now published by the National Clearing House for Mental Information, Public Health Service, U. S. Department of Health, Education and Welfare, Washington). A recent bibliography may be found in Hugo Adam Bedau, *The Death Penalty in America* (Garden City, N.Y.: Doubleday & Company, Inc., 1964), pp. 565–574. For aid in preparing a bibliography, see Thorsten Sellin and Leonard D. Savitz, *A Bibliographical Manual for the Student of Criminology* (New York: National Council on Crime and Delinquency, 1963).

Recent Official Reports

Capital Punishment. New York: United Nations, 1962.

Capital Punishment. Columbus: Ohio Legislative Service Commission, January, 1961 (Staff Research Report No. 46).

Capital Punishment: Material Relating to its Purpose and Value. Ottawa: Queen's Printer, June, 1965.

Committee on Capital Punishment, Legislative Council of Maryland, *Report.* Baltimore: Legislative Council of Maryland, October 3, 1962.

Committee on the Judiciary, House of Representatives, 86th Congress, Second Session, *Abolition of Capital Punishment, Hearings . . . on H.R. 870 to Abolish the Death Penalty . . .* , May 25, 1960 (Serial No. 21). Washington: Government Printing Office, 1960.

Commonwealth of Massachusetts, *Report and Recommendations of the Special Commission Established for the Purpose of Investigating and Studying the Abolition of the Death Penalty in Capital Cases.* Boston: The Commission, December 30, 1958 (House No. 2575).

DeMarcus, John P., *Capital Punishment*. Frankfort: Kentucky Legislative Research Commission, 1965 (Inf. Bul. No. 40).

General Assembly of Pennsylvania, *Report of the Joint Legislative Committee on Capital Punishment*. Harrisburg: The Committee, June, 1961.

Royal Commission on Capital Punishment, 1949–1953, *Report*. London: Her Majesty's Stationery Office, 1953.

State of New Jersey, Commission to Study Capital Punishment, *Report*. Trenton: The Commission, October, 1964.

Subcommittee of the Judiciary Committee on Capital Punishment, *Report . . . Pertaining to the Problems of the Death Penalty and Its Administration in California*. Sacramento: Assembly of the State of California (Interim Comm. Report, Vol. 20, No. 3), January 18, 1957.

General

Bedau, Hugo Adam, ed., *The Death Penalty in America: An Anthology*. Garden City, N.Y.: Doubleday & Company, Inc., 1964.

Bye, Raymond T., *Capital Punishment in the United States*. Philadelphia: The Committee of Philanthropic Labor of Philadelphia Yearly Meeting of Friends, 1919.

Joyce, James Avery, *Capital Punishment: A World View*. New York: Thomas Nelson & Sons, 1961.

Kirkpatrick, Clifford, *Capital Punishment*. Philadelphia: The Committee on Philanthropic Labor of the Philadelphia Yearly Meeting of Friends, 1925.

Patrick, Clarence H., "The Status of Capital Punishment: A World Perspective." *Journal of Criminal Law, Criminology and Police Science*, 56:397–411, December, 1965.

Sellin, Thorsten, "Capital Punishment." *Federal Probation*, 25 (No. 3):3–11, September, 1961.

Sellin, Thorsten, ed., *Murder and the Penalty of Death*. Philadelphia: The American Academy of Political and Social Science, 1952 (Vol. 284, November, 1952, issue of *The Annals*, published by the Academy).

Of Historical Interest

Bedau, Hugo Adam, "A Survey of the Debate on Capital Punishment in Canada, England, and the United States." *The Prison Journal*, 38:35–40, October, 1958.

Beichman, Arnold, "The First Electrocution." *Commentary*, 35:410–419, May, 1963.

Capital Punishment in North Carolina. Raleigh: North Carolina State Board of Charities and Public Welfare, 1929 (Special Bul. No. 10).

Christoph, James B., *Capital Punishment and British Politics.* London: Allen & Unwin, 1962.

Davis, David Brion, "The Movement to Abolish Capital Punishment in America, 1787–1861." *American Historical Review,* 63:23–46, October, 1957.

McCafferty, James A., "Major Trends in the Use of Capital Punishment." *Federal Probation,* 25 (No. 3):15–21, September, 1961.

Norris, William, *One from Seven Hundred.* New York: Pergamon Press, 1966. (Chapter 6, "The Rope's End," deals with the parliamentary debate of 1965 in England.)

Teeters, Negley K., *Scaffold and Chair: A Compilation of Their Use in Pennsylvania, 1682–1962.* Philadelphia: Pennsylvania Prison Society, 1963.

Teeters, Negley K., and J. Hedblom, *Hang by the Neck.* Springfield, Illinois: Charles C. Thomas, 1966.

Tuttle, Elizabeth Orman, *The Crusade Against Capital Punishment in Great Britain.* London: Stevens and Sons, 1961.

The Administration of Capital Punishment

Bedau, Hugo A., "Death Sentences in New Jersey, 1907–1960." *Rutgers Law Review,* 19:1–64 (1965).

Bedau, Hugo A., "Murder, Errors of Justice, and Capital Punishment." In Bedau, ed., *The Death Penalty in America,* 434–452 (see *General*).

DiSalle, Michael V., *The Power of Life or Death.* New York: Random House, 1965.

Duffy, Clinton T., with Al Hirschberg, *Eighty-eight Men and Two Women.* Garden City, N.Y.: Doubleday & Company, Inc., 1962.

Ehrmann, Sara B., "For Whom the Chair Waits." *Federal Probation,* 26 (No. 1):14–25, March, 1962.

McGee, R. A., "Capital Punishment as Seen by a Correctional Administrator." *Federal Probation,* 28 (No. 2):11–16, June, 1964.

Oberer, Walter E., "Does Disqualification of Jurors for Scruples Against Capital Punishment Constitute Denial of Fair Trial on Issue of Guilt?" *Texas Law Review,* 39:545–567, May, 1961.

Prettyman, Barrett, Jr., *Death and the Supreme Court.* New York: Harcourt, Brace and World, Inc., 1961.

Seagle, William, *Acquitted of Murder.* Chicago: Henry Regnery Company, 1958.

Thomas, Paul A., "Murder and the Death Penalty." *American*

Journal of Correction, 19 (No. 4):16 ff., July–August, 1957 (attitude of prison wardens).

In Favor of Capital Punishment

Allen, Edward J., "Your Protection and Mine." *The Police Chief,* 27 (No. 6):22, 24–26, 28, June, 1960.

Barzun, Jacques, "In Favor of Capital Punishment." *The American Scholar,* 31:181–191, Spring, 1962.

Gerstein, R. M., "A Prosecutor Looks at Capital Punishment." *Journal of Criminal Law, Criminology and Police Science,* 51:252–256, July–August, 1960.

Hook, Sidney, "The Death Sentence." *The New Leader,* 44:18–20, April 3, 1961.

Ingram, T. Robert, ed., *Essays on the Death Penalty.* Houston: St. Thomas Press, 1963.

Lynch, Patrick, "Scriptures and Crime." *Trial,* 1:38, 42, April–May, 1965.

The Opposition

Adamo, Mons. Salvatore J., "It's Time to Outlaw Capital Punishment." *U. S. Catholic,* 31:19-20, May, 1965.

Barry, John V., "Hanged by the Neck Until . . ." *Sydney Law Review,* 2:401–413, March, 1958.

Block, Eugene B., *And May God Have Mercy . . . : The Case Against Capital Punishment.* San Francisco: Fearon Publishers, 1962 (supplement, 9 pp., issued in March, 1966).

Camus, Albert, "Reflections on the Guillotine." *Evergreen Review,* 1 (No. 3):5–55 (1957).

"Capital Punishment." *Existential Psychiatry,* 1:7–20, Spring, 1966. (A symposium with participants Willard J. Lassers, Hans Mattick, Jordan M. Scher, and the Rev. Robert Taylor.)

Gardiner, Gerald, *Capital Punishment as a Deterrent: And the Alternative.* London: Victor Gollancz, 1956.

Gowers, Sir Ernest, *A Life for a Life?* London: Chatto and Windus, 1956.

Hale, Leslie, *Hanged in Error.* Baltimore: Penguin Books, 1961.

Koestler, Arthur, *Reflections on Hanging.* New York: Macmillan Company, 1957.

Koestler, Arthur, and C. H. Rolph, *Hanged by the Neck.* Baltimore: Penguin Books, 1961.

Playfair, Giles, and Derrick Sington, *The Offenders: The Case Against Legal Vengeance.* New York: Simon and Schuster, 1957.

Tidmarsh, Mannes, J. D. Halloran, and K. J. Connolly, *Capital*

Punishment: A Case for Abolition. London and New York: Sheed and Ward, 1963.

Williams, Edward Bennett, "Capital Punishment." *Trial,* 1:39–42, April–May, 1965.

Yoder, John Howard, *The Christian and Capital Punishment.* Newton, Kansas: Faith and Life Press, 1961 (Institute of Mennonite Studies, Series No. 1).

Some Research Studies

Campion, Donald, "The State Police and the Death Penalty." In *Appendix "F" of the Minutes of Proceedings and Evidence, No. 20 of the Joint Committee of the Senate and the House of Commons on Capital Punishment . . . ,* Second Session, Twenty-second Parliament, pp. 729–741. Ottawa: Queen's Printer, 1955.

Dann, Robert H., *The Deterrent Effect of Capital Punishment.* Philadelphia: The Committee of Philanthropic Labor of Philadelphia Yearly Meeting of Friends, 1935 (Bul. No. 29).

Graves, William F., "A Doctor Looks at Capital Punishment." *Medical Arts and Sciences,* 10:137–141 4th Quarter, 1956.

Johnson, Elmer H., "Selective Factors in Capital Punishment." *Social Forces,* 36:165–169, December, 1957.

Savitz, Leonard D., "A Study in Capital Punishment." *Journal of Criminal Law, Criminology and Police Science,* 49:338–341, November–December, 1958.

Sellin, Thorsten, *The Death Penalty.* Philadelphia: American Law Institute, 1959.

Wolfgang, Marvin E., "Murder, the Pardon Board and Recommendations by Judges and District Attorneys." *Journal of Criminal Law, Criminology, and Police Science,* 50:338–346, November–December, 1959.

Wolfgang, Marvin E., Arlene Kelly, and Hans C. Nolde, "Comparison of the Executed and the Commuted Among Admissions to Death Row." *Journal of Criminal Law, Criminology, and Police Science,* 53:301–311, September, 1962.

Index

286   INDEX

Crusade Against Capital Punish-
ment in Great Britain, The,
60
Curtis, Newton M., 116–117

Dallas, George M., 112
Darrow, Clarence, 118, 119, 120
Davis, Governor Harry L., 119
Davis, Miner, 222
Death penalty, 5, 16
abolition *de facto* in France, 7
abolition of, 5–6, 8–9; in 1917,
118–119; in Rhode Island,
113; in Wisconsin, 113
and acquittals, 193–194
and administration of justice,
189–206
in Africa, 10
in Alaska, 230
application of, 10
arguments for, 138
in Arizona, 118
in Asia, 10
in Australia, 10
and authoritarian regimes, 8
in Belgium, 10
Caesar on, 49–51
in Canada, 10
Cato on, 51
in Chile, 11
Cicero on, 46, 48, 49
in Colorado, 114, 118
in Communist countries, 240
commutation of, 10
and cost of trial, 203–205
counter-currents favoring, 7
in Cuba, 11
and degrees of murder, 202
as deterrent, 82–83
distorts administration of justice, 205–206
in Eire, 240
in El Salvador, 11
errors of justice and, 207
in Europe, 11, 240
execution of, 240–241
and fair trial, 220–226
in Germany, 101
in Great Britain, 101
in Greece, 240
in Guatemala, 11
federal law and, 112–113

in France, 11, 14, 240
in Illinois, 118
in Indiana, 118
in Iowa, 114
in Ireland, 11
irrational views on, 189–191
in Italy, 100–101
jury system and, 208–209
in Kansas, 114
life imprisonment as alternate
for, 191–193
in Maine, 114
mandatory, 191, 196–197; in
District of Columbia, 120; in
Massachusetts, 114, 118, 190–
191, 197–199, 199–200, 206;
in Vermont, 120
mental responsibility and, 202–
203
in Mexico, 11
in Michigan, 113
for military crimes in wartime,
13
in Minnesota, 118
in Mississippi, 243
in Missouri, 118, 124–131
movements to abolish, 104–122
in Nebraska, 119
in New Hampshire, 118
in New York, 118
in the nineteenth century, 7
in North Carolina, 118
in North Dakota, 118
and number of trials, 199–200
in Ohio, 118, 242
in Oregon, 118, 227
in Pennsylvania, 118, 119
and police safety, 138–154
for political crimes, 6–7
and prison homicides, 154–160
prison reform and, 114–116
problem of, 3–21
public opinion and, 15
re-introduction of, in France, 14
retribution and, 242
in Roman Republic, 47–48
and second-degree convictions,
196–199
and sensationalism, 205
sentiment against, 110–111
and social selection, 8
in South Dakota, 118

NOTES

NOTES

NOTES

NOTES